Affective Intelligence
and Political Judgment

DATE DUE

Affective Intelligence and Political Judgment

George E. *Marcus*
W. *Russell Neuman*
Michael MacKuen

The University of Chicago Press
Chicago and London

The University of Chicago Press, Chicago 60637
The University of Chicago Press, Ltd., London
© 2000 by The University of Chicago
All rights reserved. Published 2000
Printed in the United States of America
09 08 07 06 05 04   2 3 4 5

ISBN 0-226-50468-9 (cloth)
ISBN 0-226-50469-7 (paper)

Library of Congress Cataloging-in Publication Data

Marcus, George E.
    Affective intelligence and political judgment / George E. Marcus, W. Russell Neuman,
    Michael MacKuen.
        p.   cm.
    Includes bibliographical references and index.
    ISBN 0-226-50468-9 (cloth : alk. paper)—ISBN 0-226-50469-7 (pbk. : alk. paper)
    1. Political psychology.   2. Rational choice theory.   3. Voting.   4. Affect
(Psychology)   I. Neumann, W. Russell.   II. MacKuen, Michael.   III. Title.

JA74.5.M36   2000
320'.01'9—dc21   00-008392

♾ The paper used in this publication meets the minimum requirements of the American
National Standard for Information Sciences—Permanence of Paper for Printed Library
Materials, ANSI Z39.48-1992.

To our wives, Lois, Susan, and Michele,
each a professor in her own right,
each more supportive of our efforts than we deserve,
each pleased to hear, however, that the manuscript is finally done.

Contents

Figures and Tables

Tables

Acknowledgments

This project results from fifteen years of research initiated by Marcus. In 1987, MacKuen's collaboration began with the planning and execution of the 1988 Missouri Election Study. Neuman joined the team in 1994. Over the years, the list of those on whom we have depended has grown considerably. At the significant risk of omitting colleagues and friends who have lent valuable advice and counsel, we would like especially to acknowledge the generous support provided by Joseph Cappella, Jim Gibson, Dennis Chong, Stanley Feldman, Doris Graber, Milton Lodge, Jim Stimson, Diana Mutz, Laura Stoker, Ted Brader, John Cacioppo, John Tryneski, Lance Bennett, Marion Just, Ann Crigler, Jon Krosnick, Joanne Miller, Asher Arian, David Watson, John Zaller, John Petrocik, Herbert Simon, Donald Kinder, Wendy Rahn, David Sears, Donald Green, Robert Abelson, Pam Conover, Bryan Jones, Don Searing, Roger Masters, Lisa D'Ambrosio, Susan Fiske, Jeffrey Gray, Cheryl Rusting, Kevin O'Gorman, Blake Thomas, Tom Nelson, Paul Clark, Chrystalla Ellina, Jennifer Hochschild, and an anonymous reviewer for the University of Chicago Press. We would also like to thank David Bemelmans for his careful and thoughtful copyediting of the manuscript. We remain responsible, of course, for any of the book's errors and insufficiencies. Perhaps the kind and wise commentaries of our colleagues were not threatening enough to capture our distracted attentions.

Coming to Rational Choice

Affective Intelligence is a theory about how emotion and reason interact to produce a thoughtful and attentive citizenry. We focus particularly on the dynamics between feeling and thinking through which busy individuals come to pay some attention to the hubbub of the political world that swirls around them. Most of us are not policy wonks, political activists, or professional politicians. Most of the time, most of us literally do not think about our political options but instead rely on our political habits. Reliance on habit is deeply ingrained in our evolution to humanity.

So when do we think about politics? When our emotions tell us to. We posit that individuals monitor political affairs by responding habitually, and for the most part unthinkingly, to familiar and expected political symbols, that is, by relying on past thought, calculation, and evaluation. But the central claim of our theory is that when citizens encounter a novel or threatening actor, event, or issue on the political horizon, a process of fresh evaluation and political judgment is triggered.

The term *Affective Intelligence*[1] is meant to be provocative, to elicit a sense of the paradoxical, to draw the reader's attention to the possibility that affect and reasoned intelligence need not be seen as incompatible modes of human perception locked in inevitable opposition. Much of the Western tradition in the arts and especially in the sciences emphasizes the tensions and disjunctures between the emotional and the rational. Further, the

---

1. Daniel Goleman (1995) used a similar phrase, *emotional intelligence*, to title his popularly oriented book on emotional life. Goleman's usage, however, is quite different than ours. His theme is emotional self-awareness, that is, being "intelligent" about the role of emotion in human life. He draws on much of the same literature in neuroscience as we do, but directs those insights toward the strategic end of managing emotions in attaining personal and professional goals.

Western tradition tends to derogate the role of affect in the public sphere. Being emotional about politics is generally associated with psychological distraction, distortion, extremity, and unreasonableness. Thus, the conventional view is that our capacity for and willingness to engage in reasoned consideration is too often overwhelmed by emotion to the detriment of sound political judgment. As a result, theories of democratic practice proclaim the importance of protecting against the dangers of human passion and political faction by building up institutions, rules, and procedures—all intended to protect us from our emotional selves.

Drawing on extensive sources in neuroscience, physiology, and experimental psychology, our research has led us to conceptualize affect and reason not as oppositional but as complementary, as two functional mental faculties in a delicate, interactive, highly functional dynamic balance. To idealize rational choice and to vilify the affective domain is to misunderstand how the brain works. The various challenges confronting human judgment require the active engagement and interaction of both mental faculties, just as it does the contributions of the left and right hemispheres of the brain.

Opposition versus Interaction

Because the distinction between opposition and interaction is central to our argument we begin with an extended example from the physiology of sleep to illustrate our premise. Our story starts in France in the late 1970s where biochemists discovered a new stimulant called modafinil. It appeared they stumbled onto something of a wonder drug. It stimulated wakefulness without the well-known side effects and after effects of such traditional stimulants as amphetamines and caffeine. There was no evidence of anxiety from an overstimulated nervous system, no elevated heart rate and blood pressure, no crash after use or day-after hangover, no patterns of drug dependency from repeated use. What was the secret?

The chemistry of modafinil is different. As Stanford psychiatric researcher Dale Edgar puts it (Goode 1998), "Modafinil selectively promotes wakefulness in a way analogous to the way the brain naturally wakes up." Rather than stimulate the entire circulatory system, the drug selectively stimulates cellular activity in the area of the suprachiasmatic nucleus, the brain's circadian clock. The key insight here is a new understanding of the dynamic between sleep and wakefulness in the body and mind. Our traditional understanding is that after we have been awake for a long period of time we become increasingly tired and ultimately succumb to sleep. The notion is inherently one-dimensional and oppositional. There is a state of wakefulness opposed by the need for sleep. But the insight that has emerged from recent neurochemical research is that there are two sets of signals working in a delicate balance, one set of alerting signals and another of sleep pressure as illustrated in figure 1.1.

If the two were simply in zero-sum opposition, a person who experienced more alerting signals would experience less sleep signals. But in fact, the two operate independently and interactively. One can be awake with high sleep and alerting signals present. Or one can be awake with low levels of sleep and alerting signals. And sleep may come not because sleep pressure has increased, but because alerting signals have declined more than sleep pressure. Such distinctions are lost in simple zero-sum notions of opposition.

We will argue in the chapters ahead that the oppositional conception of passion versus reason derives from a similar oversimplification and misunderstanding. As a result, what has remained hidden is an important dynamic by which the human mind uses emotional evaluations of threat and novelty to engage attention and rational calculation (Gibson 1998; Marcus, Wood, and Theiss-Morse 1998).

Why Willie Horton?

In the lore of campaign advertising there are some classic exemplars of powerful emotional communication. One such ad depicted a child

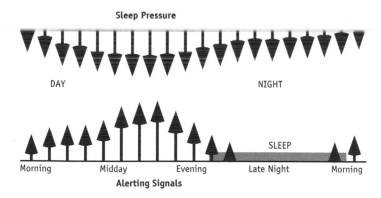

Sleep Pressure

DAY   NIGHT

SLEEP

Morning   Midday   Evening   Late Night   Morning

Alerting Signals

Figure 1.1   Sleep Resulting from Two Dynamic Forces
SOURCE: Adapted from Goode 1998.

picking flower petals under threat of nuclear disaster and was shown only once during the Goldwater–Johnson race in 1964. Because it captured the Goldwater-as-trigger-happy theme so powerfully, albeit indirectly, it has been identified as the most famous campaign ad of modern American political history. Running a close second is the Willie Horton ad in 1988.

Mr. Horton suddenly emerged from obscurity to become something of a household word, like Roe, Miranda, Rodney King, and Monica Lewinsky. In fact, for some citizens dredging through the fading memories of that presidential race, the name Willie Horton may well be recalled before the name of a colleague of ours, currently a professor of political science at Northeastern University in Boston, one Michael Dukakis. How is it possible that an obscure convict would perhaps become better remembered than the Democratic nominee for president? The answer, in our view, is that Willie Horton became narratively and visually a potent threatening symbol. Horton was a black man who had been convicted of first-degree murder. While on furlough from a Massachusetts prison during Dukakis' governorship, he escaped and stabbed a Maryland man and raped his fiancée. For the conservative PAC that sponsored the ad, Horton represented a particularly useful symbol of the threat of crime, of white racial concerns, and of Dukakis' generally "liberal" stance on those issues.

Kathleen Jamieson's careful analysis of the ad and its political context in *Dirty Politics* (1992) makes similar observations. She points out that the campaign ad clearly implied that 268 first-degree murderers were furloughed by Dukakis to rampage, rape, and kidnap. But in fact, no other furloughed first-degree murderer, black or white, either murdered or raped. Of 67,378 furloughs for 11,497 convicts during Dukakis' tenure, 268 did escape, a figure roughly equivalent to that for the Republican predecessor of Dukakis in Massachusetts who had actually established the furlough program. Jamieson (1992, 16) is concerned about this use of deception and distraction in the campaign process and labels the visceral potency of Willie Horton as one of the "psychological quirks that characterize humans." We share her concern that fear makes people and events memorable; but now that the issue is raised, we want to explore whether this aspect of human perception and memory is more than just a quirk. If, following Jamieson, we aspire to raise the level of campaign discourse and meaningfully confront the cycles of public cynicism and political withdrawal, we need to better understand why Willie Horton ads work, why such ads sometimes backfire, and how we can better ground our aspirations for civic virtue in a realistic understanding of human emotion.

The Civic Ideal of Rational Choice

The reasons that scholars and pundits have been uncomfortable about and reluctant to tackle the dynamic interactions of passions and politics represent in themselves a relatively complex puzzle. We will take some time at various points in this book in attempting to unravel these strands as they are important to our thesis. We will not attempt an exhaustive literature review or an intellectual history. We are strategic in our analysis of the fashions and themes of recent social science. Indeed, we will turn to the rational choice school of modern social science as a contrasting case study to help understand the nature of Affective Intelligence.

The rational choice perspective is a widely recognized model of coherent, theoretically grounded, empirically informed, and productive scholarship. In the social sciences and especially within recent political science, the rational choice perspective is a paradigm of paradigm building. We use the word *paradigm* in the traditional Kuhnian sense—a set of theory-based assertions about human behavior matched with a methodological design to test various hypotheses derived from the overarching model (Kuhn 1982). This is normal science. The rational choice literature identifies a set of variables, a set of propositions about their causal linkage, and a set of empirical indicators. There is much debate about what the numbers mean and how the numbers relate to the theory. And, at the margins, some scientists argue about whether the right variables have been included in the model.

From the beginning the rational choice school has been subject to criticism by outsiders who are uncomfortable with its disciplined and narrow focus on human behavior as interest-calculation (Somit and Peterson 1999). Rational choice theorists are familiar with and more than a little weary of this critique, and are apt to testily respond "Yes, yes, we know, but our parsimonious model rewards us with testable hypotheses and the prospect of theoretical refinement." The rational choice response is, in effect, if you have a better model, let's see it. That is the challenge to which we respond. Whether the resulting integration of rational and emotional factors in studying human choice and political behavior is by any chance "a better model" we leave for our critics and successors to decide.

But why is the rational choice model so influential, increasingly exerting its influence beyond neoclassical economics to sociology, political science, and even psychology? Why is the rational choice perspective so self-disciplined in consistently excluding affect-related variables from its models? Is there any history of rational-choice researchers trying to draw insights from the psychology of emotion into their modeling of human choice behavior?

We will develop a response to the first two of these questions in the pages ahead. But the surprising answer to the last of these questions is yes, indeed. Herbert Simon (1967) anticipated many of the arguments of this book in a seminal but somewhat obscure article published in the *Psychological Review* in 1967. Simon is a Noble-prize-winning social scientist of extraordinary stature, one of the founding fathers of the rational choice school, and an active scholar in the fields of economics, political science, administrative science, and psychology. The fact that his article and his continuing references to its central insight in numerous subsequent publications have not attracted much attention provides a clue to the continuing disjuncture between our understanding of rational choice and affective choice.

Simon came to this issue from a very different intellectual starting point. He was interested in what could be learned from comparing human and machine intelligence. One of the most interesting distinctions, of course, is the observation that human thought arises "in intimate association with emotions and feelings which is never entirely lost" (Simon 1967, 29, quoting Neisser 1963). This contrast between human and machine intelligence is a deeply situated theme in artificial intelligence theory and as well a frequently repeated motif in popular culture and science fiction. (One thinks, for example, of the Mr. Spock character and his successors from the *Star Trek* series.) But Simon's seminal paper is in a psychology rather than computer science journal and he quickly sets aside the man–machine comparison to turn to human psychology itself. One reason we cannot model the emotion–cognition link in our software, he argues, is that we have such a limited understanding of how it works in humans. Simon noted in 1967 that theories of human information processing were generally silent on the interaction of cognition and affect. The same was true when he returned to this issue in 1981 at the Seventeenth Carnegie Symposium on Cognition, and still true when he gave a similar address to the American Political Science Association a few years later (Simon 1985; Simon 1982). Each time he notes the lack of theory and posits what he describes as a starting point for a theory of affect–cognition interaction.

The human nervous system, according to Simon, is primarily a serial processor of information. He reviews research on attention, temporal response intervals, and memory to support this contention. Such serial processors require two support mechanisms, first a goal-terminating mechanism (Simon's term is *satisficing*) to redirect attention when goal-oriented behavior has reached a satisfactory state in terms of an initial goal. Second, the human organism living in a demanding environment requires an interrupt mechanism to redirect human attention to higher priority real-time needs, no matter the ongoing effort to secure some antecedent goal. It is this second mechanism that lies at the core of our conception of Affective Intelligence.

Although Simon's own subsequent research focused on satisficing, he did not himself return to elaborate and test the interrupt-mechanism theory. Given his prominence and persuasiveness, it is puzzling why no one else has done so. We contacted Professor Simon and posed the question to him. He noted that despite now seven articles on these themes by his count,[2] there has not been a noticeable reaction in the literature. He speculated that because most of his work has focused in other areas of economics and psychology and because he did not maintain personal relationships with the subset of researchers "in the emotion field," not much of a scholarly response should be expected. For us, that was the key to the puzzle. The interface between emotion and cognition falls outside the paradigm of each field of research.

Looking back on the 1981 Carnegie Symposium on affect and cognition, organizer Susan Fiske, now at the University of Massachusetts, mused that the "affect people in political science were just not interested in the functional impact of emotion on cognition, or on an evolutionary perspective. The cognition people primarily viewed emotions as excess baggage" (Fiske 1998). Yale psychologist Robert Abelson (1996) takes the argument further, noting what he calls the "tyranny of instrumentalism." Western political culture exalts rational, unemotional, means-ends calculation. Researchers look for it first, find it easier to measure and manipulate in experimental settings, and, when asked, subjects naturally justify their behavior in the instrumental terms their culture values.

The inattention to these issues that Simon and others have sought to point out is systematically reinforced and deeply grounded in Western culture and in the dominant research paradigms. Our task is to understand why behavioral research in political science and especially the dominant rational choice perspective is so persistent and successful in setting aside, subordinating, or simply ignoring human emotion. The better we understand why such questions have been ignored thus far, the better we can stimulate attention and much-needed debate concerning what is in effect a theory about theory-building. We will address this issue at length in chapter 2.

2. Simon 1967, 1982, 1985, 1986, 1987, 1984.

Table 1.1 Comparison of Key Elements of the Traditional Paradigm and Affective Intelligence

Traditional Paradigm	Revised Concepts
Static concept of political attentiveness	Dynamic concepts of affect and attention
Thoughtful and habitual behavior blurred in concepts of attitudes and party affiliation	Habitual behavior theoretically central
Opposition between affect and cognition	Interaction between affect and cognition
Instrumental orientation to political behavior	Mix of thoughtless reliance on habit and explicit calculation of interest
Idealized notion of citizenship	Political ideals and institutions informed by realism about psychological dynamics
All political issues equivalent	Issue type a variable
Survey research dominates	Multimethod
Attentiveness assumed	Attentiveness a variable
Self-interest assumed	Self-interest a variable

A summary of how modeling Affective Intelligence points research in new and difference directions is presented in table 1.1.

A central problematic is to better understand the interactions between momentary psychological states and accumulated psychological traits that give individual citizens their unique political personality. We know that Republican and Democratic voters (traits, habits) sitting next to each other watching a presidential campaign debate may come away with very different emotions and impressions (states) concerning who won and indeed what the debate was really about. We know that an image or phrase in a campaign commercial or political speech can powerfully alert voters to pay more attention to a candidate (state) and over time change their political activism or their standing vote choices (trait). We seek to understand how that dynamic process works.

A Brief Summary of the Theory of Affective Intelligence— The Dual Emotional Systems of Disposition and Surveillance

Our research leads us to conceptualize affect and reason as two complementary mental states in a delicate, interactive, highly functional dynamic balance. It is common parlance to describe an individual confronting something new, say a new candidate or policy issue, as first thinking about the choice (cognition) and second coming to an emotional judgment (affect). Similarly, it is a long-standing presumption associated with the founding research of William James that, even when dealing with the familiar and comfortable, recognition must precede emotional reaction (James 1894). This think-first-and-feel-second ordering turns out to be a central issue of some controversy in the psychological literature on emotion.[3] Psychologist Robert Zajonc (1980) was the first to openly challenge this ordering, arguing that affective reactions often arise before conscious—that is to say, cognitive—awareness. We agree and argue that the ordering actually works the other way around: affective systems manage both our response to novelty or threat and our reliance on established habits. More importantly, our work suggests that in addition to managing our *emotional* reactions to things that are novel, threatening, and familiar, affect also influences when and how we *think* about such things.

We begin by focusing on two systems associated with the brain's limbic region, the disposition and the surveillance systems, which are discussed more fully in chapter 4. These two brain systems manage "reinforcers," that is, stimuli that people learn to associate with either good or bad consequences and thus guide (often unconsciously) strategic choices about behavior. The most important point to make about these dual system functions is that they are mutually engaged in governing both thought and behavior. Although they often function below the level of consciousness, they are distinct information processing systems in their own right.

The Disposition System

The most commonly understood system of the limbic region governs behavior by monitoring primarily positive reinforcers and establishing dispositions. Strategic action, behavior designed to achieve a purpose, requires an ongoing evaluation. That is, it demands an assessment of the effort, the prospects of success, the current stock of physical and psychic resources, and feedback on the success and failure of the sequence of actions. For humans, these strategic considerations are only occasionally governed by conscious calculation. More often, these executive functions are done subconsciously.

Importantly, the emotions of the disposition system provide precisely this guidance. When our feelings are focused on ourselves, changes in mood from gloomy to enthusiastic tell us that we are bursting with confidence, energy, and eagerness. Alternatively, when our mood changes in the direction of depression, we conclude that we are exhausted and beaten.

---

3. As Sniderman observes, "Discussions of affect and cognition seem to excite a cat-and-dog fight over ontological priority" (Sniderman, Brody, and Tetlock 1991, 262).

Shifts in the direction of increased elation strengthen the motivation to expend effort and strengthen confidence in a successful outcome. Shifts in the direction of increased depression weaken the motivation to expend effort and undermine confidence that the outcome will prove successful. Accordingly, this emotional calculus is translated into a summary disposition toward the action.

The constellation of dispositions attached to previous experiences governs people's behavioral repertoires. People learn habits most profitably to get through their everyday lives and to deal with ordinary recurring situations. As they develop their skills, these repertoires become increasingly well stocked to deal appropriately with more complex and differentiated circumstances. The disposition system relies on emotional assessment to control the execution of habits: we sustain those habits about which we feel enthusiastic and we abandon those that cause us despair.

In the course of growing up we learn to walk without thinking. Some of us learn to dance, swing a tennis racket, and throw a baseball. Similarly, we learn to pick out our clothes, to order in a restaurant, and to move about a bookstore without having to think too hard about how to actually execute such routine tasks. And in politics, we learn which newspapers, which ideas, and which political loyalties will reward and which ones will not. So, it is not surprising that empirical work shows that these dispositions are powerful predictors of the willingness to engage in previously learned actions.

The Surveillance System

Life, however, is full of surprises and two kinds of surprises are crucial. As we confront the world we come across new and unpredictable people and circumstances. And, at various times, there are people and circumstances that may be threatening. The disposition system provides people with an understanding, an emotional report card, about actions that are already in their repertoire of habits and learned behaviors. The second system, the surveillance system, acts to scan the environment for novelty and sudden intrusion of threat. It serves to warn us when we cannot rely on past learning to handle what now confronts us and to warn us that some things and some people are powerful and dangerous. This system uses emotion to signal the consequences of its ongoing analyses. It generates moods of calmness, on the one hand, and anxiety, on the other. Here we focus on its attentional properties.

Identifying two systems in the limbic region of the brain suggests that people rely on their feelings to assess how well they are doing, and they rely on their feelings to scan for signs of threat and uncertainty. What is interesting about this second emotional system is that the onset of increased anxiety stops ongoing activity and orients attention to the threatening appearance so that learning can take place. This turns out to be a particularly important dynamic process for understanding political judgment.

The surveillance system, like the disposition system, is a learning system. It is an active information processing, but not conscious, system. It produces behavioral and affective responses, not conscious thoughts (though, as this system is linked to "higher" conscious systems, it will provoke thinking). This system cycles continually to compare sensory information about the world with expectations obtained from the behavioral system. So long as the comparison shows no discrepancy between expectation and reality, the system generates a sense of calm and remains unobtrusive. When the system detects unexpected or threatening stimuli, however, it evokes increasing anxiety, it interrupts ongoing activity, and it shifts attention away from the previous focus and toward the intrusive stimuli.

The Organization of the Argument

Chapter 2 provides the context for our analysis by tracing the evolution of the intellectual polarity between passion and reason in the Western tradition. We also briefly review how these tensions have been incorporated in current research in political science. The persistence and richness of this polarized conception strike us as remarkable.

Chapters 3 and 4 turn to the neuroscience of the brain in an effort to develop testable models of the dual emotional systems of surveillance and disposition and their interaction with political judgment. As this may be new terrain for many readers, we take some time at this point to carefully develop the linkages between physiology, psychology, and political thought in practice.

In chapters 5 and 6 we lay out the accumulated research findings in the political science tradition—primarily survey research but also some experiments and aggregate time series to test the model and the conditions under which it is operative.

The final chapter draws the strands together and sets forth an agenda for further research given our collection of preliminary conclusions and, as yet, unsolved mysteries.

Human Affect in the Western Tradition

For thousands of years in the Western world, we have believed that emotion is an unpredictable response to life's events, incompatible with intelligent judgment.

—Richard S. and Beatrice N. Lazarus, *Passion and Reason: Making Sense of Our Emotions*

The nature, causes and consequences of the emotions are among the least well understood aspects of human behavior.

—Jon Elster, *Nuts and Bolts for the Social Sciences*

To be passionate about politics [is] to be some kind of nut.

—Ira Roseman, Robert P. Abelson, and Michael F. Ewing, "Emotions and Political Cognition: Emotional Appeals in Political Communication"

The ancient Greek philosopher Anaxagoras, advisor to Pericles, suddenly finds himself in a modern American academic library. He sits down to read up on what humankind has learned about democratic politics in the two and a half millennia since his day. He is surprised and a bit disappointed to discover that the analysis and political rhetoric sound strikingly familiar. It is not that we haven't learned a few things. The technologies are new and amazing. Economics has come a long way. But the basic conceptions of citizen deliberation, political dialogue, and democratic participation have survived in surprisingly familiar form. His doctrine of *Nous*, the concept of the rational mind that inspired Plato and Aristotle and became the cornerstone of Stoicism, the ideal of rational control over emotional impulses, would also influence Roman philosophy, medieval Christianity, and the Puritans, among others, in American political culture.

That is a pretty long run for a fundamental idea. Indeed, it has become so deeply embedded and widely accepted that it is rarely challenged. We intuitively sense the tension between the emotional demands of our bodies and the socialized values of our "rational" minds. We deal with our successes and failures in what we often interpret as a battle of mind versus body. The primacy of rationality may be so well accepted that it appears to us in Western culture as axiomatic. But Anaxagoras would do well to read a little further in modern physiology and neuroscience to discover the beginnings of a new understanding. Increasingly in recent years, research on the functioning of the brain rejects these deeply ingrained notions and concludes that they dramatically distort our understanding of how thinking and feeling really interact (Damasio 1994; Gray 1987b; LeDoux 1996).

As we begin to outline a theory of Affective Intelligence, we will take a brief look at the extraordinary perseverence of fundamental beliefs about passion and politics throughout the evolution of Western thinking. We will identify a number of recurring themes in philosophy and literature that manifest the tension between emotion and rational thought and briefly demonstrate the continuing resonance and influence of these ideas in modern political science research.

The Paradox of the Present

It is easy to make fun of primitive ideas and misconceptions of our forebears. We remark with curiosity about the fervent belief in a flat earth, in the power of magic spells, and in the existence of various ethers and spirits. Science and human understanding have come a long way. But they had already come a long way in the nineteenth century when bloodletting was still common and the science of phrenology, based on the belief that bumps on the skull revealed detailed information about underlying brain functions, was widely popular. Bloodletting, the medical practice of extracting blood to purge the body of excessive bad "humors," had been practiced for centuries. Although today it is demonstrably detrimental to the health of already weakened patients, to medical science of earlier days it made intuitive sense. Indeed, George Washington was probably killed by the excessive bloodletting he received after coming down with fever following a rainy ride. Not all patients so treated died. It was thought necessary that they get worse before they get better. Unfortunately, it was also believed that the more serious the health problem, the greater the need for even more heroic bloodletting.

Is it possible that similar misconceptions continue to persist in present-day medical, political, social, and economic practices? Of course they do. But by definition, they do not appear that way to our modern eye. That is the paradox of the present. Our sense of the world around us is itself socially constructed. As Walter Lippmann put it, it is not that we see and then understand; we understand first, and then see. So our present inquiry is more than an instructive digression. We need to better understand the roots of Western conceptions of affect and intelligence to be able to take advantage of the latest advances of understanding in neuroscience.

The Culturally Embedded Concepts of Affect and Intelligence

The word *emotion* is derived from the Latin *e* and *movere*, meaning to set in motion, to motivate, or to be in a state of agitation or perturbation. So the idea of arousal and stimulation are reflected in the etymology of "emotion." But more importantly, for most of the common era the term typically used to identify the political impact of affect has been *passion*, derived from the Latin *pati*, meaning to suffer or endure, and related to the Greek *pathos*, or suffering. These roots are reflected in such modern English words as *passive, patient, sympathy, empathy,* and *pathetic*. It might seem odd that these two central root words have contrasting meanings of activity and passivity. But the two reflect the fundamental tension between affect and intelligence that is a central theme in Western cultural heritage. To be passionate is to be gripped, seized, or possessed by primordial forces beyond one's rational control. Thus it is hard to imagine thoughtful actions resulting from a passionate state. We see this understanding reflected in the special mitigating and aggravating circumstances of "crimes of passion" that the legal system invokes for juries to assess in weighing such crimes.

Western literature and poetry resonate with numerous variations on passion as madness or intoxication. The character Acrasia in Edmund Spenser's (1989 [1590]) *Faerie Queene* was the personification of uncontrolled passion that transformed her captive lovers into monstrous shapes. Spenser's choice of character names was no doubt playing off the Greek *akrasia*, lack of self-control. The term *acracy* for out of control or out of balance came into use later in medieval medicine. Madness itself was defined by medieval physicians as an imbalance of the four elements of fire, air, water, and earth in the body's humors. The misunderstandings of human physiology and biochemistry in Hippocrates and Galen were passed down to guide medical practice for sixty generations virtually without challenge or refinement. Treatments included magic spells, primitive medications, and dietary regimes. A medical treatment introduced by Asclepiades in the first century prescribed long baths and copious wine and was revived periodically in various forms as late as the eighteenth century in response, we would assume, to the understandable enthusiasm of many generations of patients. At least the Greeks had identified the brain as the physiological source of mental functioning. The Mesopotamians were convinced that the liver was the seat of the soul and produced liver-shaped religious totems.

Enduring Oppositions

One enduring principle throughout this cultural progression of evolving scientific understanding was the ideal of keeping emotions "under control."

Controlling Emotion

Psychologist Carroll Izard's seminal *The Face of Emotion* (1972) builds its argument in part on an historical analysis. He traces two themes that have continued from the time of the Greeks, the denial of the importance of emotion and culturally reinforced norms of emotional control. Izard finds that in the celebration of the ideal of human rationality from the Greeks to the modern Age of Reason, humankind has unintentionally and systematically distorted the meaning and significance of human emotion. He calls this the "rational man ideology," a collection of beliefs and values codified in socialization practice and passed on from generation to generation. It represents, he argues, a fundamental misconception of potentially devastating consequence.

> These socialization practices emphasize the importance of personal characteristics, skills, concepts and purposes mistakenly thought to be pure functions of intelligence or cognition. They de-emphasize or deny any important function to the emotions. In general, psychologists and non-psychologists alike view the emotions as transient and troublesome states serving no really important purpose. . . . The rational man ideology has succeeded in hiding man from his full nature. (Izard 1972, 396)

Izard takes particular interest in cultural practices that attempt to manipulate conscious control of the striate muscle system as a means of emotional control—a practice reflected in such admonitions as "keep a stiff upper lip" and "keep your chin up." Diverse religious beliefs and socialization practices worldwide assert that willpower combined with focused control of the voluntary muscles is the key to emotional maturity, which indicates how widespread, if not universal, such an outlook is. These ideas are sustained today in serious therapeutic approaches to mental illness (Pesso 1969; Pesso and Crandell 1990). A central idea throughout is opposition—the raging emotions misdirecting, distracting, and misleading the mind that if only left alone could more properly make sound decisions. Not surprisingly, Western society developed ideals that emphasize the need for sustained willpower to focus attention on thoughtful consideration of valued goals and for training to overpower the distractions of emotion.

Emotion and Institutions of Constraint

Another enduring theme is that the power of emotion is perhaps most obvious and dangerous when it is public. Echoing the medieval skepticism about unrestrained human nature, emphasis is placed on the central importance of norms and institutions. This is a view not just held by conservatives, but is also resonant within liberal perspectives (Bessette 1994; Holmes 1995).

Le Bon's 1896 classic *The Crowd*, for example, founds its argument on the distinction between an unorganized and dangerously primordial crowd and the organized and norm-managed collectivities represented by modern institutions. The character of the crowd, Le Bon asserted, is "impulsiveness, irritability, incapacity to reason, the absence of judgment and the critical spirit, the exaggeration of the sentiments . . . —which are almost always observed in beings belonging to inferior forms of evolution—in women, savages, and children, for instance" (Le Bon 1986 [1896], 35–36). Le Bon's view, although characteristic of his time, reflect longstanding skepticism about pure democracy and the need for the collective constraints and cushioning effects of representative institutions. These are core elements of the theory of representative democracy. To Madison in *Federalist* 10, the evil of faction was defined as a group of citizens united by "common impulse of passion."

> The latent causes of faction are thus sown in the nature of man . . . human passions have in turn divided mankind into parties, inflamed them with mutual animosity and rendered them much more disposed to vex and oppress each other than to cooperate for their common good. So strong is this propensity of mankind to fall into mutual animosities that where no substantial occasion presents itself the most frivolous and fanciful distinctions have been sufficient to kindle their unfriendly passions and excite their most violent conflicts. (Madison, Hamilton, and Jay 1961 [1787], 58–59)

The cure for the human vice of faction and the zeal to which it is attached, Madison avers, is representative democracy and well-constructed union.

The Savage and the Civilized Citizen

In understanding the social contract between the modern citizen and the modern state, we continue to draw on the philosophical underpinnings of Hobbes, Locke, and Rousseau. Although our philosophical forebears each had a different conception of life before the development of civilization, they recognized that social and political institutions evolved slowly and unevenly. But the notion of life in the wild without enforceable rules or central authority remains powerfully symbolic. In Hobbes' (1968 [1651]) classic description of that life,

> [t]here is no place for industry; because the fruit thereof is uncertain: consequently no culture of the earth, no navigation, nor use of the commodities that may be imported by sea; no commodious building, no instruments of moving and removing such things as require much force; no knowledge of the face of the earth; no accounting of time, no art; no letters; no society and which is worst of all, continual fear and danger of violent death; and the life of man solitary, poor, nasty, brutish and short. (Hobbes 1968 [1651], 82)

What makes this particularly relevant to our present inquiry is the notion of the state of nature evolving into the modern political state. We come to understand when the noises of the jungle must be constantly monitored for signs of threat and danger. We understand that those early humans who exhibited particularly sensitive skills at surveillance and the quick replacement of habitual behavior with attentive caution were more likely to survive and reinforce such behavioral patterns in the gene pool.

In responding to the symbolic and political and economic behavior of the king or the president in succeeding years, the modern citizens continue to draw on their evolutionary and animal roots in balancing attention among the many stimuli that might call for attention and rational calculation.[1]

---

1. We have made repeated reference in these pages to the Western tradition of thought that tends to polarize emotion and cognition, as if they were locked in zero-sum opposition. While we wish to stress the prominence of that strain of thought, we do not mean to exaggerate its influence in intellectual history to the exclusion of enlightening and interesting exceptions. One thinks of Jewish mysticism, elements of Christian theology and liturgy, and cultural romanticism in the nineteenth century, in each of which there is a celebration of the unique linkages between human emotion and cognition. Also, perhaps we would do well to acknowledge the influential conservative tradition characterized by Burke and Hume among many others who counseled reliance on emotionally grounded and historically evolved traditions in the calculation of political choice.

Models of Political Emotion

How might we make sense of this enduring thematic common to political philosophy, myth, and literature? In our discussion of the paradox of the present, we noted how easily we reject as naïve our ancestors' understanding of the nature of the individual and our collective institutions. A flat earth and a geocentric universe make perfect sense to the unaided eye and dominated human understanding for millennia. The polar opposition of passion and reason makes similar intuitive sense. But it may well take several generations before research now on the frontiers of neuroscience becomes part of the fundamental norms and practices of our collective culture.

Before proceeding with that aim, we take stock and attempt to outline the underlying cultural causes for the opposition of passion and reason so we might explicitly compare older and newer models in experimental, field, and survey research.

Four Underlying Pathologies

The mythologized battle between passion and reason in the Western tradition is an inventory of human psychopathology. As it was fashionable from the seventeenth to the early-twentieth centuries to diagnose illness in women and children as some form of predictable hyperemotionality or hysteria, it remains fashionable today to characterize the subtle dynamics between different neurological systems in pathological terms. So the modern equivalent of a diagnosis of hysterical illness is the presumption that if the amygdala communicates with the cerebrum, bad things will happen. Characterized in this way, it sounds like a pretty primitive conceptualization of human psychology, which is indeed what we hope to show. But first let us analyze the presumed mechanisms of pathology that have developed in the course of the Western tradition.

THE DISPLACEMENT PATHOLOGY

The principal argument here is that emotionally charged inputs overstimulate the individual, distort judgment, and inhibit or displace reason and evaluation. Reasoning requires calm deliberation. Affect leads to impulsiveness and inconsiderate judgment, perhaps something like hysteria.

Part of the mechanism presumed to be at work in this case is extremeness and imbalance. It is a common theme in the literature, the subtle equation of emotional input with extreme or overpowering emotional input. The metaphors tend to involve heat, overheating, boiling. One's blood boils; one is in the heat of passion; one blows one's top; one is subject to hot cognition. With electricity came other metaphors—short-circuiting and blowing one's fuse.

Another component of this hypothesized pathology is hurried judgment, the absence of a calm consideration of alternatives. The common cultural solutions of having a cooling-off period, of counting to ten, of sleeping on it, and the like all speak to this element. Then there is the presumed zero-sum relationship between affect and reason. The brain has limited capacity. Emotionality takes up capacity and suppresses or displaces cognitive functioning.

A final element is the passivity of the individual in response to emotional stimuli. We don't consider emotional stimuli, we are in their grip; we are taken over by, or consumed by them. It is a one-way causal linkage between passion and reason.

THE DISTRACTION PATHOLOGY

The presumption here is that emotional symbols distract the mind from weighing relevant evidence and draw attention to irrelevant matters. Thus we are concerned in politics that emotional appeals draw attention to personal qualities rather than more meaningful political issues.

Consider a debate or discussion among individuals in search of a collective decision. Participants ideally put forward their reasoned assessment of alternatives, their view of likely consequences, their sense of critical values at stake. A visceral approach, as the stereotype would have it, appeals to the heart rather than the head, to hot buttons (heat again), to vague symbols.

The term *ad hominem* captures this presumption. The phrase refers to the logical fallacy in rhetoric when one argues "against the man," attacking the individual or individual characteristics rather than establishing pertinent fact.

THE INTRANSIGENCE PATHOLOGY

An emotionally charged stimulus is presumed to lead to such an extremity of belief that the person is unwilling to compromise or to adjust their belief in the light of new information.

Several mechanisms are seen to contribute to this phenomenon. One is that the intensity of belief and feeling preclude attentiveness to the arguments of the "other side." In the political world this is associated with conceptions of partisanship, fragmentation and polarization, and to identity politics.

Another is the notion that fixation on a particular issue becomes so intense that it precludes attention to other issues, thus resulting in single-issue politics. Research on the psychology of ideology and authoritarianism is also relevant here. The strength of the organizing schema is so strong that all incoming information is distorted to fit the schema and, of course, compromise is characterized as selling out, lack of will, weakness, and lack of principle.

THE SELF-ABSORPTION PATHOLOGY

It is presumed that individuals in a state of anxiousness and emotional arousal will rely heavily on instincts for base self-interest and primordial self-preservation and will emphasize these interests of the self over collective or sociotropic interests when evaluating political alternatives.

This may be the least well developed of the four hypotheses. Basically it equates emotionality with desperation. The calm generosity of the well endowed who can afford to compromise when the spirit strikes them is contrasted with the anxiety of the critically impoverished. It harks back to Plato's observation that the thirsty man thinks of nothing but to quench his thirst. Emotionality is associated with basic issues of survival, the lowest level of Maslow's (1954) hierarchy of needs. Altruism is the prerogative of only those who enjoy abundance.

In reflecting on these four possible pathologies, several themes can be seen to recur, each of which will be addressed again in the pages ahead. One such theme is the conflation of emotion and extreme emotion. This is especially evident in displacement pathology but is present in different ways in each of the others. Extreme levels of any stimulus or even any habitual behavior can have pathological effects. It is important, however, to make sure our language and our analytic approach allow us to distinguish the phenomenon from its possible level of intensity.

A second common theme is that there is a one-way causal influence from emotion to cognition. But much of the advances in neuroscience in recent years emphasizes the complexity and multidirectionality of synaptic communication within the brain, for example, the co-orientation of left and right hemispheres. As our understanding of neurophysiology deepens, we may be able to make more sense of how dynamic and complex these interactions between neural systems actually are. The one-way conception is also reflected in the notion of cognition as the passive and at times helpless recipient of emotional stimuli.

A third common thematic is some level of confusion between state and trait, that is, between temporary and enduring phenomena. Most conceptions of an emotional state recognize that it is transitory, the immediate response to an emotional stimulus—thus such notions as temporary insanity. What is missing from the hypotheses is clear and testable mechanisms that relate an immediate psychological state to longer term and enduring patterns of belief and cognition.[2]

Current Research on Political Choice

In reading the modern literature of political science and political communication, we find a strong filtrate of the traditional Western polarization of emotion and cognition. Their presumed opposition permeates the normative conceptions of democratic process and citizenship, the measurement of political attitudes and behavior, and even the spatial modeling of rational political choice. We will return to these issues in the final chapter, but briefly highlight two examples here before turning to the underlying neuroscience of thinking and feeling. The first is the debate about citizen competence, the second is the spatial modeling of rational choice, both closely associated with the National Election Study series that we will explore in chapters 5 and 6.

The Debate Over Citizen Competence and the Notion of the Normal Vote

For the last half century, the American National Election Studies initiated originally at the University of Michigan and now managed by an interuniversity board have become the gold standard in the empirical study of the dynamics between voters, issues, and candidates. One central and enduring controversy about how citizens respond to and understand issues and candidates has focused on the levels of information and sophistication possessed by the typical voter. Philip Converse (1964) of the University of Michigan became a principal player and a bit of a scholarly lightning rod as the debate over citizen competence heightened. This literature is of special importance to us because it deals with political attentiveness, information processing, and voting calculus. The notion of habitual behavior is captured in the concept of the "normal vote," which posits a standing vote decision based on party affiliation and a dynamic process of possible party defection and rational calculation based on the short-term forces of candidate qualities and the current issue agenda.

2. Again, we do not wish to overclaim or weaken our case by reliance on a straw man. We identify here a set of recurring themes of pathology and opposition. In our view they accurately reflect a very influential strain of Western thought. Of course, many scholars and philosophers over the years have recognized the awkwardness of the simplifying opposition and struggled both to understand it and transcend it. Perhaps the most thoughtful effort to explore the possibility of cooperation between emotion and reason are Hume's A *Treatise on Human Nature* (Hume 1739–40) and Adam Smith's *The Theory of Moral Sentiments* (Smith 1959). These, and other views, are explored in Marcus forthcoming.

Emotion plays two roles in the normal vote model. First, it is the foundation of the "long-term" forces, namely, the partisan affiliations formed early in life that result in stable cues for contemporary and future use. Emotion, as used here, seems an example of the intransigence pathology. The stronger the partisan loyalty, the more committed are voters to their historical attachments and the less they are willing to consider alternatives. Second, emotion serves as the basis of the "short-term" forces. Less partisan and ironically generally less well-informed voters represent a swing vote, picking up on short-term candidate cues and current events. In this case, emotion is modeled as a contemporary, though cursory, reaction to current political symbols and personalities rather than ideologically grounded issue positions. Short-term forces, thus depicted, represent an example of the displacement pathology—emotions serve as an alternative to judgment, if by judgment we mean a careful attentive and considered comparison of the available choices.

The debate over citizen competence drew in large measure from Converse's disappointment at the initial discovery of a large number of voters who employed an unsophisticated and apolitical nature-of-the-times calculation in comparing Eisenhower and Stevenson as presidential candidates in 1956. "The economy is healthy, there is no foreign policy crisis, and we seem to have successfully extricated ourselves from Korea," this hypothetical voter calculated. "I'll stick with Ike." But what about issue calculations, the evaluations of conservative and liberal ideologies? A small army of survey researchers adjusted and reinterpreted estimates of measurement error, inter-item correlations, and open-ended utterances in an attempt to salvage the casually attentive voter from disparagement as incompetent (Ferejohn and Kuklinski 1990; Neuman 1986). But in our view the original finding need not be characterized as contrary to democratic theory or as a challenge to the premise of citizen competence. Searching the political horizon for signs of novelty or threat, concluding they are absent, and relying on the status quo might be seen as a most reasonable calculation for a voter in 1956. The normal vote model is dynamic at the level of collective decision, but it lacks a parallel microlevel theory of voter psychology, attentiveness, and issue calculus. The brouhaha over citizen competence may be in part a victim of an unexamined legacy of polarized concepts of emotion and reason.

Rational Choice Modeling—Emotion as an Endogenous Variable

Another predominant perspective, as we have noted, is spatial and rational choice modeling of electoral behavior. Here a resolution to the persisting nuisance of human affect is to simply define it as endogenous. We have puzzled over why the rational choice model is so influential, increasingly exerting its influence beyond neoclassical economics to sociology, political science, and even psychology. We wonder why the rational choice perspective is so self-disciplined in consistently excluding affect-related variables from its models. Four patterns are evident in this growing component of modern rational choice literature, each resonating in its own way with the Western tradition of opposing rationality and emotions.

THEORETICAL PARSIMONY

The argument here is that rational-choice style spatial models work pretty well. Available data generally support the thesis of utility maximization. If it ain't broke, why complicate things unnecessarily? In the introduction to his text *Public Choice*, for example, economist Dennis Mueller (1979, 5) reviews the central tenets of the rational choice perspective and notes:

> To many political scientists the public choice models seem but a naive caricature of political behavior. The public choice theorist's answer to these criticisms is the same as the answer economists have given to the same criticisms as they have been raised against their "naïve" models of economic behavior down through the years. The use of the simplified models of political behavior is justified so long as they outperform the competitors in explaining political behavior.

Our interest focuses on the debate over possible refinement. Defenders of the faith tend to assert that attempting to add additional variables to account for institutions—like values and especially emotional states—muddies the water and actually reduces the scientific value of the modeling.

Dennis Chong (1996), in a discussion of rational choice critics, asserts that rational choice theory cannot be set aside because of disconfirming facts, it can only be supplanted by a superior theory, which thus far, at least in his view, the critics lack. Or in Elster's (1986, 27) more direct summation of this viewpoint, "you can't beat something with nothing."

Fiorina (1996), for example, argues that rational choicers should stick to their knitting, focusing on that subset of issues their tools are designed to address and avoiding such things as political psychology where they have, as he puts it, no comparative advantage.

MEASUREMENT DIFFICULTIES

Leave affect to the poets, the argument goes, they don't have to concern themselves with the replicable measurement of emotion and the assessment of its potential correlation with behavior. Economists traditionally are suspicious of individual explanations for personal behavior. Most of us are socialized to invent explanations for our behavior *post hoc* (Elster 1993, 14). Why waste time trying to make sense of these rationalizations when we can focus on the behavior itself, or in Paul Samuelson's now famous choice of words, on "revealed preferences" (Sen 1973). Economists take seriously the aphorism "Pay attention to what I say, not what I do" in reverse, and for the obvious reasons.

Economists have no tools for investigating the origins of the utility functions they assess, and no taste for such an inquiry (Simon 1987). Such functions are givens, the products of a psychological black box. In part it contrasts the rational choicer's interest in outcome contrasted with the psychologist's fascination with process (Hogarth and Reder 1987, 10).

The rational choice tradition in political science emphasizes legislative and voting behavior rather than public opinion research (Chong 1996, 44). It is a natural outgrowth of its roots in economic modeling and not without a legitimate rationale, but this methodological rejection of the susceptibility of attitude, opinion, and affect to precise measurement reinforces the theoretical aversion.

COLLECTIVE SIGNAL VERSUS IDIOSYNCRATIC NOISE

Although affect may be immensely important in individual political behavior, the argument goes, it tends to be idiosyncratic. And the influences of idiosyncratic affect cancel each other out at the collective level. They are perhaps best ignored as simply behavioral noise.

Cornell economist Richard Thaler (1991, 97) put it most succinctly and grandly: "In the aggregate, errors will cancel." It is grandly put because such language implies that if humans behave contrary to the theories of economists, they behave in error. But there is more to the argument.

Kenneth Arrow (1987, 201) in a fascinating but obscure paper develops the argument that although rationality is usually presented and understood as an individual-level phenomenon, it really isn't. "Rationality is not a property of the individual alone, although it is usually presented that way. Rather, it gathers not only its force but also its very meaning from the social context which it is imbedded." He proceeds to note that assumptions of rationality at the individual level are seldom justified in real world conditions, especially concerning the information gathering and processing expected of the consumer in the marketplace. But in the aggregate, in the behavior of the marketplace as a whole, rational and self-interest calculations are demonstrable and consistent. Perhaps it ultimately reduces to the primordial notion that affect is the evil seductress, constantly distracting attention, distorting perception, and tugging the individual away from calm and rational deliberation.

EPHEMERAL VERSUS ENDURING EFFECTS

Emotions, we are told, are ephemeral, even volatile. Self-interests endure. Why devote energy to building models of chimera when we have alternative variables that are more clearly defined and less variant over time? The edifice of economic science is built on a solid foundation of primary concepts, perhaps the most central of which is the notion of clearly ordered and semipermanent human preference functions. In a classic review of the evolution of decision and management science, for example, James March (1978) walks his readers through the central assumptions of the field. He works his way up to choice behavior and pauses to note how important "stable preferences" are to the theory. He acknowledges that preferences do vary over time and focuses attention on the need to study behavior over relatively short time periods, because unstable preferences make the math virtually intractable.

Chicago economist Gary Becker (1976, 5) makes the point even more directly. "The assumption of stable preferences provides a stable foundation for generating predictions about responses to various changes and prevents the analyst from succumbing to the temptation of simply postulating the required shift in preferences to 'explain' all apparent contradictions to his predictions." This is experience speaking. One can appreciate how shrewd theorists carefully postulate around some of the more volatile aspects of the human condition. But, as we argue at some length in the pages ahead, such tactics have costs.

Our approach to this issue is to draw on a fundamental distinction in psychology—the difference between a psychological state and a psychological trait. Humans exhibit both states and traits and there are systematic linkage structures connecting them. A careful distinction between them allows each a role in theory development. A long tradition of research in experimental psychology attempts to build extensible and broadly applicable models of real-world human behavior based on careful observations of fleeting choices and instant reactions in the laboratory. Some of the most promising new work in political communications focusing on framing and priming effects deals with state–trait interactions of this sort (Ansolabehere and Iyengar 1995; Cappella and Jamieson 1997; Iyengar and Kinder 1987). Our colleagues in economics have shown wisdom in the selection and ordering of the variables they study. We hope to learn from their accomplishments. But, in the long run, it may not be necessary to rule out affect variables on grounds of intractable volatility.

Affect as a Component of Modern Behavioral Research

The good news from our point of view is that as some rational choice models have been gaining attention by setting aside the complexity of emotional dynamics, other approaches that draw attention systematically to emotional–cognitive dynamics have been gaining ground as well. Affect as the end state of cognitive processes, for example, is central to the online model of political judgment (Lodge, McGraw, and Stroh 1989). It is also well represented in psychology where emotion is treated as an "affective tag" storing evaluative assessments (Fiske and Pavelchak 1985), as a crucial element in schema theory (Hastie and Park 1986), and as a summary evaluation in voter evaluation processes (Rahn et al. 1990).

Similarly political communication, especially in the area of campaign politics, also has devoted increasing attention to affective dynamics, though it is "negative emotion" that is thought here to be important as a catalyst for new positions rather than simply an anchor of earlier values, interests, or attitudes (Jamieson 1992). Emotion in this context is not passive but a potent, volatile, instigator of action.

On the one hand, emotion seems to give us summary evaluations that persist to dominate our decisions irrespective of contemporary considerations (emotion as disposition). On the other hand, emotion seems to be necessary to capture our attention and make us capable of changing our views (emotion as momentary response to dramatic appeals, events, or circumstance).

As different as these conceptions are, they nonetheless share an important common presumption in their treatment of emotion. Two conceptions of evaluation are in play. In the first, evaluation is conceived as a single summary dimension (liking versus disliking). The second conception of evaluation is that emotional reactions result from a unitary cognitive process. Various discrete model theorists posit a number of cognitive discriminations that when applied yield the various discrete moods (Davies 1980; Ekman 1982; Ekman 1992; Izard 1977; Izard 1992; Roseman 1979, 1984, 1991). There is as yet little agreement among discrete, or attribution, theorists either as to the underlying cognitive distinctions (or attributions) or as to the number of discrete emotions (Elster 1999). In any case, emotion is often understood as a single summary evaluation, as an end-state of prior evaluative processes that are cognitive in nature.

We are active readers of this growing literature and agree that evaluation is central to the influence of emotion. However, we will argue that emotion is neither a single evaluative process nor necessarily an automated summary of preferences. Rather, we argue that emotional evaluations are at least two-fold with each devoted to a strategic purpose: a surveillance task and a habit-enabling task. As a result, emotion, rather than being a single process or a single dimension of evaluation, is constituted by multiple evaluative processes and multiple dimensions of emotional appraisal. We are not the first to suggest this division of affect into multiple channels. Abelson and his colleagues (1982), in their analysis of the original measures of the emotions evoked by presidential candidates, were surprised to find that their analyses supported neither the single dimension view of evaluation nor the discrete model differentiation of emotion. And Roger Masters and Denis Sullivan have consistently found in their research, and have argued for, a differentiation between multiple dimensions of emotional response to politicians (Sullivan and Masters 1988). We examine the history of valence and discrete approaches to emotion in greater detail in appendix A.

The new energy in research on affective dynamics in the psychology of political judgment encourages us. Some of this work seems to build theory very much within the Western tradition that sets up emotion and cognition as polar oppposites, other research challenges that premise. The key to sorting this out, in our view, lies in new findings and insights about brain physiology in neuroscience.

Chapter 3

Drawing from the Neurosciences

In this chapter we will add another potent ingredient to the brew—some recent discoveries in neuroscience that demonstrate how emotion is not the result of a single psychological process but rather the engagement of two physiological subsystems or pathways in the brain. There is an important linkage between the two emotional systems, but they operate with demonstrable independence. By modeling emotion as two parallel subsystems, each independently evaluating sensory input, we come to better understand how these dual affective systems interact with thinking even before conscious perception comes into play. This turns out to be an important element in our model and our strategy of measurement. We will review a series of seminal studies that illustrate these key ideas.

We rely primarily on three themes in this analysis. The first is the affective primacy argument—that emotional evaluations of and reactions to symbols, people, groups, and events, are generated before conscious awareness. The second is that a great deal of emotional processing never reaches the level of conscious awareness. This is important in political science because so much of our research depends on surveys and interviews in which respondents are asked to recreate and interpret emotional cues—a delicate phenomenon of respondents often telling "more than they can know" (Wilson 1979). The third theme focuses on how the usefulness of habits depends on our ability to connect our emotions and actions.[1]

1. Psychologist John T. Cacioppo has modeled a single emotion system that has two "channels," one to process positive signals and one to process negative signals (Cacioppo and Berntson 1994; Cacioppo and Gardner 1999). While we characterize these neurodynamics as two subsystems rather than channels, our analysis is highly convergent with Cacioppo's approach. His work focuses on the differential metrics of each channel's response to sensory stimuli while our work focuses on the differential output consequences of each subsystem.

The Hardwired Brain—Emotions Precede Thoughts

We begin by reviewing what is for some a rather radical assertion. Rather than focusing on the subjective phenomenon of feeling and how we come to interpret the meaning of the subjective states associated with emotion, a tradition that goes back to William James, we note that emotions are generated by affective processes that precede conscious awareness. Emotions, it turns out, prepare and direct conscious awareness as well as behavior.

Since the argument that emotional responses are authored by emotional systems prior to and outside the ken of conscious awareness is somewhat counterintuitive, we offer two reports—one narrative and one experimental. These examples illustrate both the modular character of the brain and the subtlety and swiftness with which emotional systems operate outside the realm of consciousness. A crucial insight lies in the distinction between procedural memory and declarative memory.

Dr. Claparede's Discovery

Joseph LeDoux recounts a revealing story of how the brain makes associations and develops patterns of likes and dislikes. He tells of a lesson in learning performed by an early twentieth-century French physician, Eduoard Claparede:

> [Dr. Claparede] examined a female patient who, as a result of brain damage, had seemingly lost all ability to create new memories. Each time Claparede walked into the room he had to reintroduce himself to her as she had no recollection of having seen him before. The memory problem was so severe that if Claparede left the room and returned a few minutes later, she wouldn't remember having seen him
>
> One day, he tried something new. He entered the room, and, as on every other day, he held out his hand to greet her. In typical fashion, she shook his hand. But when their hands met, she quickly pulled hers back, for Claparede had concealed a tack in his palm and had pricked her with it. The next time he returned to the room to greet her, she still had no recognition of him, but she refused to shake his hand. She could not tell him why she would not shake hands with him, but she wouldn't do it. (LeDoux 1996, 180–81)

This woman, who was unable to remember anything for more than a second, could nonetheless learn that she had been hurt, how she had been hurt, who had hurt her, and what she specifically needed to do to avoid being hurt in the future. She created and implemented an effective solution:

she refused to shake the hand of the one person who had previously caused her pain. She mastered all of these tasks—recognition, attribution, and adaptation—after only the one painful occasion. How was she able to accomplish this? By relying on her emotional abilities, abilities that grasped the situation and implemented an effective strategy to deal with any reoccurrence.

This story illustrates a key understanding. Our capacity to recall observations into conscious awareness, the stuff of declarative memory, is not the only or even the primary means by which we learn.[2] Learning is principally at the service of doing. And doing is guided by procedural memory, not by declarative memory. While declarative memory makes what we know available to consciousness, thus aiding introspection, it has very limited abilities as far as the actual execution of behavior is concerned. So limited that it cannot directly control much of what we do. Procedural memory, not declarative memory, controls much of our daily activity.

Bechara's Card Game

Our second report is drawn from Antonio D'Amasio's research group at the University of Iowa. The team designed a card game that reveals how the dual emotional subsystems of the brain interact with learning and rational choice (Bechara et al. 1997).

In this study, ten normal subjects were each given two thousand dollars of token money for the game, which began with each player's selecting a card from one of four decks of cards (A, B, C, and D). The first card of each deck gave a reward of either one hundred dollars (decks A and B) or fifty dollars (decks C and D). Some cards in each deck imposed a monetary penalty (larger in decks A and B, smaller in decks C and D). Thus each set of decks provided cards each of which gave either a reward or penalty. Subjects were instructed to take their first cards from decks A and B. Thereafter, subjects selected cards from whichever deck they fancied.

Continued selection of cards from decks A and B led to an overall loss, while continuing to select cards from decks C and D led to an overall gain.

---

2. It is important to note that most political science and communication research focuses on declarative memory. When researchers ask such questions as "Did you vote last election?" or "Are you better or worse off now than last year?" we are probing declarative memory. Procedural memory is different, however, and the connection between the two is not especially robust. For example, most of us can readily sign our signature, an ability stored in procedural memory. But we cannot say precisely how to accomplish this task. If you doubt this try to sign your signature using your nondominant hand (since handwriting is commonly highly lateralized, most of you will find this difficult to do with any dexterity). You "know" how to sign your signature. Why can't "you" tell your nondominant hand to execute that same task? Because the task is stored in procedural, not declarative, memory.

Since this crucial difference between the four decks was unknown to the players, they would have to deduce the difference, if they could, by observing the play of the cards as each of the subjects turned them over, one by one. Each player continued the game by trying to pick the most rewarding deck.

To assess why each person chose from this or that pile of cards, each subject was stopped after twenty cards were played and asked "What do you know about what is going on in this game?" and "Tell me how you feel about this game?" These questions were asked again after each additional ten cards were played. Thus, the two questions were repeated after the thirtieth card played, the fortieth card played, and so forth until the end of play (the hundredth card played).

In addition, players had their skin conductance responses monitored. The galvanic skin response, or GSR, provides one method of assessing whether an emotional association has been formed—one of the measures used in lie detector machines. GSR monitoring provided a moment-to-moment recording of any emotional response each subject experienced as the play of cards unfolded.

This design enabled D'Amasio's group to see if and when people had a "hunch" that some decks were better, or worse, than others. Further it could ascertain if and when the card players could explain the differences between the decks A and B, on the one hand, and decks C and D, on the other. Seven of the ten players did eventually catch on and correctly conceptualize the game. By noting the play of cards, that is, which decks were played, the researchers could tell if and when the players adjusted their behavior, switching away from the "bad," penalizing decks, and toward the "good" or long-term rewarding decks. Finally, the GSR responses would reveal if and when subjects experienced emotional reactions.

At the very beginning players selected additional cards from the "bad" decks, decks A and B, no doubt influenced by the first cards turned. The $100 reward was noticed. After twenty plays, players began to move away from selecting cards from these decks and played the "good" decks with greater frequency. In this first period, however, from first to the twentieth card, none of the players reported a "feeling" about any of the decks and none could correctly conceptualize the game. During this phase the players experienced significantly elevated GSRs to the penalty cards selected from decks A and B. Players had formed an emotional association with the larger penalties. All players selecting a penalty card from these decks had begun to experience an emotional response though they could not, as yet, say they had.

In the next series of plays, the phase that Bechara's group call the "hunch phase," subjects reported "liking" or "disliking" certain decks, though they could not say precisely why. In this period all ten of the subjects report a good feeling about the "good" decks, as compared to a bad feeling linked to the "bad" decks. However, they could not give a conceptual account of the game, that is, they were unable to identify the actual difference between the cards in the "good" and "bad" decks, respectively. Thus, the correct "hunch" came after subjects had already begun to shift away from selecting cards from the "bad" decks and toward selecting cards from the "good" decks. Further, the correct "hunch" arose after heightened GSRs properly differentiated between the decks.

Finally, most (but not all) of the subjects achieved a correct conceptual understanding of the game: while decks C and D had smaller reward cards, they had even smaller penalty cards than decks A and B. This phase, called the "conceptual phase," was reached by seven of the ten subjects by the time the last card was played.

Each of the ten subjects adjusted their strategic behavior before they had either a hunch or a proper understanding of the game. Even the three subjects who did not figure out the game nonetheless adjusted their behavior to improve their play.

Interestingly, the researchers also asked some patients who had bilateral damage to the prefrontal cortex, the area of the brain where procedural memory is most active, to play the game. As these patients played, they came to properly understand the game. However, they did not experience the heightened GSR to the "bad" decks and they did not adjust their play *even after they came to understand the game*. They picked cards randomly without regard to the sequence of rewards and punishments. Because they could not associate the outcomes as they occurred with the proper emotional response, they were unable to adjust their play of cards to improve their winnings even though they understood the game.

Clearly, because we expect people who play this game to act on the basis of what they understand and can verbalize about it, we should be quite perplexed about the play of cards in both groups of subjects. In the case of the first group, they adjusted, correctly, their play of the game well *before* they came to understand the game. In the case of the second group, they did not adjust how they played the game even though they learned what to do in order to win. Conscious awareness of the correct strategy was not instrumental to either group of players' ability to play the game to win.

But why is emotion so essential to winning? Why was gaining an understanding of the correct strategy not enough? How did players change their behavior to a winning strategy before they gained an understanding? Let's return to the issue of procedural memory and how it differs from declarative memory. We are now in a position to explain more precisely why learning to do things, recurring actions that become efficient habits, requires emotion. Consider a very "cognitive" task, say, writing a postcard to a friend. Letters have to be formed and grouped into words, phrases, and sentences. This seems hardly to be a task that would require emotion. Yet it does, though not of the manifest kind.

The writer might begin with the simple task of writing "Dear . . . ." Take the smallest part of that small task, writing the first letter, the cursive capital letter "D." Each of us can do this without difficulty or hesitation. It is, after all, just one letter among the many others that will fill up the postcard. We just write out the letter, whether we are using a pen or a pencil. Yet writing a cursive letter "D" is a very complex task that has a beginning followed by a smooth line of ever-changing, curving trajectory. The letter begins at the top of a box, loops down and back up, then swings out, around, and down, and back to the left to close the letter. We do the movements naturally and seemingly without emotion. In one sense of the word, these are "automatic" actions. They are actions we don't have to think about, we just do them because we already know how to do them.

But emotional processes are crucial in this task as they are in most other habituated tasks. We generally master the template for writing a cursive letter "D," as we have for all other letters of our own alphabet, when we are young. But to execute this specific action, as in all instances of writing a letter, we must link together a series of subtle movements. And before we can begin the next movement in the series we must successfully complete the prior movement. Emotional processes monitor how well we execute each task as well as how well it matches the expectations of success. Emotional processes also provide the feedback that success in the first pen stroke means we can now begin the second. Habits, such as writing, require that we make many small adjustments that require eye–hand coordination and application of the template to the immediate specifics. What is the specific flow of ink or lead from our pen or pencil? How smooth or rough is the postcard? How much room is our writing consuming of the space available? Is our writing drifting up or down rather than following a horizontal line? How much pressure do we need to apply to the paper? Each of these accommodations, and others, are managed outside of consious awareness. And emotional processes that enable us to make the necessary subtle adjustments to the needs of any given situation manage these adjustments. Even the most "automatic" of habits depends on emotional processes. Because most habits are easy to execute in any given moment, they rarely generate feelings that reach consciousness. It is primarily when habits fail or when habits become more strategically salient than normal that feelings become manifest. Consider our feelings when, on the first strokes in forming the letter "D," our pen leaks and spurts ink all over the page! Noting that manifest feelings are rare in the execution of typical habits should not be taken to mean that variation in emotion, below the threshold of conscious awareness, is not critical to the successful execution of the task.

We can see this unobserved role for emotion when we consider what happens when emotions are "out of the picture," as it was for the patients with bilateral lesions that prevented emotional responses to the flow of the card game. Those patients, through no fault of their own, were compelled to follow the traditional advice about not allowing dispassionate analysis to be tainted by emotions. Consequently, although they clearly could understand the game, they were unable to form an emotional association between each event and its consequences as reward or punishment, with the result that they could not act on their understanding.

This study demonstrates the importance of the distinction between procedural memory and declarative memory. These two systems of memory are each crucial, but they perform different functions. Procedural memory manages the learning and execution of habitual behavior. Declarative memory enables us to recall the "what" and "when" of things, most often in semantic fashion. Each of these is vital, but clearly procedural memory, which relies heavily on emotional processes, is central to the execution of learned behavior (habits). Declarative memory and conscious awareness, in the absence of the proper emotional linkage of behavior and anticipated outcome, leaves behavior unaffected even in the presence of the correct understanding of the best choice.[3]

Thus, emotional systems manage information. They enhance the brain's essential ability to assess the state of one's immediate environment, to assess the state of one's mental and physical being, to evaluate the ongoing execution of learned behavioral routines, stored in procedural memory, and to assess and redistribute resources, both conscious and behavioral. Without these appraisals we are severely limited in our ability to modify our behavior in light of the information provided by our senses.

Studying the emotions enables us to explore the role of procedural memory in relation to behavior, with which it is far more engaged than

---

3. For more on the differences between declarative and procedural memory, see Wilson and Dunn 1986; Wilson et al. 1984; Wilson, Hodges, and LaFleur 1995; and Wilson and Schooler 1991. We are ignoring the role of implicit and other systems of memory in order to keep the analysis as simple as possible. See note 5.

the more commonly explored declarative memory. However, declarative memory is also quite important, especially in politics. Declarative memory, sometimes also called "semantic memory," is where our beliefs, thoughts, values, and other semantic understandings are stored. Declarative memory enables recall of prior events or "facts" or prior thoughts in conscious awareness. Moreover, our habits are often justified in semantic terms. Habits can come to be described as "values" and their existence identified as "attitudes." Habits have value because they perform strategically important functions and we can label and identify the most salient of them, giving them semantic expression.

Neuroscience offers new details about how the brain manages the activities of daily life, how humans behave, learn, make choices and, of central interest here, think and feel. One of these findings revises the traditional relationship between emotion and thought. As a result of recent research in neuroscience we have come to understand that emotional reactions actually *precede* rather than follow conscious perceptions. This means that conscious reflections on the emotional displays we experience or observe are *post hoc* interpretations that are often not themselves part of the mental processes that give rise to the initial manifestation of emotion.[4] As a result, though people often cogitate about their feelings to make sense of the emotions they feel and though people readily apply semantic labels to various subjective feelings, these labels do not explain how these feelings originate.

Pathways in the Brain

If emotional perceptions precede conscious awareness, how is it that consciousness appears to provide an instantaneous grasp of the sensate world? The work of Benjamin Libet (Libet 1985; Libet et al. 1983, 1991, 1979) measured the amount of time that the brain requires to represent sensory data in conscious awareness. Libet's estimate was that it takes half a second for these neural processes to extract the information that we experience as consciousness. This estimate is widely shared and supported by a considerable literature in neuroscience (Gazzaniga 1998; Nørretranders 1998). Moreover, the capacity of the sense organs—eyes, ears, nose, skin, and tongue—to gather information is far in excess of the capacity of the various primary sensory cortex regions to display in consciousness. For example, the information that the retina gathers is far in excess of what we

4. There are, no doubt, reciprocal relationships, with thoughts generating emotional responses and with thoughts refining or modifying already existent moods and feelings.

consciously see. The current estimate for all the sense organs is that they collect 1 million bits of information for every one bit of information that is displayed in conscious awareness (Zimmermann 1989). It is in this one-half second gap of time that other brain mechanisms speedily operate to evaluate the sensory stream enabling the brain to determine how best to reduce the information stream to what can and ought to be displayed in conscious awareness (Nørretranders 1998).

In 1987 Mortimer Mishkin and Tim Appenzeller published an important article entitled "The Anatomy of Memory." The principal finding was that sensory information did not flow in just a single pathway to a final destination in the cortex where representation in conscious awareness is generated. Rather, sensory information flowed along a pathway to the thalamus, buried deep within the brain. There, sensory information divides into two separate pathways. One pathway continues on to the various regions of the cortex, the surface regions of the brain that process these sensory streams—for example, the visual cortex for sight and the auditory cortex for sound—and support conscious awareness. The other pathway goes to the limbic area, most notably to the amygdala and hippocampus. Mishkin saw that the neural apparatus existed to support two means of learning, the first pathway goes to the various regions of the cortex for final sensory processing. The second pathway goes to the limbic region for initial emotional processing. Thus, the brain has two ways of examining sensory information and two systems of storing the results in memory, procedural memory (the pathway to the limbic system) and declarative memory (the pathway to conscious awareness).[5]

In figure 3.1 we present a highly simplified view of the major pathways to the key areas of the brain we have been discussing. The conventional understanding of vision is that we see when the optic nerve reports the activity of the cells of the retina to the visual cortex (located at the back of the brain). However, as the figure shows, the pathways go first to the limbic

---

5. There is much more to be said about memory. Procedural memory is not semantic but does have ability to manage the many repetitive tasks that form the behavioral repertoire on matters large and small. Declarative memory is semantic; it handles our capacity to reconstruct what we have seen or experienced in thoughts and articulate statements. Thus, they serve very different functions: procedural memory supports learned behavioral routines, while declarative memory supports conscious awareness and the capacity for reflection. Moreover, there are yet other important memory systems, such as implicit memory. A fuller discussion of the multiple systems of memory, however, is beyond the scope of this work. Read Schacter 1996 and Squire 1987 for sound and current introductions.

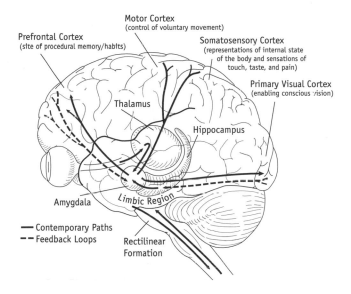

Motor Cortex
(control of voluntary movement)

Prefrontal Cortex
(site of procedural memory/habits)

Somatosensory Cortex
(representations of internal state
of the body and sensations of
touch, taste, and pain)

Primary Visual Cortex
(enabling conscious vision)

Thalamus

Hippocampus

Amygdala

Limbic Region

— Contemporary Paths
- - Feedback Loops

Rectilinear
Formation

Figure 3.1   Mapping Pathways in the Brain

NOTE: The figure is highly simplified. The figure is not meant to depict all the pathways involved in visual information processing. The pathway from the Thalamus to the Primary Visual Cortex is not indicated, nor various pathways to other areas involved in generating a conscious vision.

region of the brain. Indeed, all the major senses initially project, via the thalamus, first to one part of the limbic region, the amygdala, where the emotional import of the incoming sensory streams can be determined well before the sensory streams continue on to the various cortex regions for sensory processing. We have also marked the crucial pathways that report on the body (through the rectilinear formation and to and from the sensory and somatosensory cortices) and on how we do things (the prefrontal cortex). Thus, the emotional systems that reside in this region of the brain are well placed to get first crack at sensory information not only about what's "out there" but also on the current state of the body and its various components. Moreover, these emotional systems are well placed to connect this information and the related analyses to the learned abilities stored in the prefrontal cortex. Emotional systems are thus able to influence not only feeling states but consciousness and its related faculties and behavior.

The two pathways differ in one very important respect. The pathway to the limbic region is capable of yielding an appraisal in less than half the time it takes for sensory data to become available to conscious awareness

(Damasio 1994; Gray 1987b; LeDoux 1992, 1993). So the outputs of the limbic region pathways, the pathways that among other capabilities yield
emotional states, are well positioned to influence conscious attention as
well as behavior, especially habitual behavior.

Neuroscientists (Cloninger 1986; Damasio 1994; Gray 1987b; LeDoux
1996, 1987; Panksepp 1989, 1991) have changed how we understand emotion. Almost without exception, the focus of earlier research examined
emotion as an end state. Emotion was understood as emotional expression, whether as visual displays that could be observed (a facial grimace,
body posture), or as subjective experience (how we feel—joyful, angry, and
so on). Now the focus has shifted to understanding how the human brain
processes information thereafter expressed as emotional states. This
change in focus opens up the possibility that there are other consequences
that result from these appraisals, in as much as emotional processing is attendant to a wider array of sensory information than is available to conscious awareness and because emotional processing precedes conscious
awareness.

That the power of emotion has for too long been underappreciated is
underscored by these new findings in neuroscience. The effects of emotion
go beyond the shaping and shifting of emotional states. Neuroscience now
implicates emotion not only and obviously in what we are feeling, but also
in how and about what we think, and what we do. Moreover, emotional reactions have important effects even in their quieter states—an insight that
has been rarely explored because of our culturally inherited prejudice concerning the dangers of passion and the inability to measure these weaker
reactions.

It might seem that by dividing sensory information (what we see, hear,
smell, touch, and taste) into two pathways—one that operates outside of
and prior to the conscious realm and one that prepares for conscious
awareness—we are reproducing the traditional sharp division between affect and cognition. One pathway handles feeling; the other pathway handles awareness and thinking. But the brain's organization and function is
not so simple. Affect is also involved in the other pathway, the one that
goes to the visual, auditory, and other sensory cortexes.

Neuroscientists have confirmed and provided additional detail to Zajonc's (Kunst-Wilson and Zajonc 1980; Moreland and Zajonc 1979; Zajonc
1980, 1982) argument that emotional systems evaluate sensory information before and without the involvement of conscious awareness. Indeed,
these systems perform this task before conscious awareness gets a crack at
even a reduced portion of that same information. More importantly, the

processes that yield emotional appraisals also have consequences beyond the generation of mood states. Affective Intelligence describes how two different emotional systems drive quite different neural processes, processes that have different consequences for the emotions we experience, for behavior, and for the way we make use of the faculties displayed in conscious awareness.

Constructing Consciousness

Consciousness is the last word, not the first. It represents only the perceivable tip of the iceberg. The subjective world of conscious awareness presents the appearance of an immediate and objective world defined by our senses of sight, sound, smell, touch, and even taste. But it takes time for sights, sounds, and smells to travel from their sources to our senses. And it takes time for the brain to make use of these sensory flows.

Evolutionary biology rewards species that are able to get sensory information "up and running" as soon as possible. Important consequences result from getting this information "too late." So the fact that emotional systems have the first word in comprehending the rich and diverse buzz of information provided by our senses is critically important to understanding resultant thought and behavior (Rolls 1999).

Figure 3.2 provides a conservative estimate of the "tip of the iceberg" phenomenon in terms of the brain's rich emotional and sensory processing yet relatively small window of conscious awareness. The figure illustrates the point that only sufficiently robust and enduring sensory signals will be expressed as manifest self-conscious feelings. Emotional processing of sensory signals that are too transitory or weak to be subjectively experienced are, nonetheless, still influential. Hence, emotional processing before and below the level of consciousness will still be effectual.

Figure 3.2 further illustrates that there are two ongoing strategic appraisals for each emotional system. When these appraisals result in sufficiently robust conclusions that command the involvement of conscious awareness, they will become manifest as "feelings." Most habits do not require self-conscious attention. Hence, most of the time the execution of learned routines, or habits, does not have apparent emotional content. When the execution of a learned routine is strategically salient, however, the success or failure of that habit will be manifest in variation in enthusiasm. The manifestation of the strategically important conclusions reached by the surveillance system is variation in anxiety. This dimension of variation

Figure 3.2 Affect, Mood, Emotion, and Conscious Awareness

in emotional response constitutes an ongoing evaluation of the degree of normality of the immediate environment. When such expressed variations in emotion reach the level sufficient for our experiencing them as "feelings," we can give them subjective labels such as "elated" or "inspired" (variation in enthusiasm) and "worry" or "anxious" (variation in anxiety). Further, these stronger and less fleeting expressions of emotion can often be linked to the stimulus or situation that is their focus. But often, at the margin of conscious awareness, emotional processing will not clearly target their source because the emotional processes yield variations in emotion that are too transitory or fleeting. The experience of such changes in

6. It is common in treatments of emotion (Schwartz and Clore 1996) to distinguish between "moods" as enduring feeling states that do not have a clear stimulus source and emotions as feeling states that are more fleeting but clearly attributed to some target stimulus (as in "I am angry at or with . . . "). This distinction is less useful, in our view, because it implies that different emotional processes underlie emotion than underlie mood, though most such accounts do not explain what might produce such differences.

emotion at the boundary of conscious awareness are often labeled "moods," "intuitions," or "hunches."[6] Most importantly, affective processes determine which sensory information is represented in conscious awareness; that is, affective processes shape what we pay attention to, what is available to us in conscious awareness.[7]

What Neuroscience Tells Us about Habit and Reason

Understanding the role of emotion as learning systems brings us to our next topic: the enduring influences of emotional appraisal. Previously learned emotional responses are stored in procedural memory to retain earlier-formed associations for future use. It is well established that people often make use of their habits, rely on predispositions, when making many choices. People often make the same recurring political "decisions" by relying on previously learned symbols without regard for their currently assessed usefulness, a finding that David Sears (1990, 1993a, 1993b, Sears et al. 1980) has been researching for many years. Complete reliance on habits presumes that success in the past is the best predictor of success in the future. But what if circumstances change? What if this Democrat is different from those that have gone before? What if the economy unexpectedly has a long and enduring downturn? Reliance on yesterday's successes makes us vulnerable to novel events and unexpected changes in circumstance. How do we learn to identify and respond to such situations? Again, emotional processing is central.

Emotionality as state, the continual flow of affective appraisals reporting on the immediate state of affairs, and emotionality as trait, the availability of previously learned associations, provide us with alternative methods for making decisions and enacting behavior. Emotion as state enables us to swiftly extract useful information that we can use for an explicit consideration of the options that confront us. Emotion as trait enables us

7. We have not said much about how feelings are made manifest. This has yet to be resolved either in psychology generally or in neuroscience. An older view is that emotion is expressed as physiological states, as in "gut" feelings or heightened heart rate (James 1883). If so, different patterns of emotion could be distinguished by their unique patterns of physiological and cardiovascular arousal (Levenson and Reuf 1992). But recent work does not establish that emotions can be distinguished in this way (Cacioppo et al. 1993). A more recent view is that feedback from facial muscles provides the necessary pathway for self-identification of manifest feelings (Cacioppo, Bush, and Tassinary 1992; Cacioppo et al. 1986; Cacioppo et al. 1988; Dimberg 1990; Haggard and Issacs 1966; Hess et al. 1992; Wagner, MacDonald, and Manstead 1986; Zajonc, Murphy, and Englehard 1989).

to thoughtlessly enact previously learned routines, relying on habitual choices without much contemporary consideration or effort.[8]

While it is tempting to assert the universal superiority of reasoned, thoughtful, and explicit choice rather than reliance on habit, in fact there is substantial value to each. And we are better served by having both capacities. Reliance on habit recognizes the value of prior learning. Without the ability to secure what we have learned, we would soon overwhelm our conscious capacities with the multiplicity of choices and the repetitive reconsideration of recurring tasks.[9] Reliance on prior learning is clearly best suited for circumstances in which there is a continuity of goals, of means, and of the environmental context. If any of these change, either the goals we seek or the character of the immediate context, then our habitual choice may become not only ineffective but even dangerous. In such circumstances, setting aside the effortless and thoughtless reliance on disposition may well be a strategic imperative.

Uncoupling behavior from habit permits learning something new, a capacity of special importance to democratic politics. By having the ability to shift from reliance on affective appraisals to conscious thoughtful consideration, people gain two ways of determining what to do. It would be consistent with Western cultural presumptions to assert that conscious and explicit appraisals are always better relied on than feelings that automatically engage our habits. But if our emotional reactions guide us by providing previously stored associations between events, persons, and circumstances, then feelings provide the means by which we can understand our past, present, and future. As these associations are retained for guidance, they can be modified when new information suggests that the established habit is no longer viable.[10]

---

8. And, of course, most democratic theorists recommend that we give any significant problem of choice thoughtful and fulsome explicit consideration (Arkes 1993).

9. In assessing the profound impact of Darwin on our understanding of our species, we too often fail to consider the first principle of evolutionary thinking. A species must have the robust means for securing stable routines to manage the challenges of life in their circumstances. The second principle of evolutionary change explains how species adapt to changes in the environment that make the repertoire of learned routines no longer effective.

10. Access to stored feelings that associate events, people, and circumstances, is via implicit memory, see note 5.

Social psychologists have long noticed that people often respond to persuasive messages either by careful consideration or by a more careless response to whatever contemporary cues are manifest. Richard Petty and John Cacioppo (1986, 1996) developed the elaboration likelihood model to account for when and why people rely on the two modes of response they call "central" (careful consideration) and "peripheral" (responses are

Consider a middle-aged man who has always bought Chevy trucks. He's been happy with that choice. The Chevy trucks he's owned have worked out fine and he has never had reason for complaint with his local Chevy dealer. He's always been able to trade in each truck and replace it with a newer model, and his friends and colleagues never fail to say the appropriately encouraging things when he shows up with his latest purchase. How might this fellow go about buying his next truck? Since he's been satisfied in the past with Chevy trucks, he gives some note to contemporary information. Perhaps he is pleased by the current Chevrolet ads he sees on television or in print. If he happens to see any of the ads of competing manufacturers, he quickly dismisses their claims about the superiority of Ford or Dodge trucks. He pays some attention to current information but quickly accommodates what he hears and sees to his preexisting dispositions.

But what if this situation was unexpectedly disrupted? A few years ago General Motors took a lot of heat from the media and the federal government for selling trucks that had their gas tanks located outside the main frame of their trucks. Critics held that this design made the trucks more hazardous, specifically that their gas tanks were likely to explode in an accident. Consider how our satisfied owner of Chevy trucks might go about deciding what truck to buy after seeing news stories about poor design, graphic images of trucks exploding, and interviews with burn victims. He might still end up purchasing his favorite, the Chevy, but he might give considerable thought to the decision before heading down to the dealership.

Having two emotional subsystems enables us to rely on habit *and* to activate reasoned consideration, each in appropriate circumstances. We are not solely creatures of habit. Nor are we always inclined to calculate carefully each and every choice before us. We can and do rely on both capabilities, capabilities that derive from our emotional faculties.

---

driven not by consideration of the issues in the message but by peripheral concerns such as the message's source). Our model differs from theirs in two respects. First, our model contrasts reliance on *preexisting* dispositions, which is likely to be quite casual and lack thoughtful consideration, with reliance on careful and thoughtful consideration. That is, we contrast past reliance on habits with current thoughtful consideration while the elaboration likelihood model contrasts two modes of response to contemporary persuasive messages. Second, the trigger that shifts people from reliance on established dispositions (habits) to thoughtful consideration resides, in our model, on the surveillance system. The elaboration likelihood model of attitude change recognizes no such role for emotional influences.

Toward a Theory

The theory of Affective Intelligence makes three crucial claims about emotion and its general relationship to judgment.

First, emotional appraisals are completed before conscious awareness occurs, which enables emotion systems to take on tasks that exceed the capacity of consciousness and to influence how we use our minds.

Second, each of the two systems of emotional appraisal has distinct effects on conscious awareness and on behavior.

And, third, we have the ability to rely on two modes of decision making. One is reliance on habits, associations that have proven successful in the past. The other is reliance on explicit consideration of the contemporary situation and the alternatives before us. Each mode depends on emotional appraisals to guide our choices and actions—though in quite different ways.

Collectively, these assertions, if supported by sufficient evidence, would place emotion at the center of many features of democratic politics, including how the public and leaders communicate, how leaders and followers make choices, and which choices they make. In chapter 4 we will describe each emotional system, the disposition system and the surveillance system, in greater detail. We also will enumerate each system's specific connections between emotional appraisal, conscious awareness, and behavior so as to make a full inventory of testable claims about how specific changes in levels of anxiety and enthusiasm alter the manner of political judgment.

Dual Affective Subsystems: Disposition and Surveillance

Consider a rather mundane example of political behavior—the simple action of waving a sign at a political rally. Our political actor wags the sign enthusiastically back and forth, first toward the crowd and then toward the press and television cameras. But suddenly, a large campaign banner is unfurled that blocks the sign waver's sight lines to the cameras. Without really thinking about it, our actor moves adroitly through the crowd to search out a better position. The many muscles in the legs, hands and arms, and back will tense and relax in harmony to manage these many linked movements. The skeletal system adjusts as limbs move and weight shifts.

This description of a rather routine set of movements is far too brief an account to be precisely descriptive of the thousands of movements with millisecond timing necessary for any fluid and deft movement to be executed. Nor does it describe all the small, often imperceptible adjustments that are frequently made to maintain balance and adjust to the jostling crowd. If our actor had to think much about such matters it would slow her down, undoubtedly make her movements more awkward, and distract her entirely from the content of her candidate's long-awaited keystone speech on foreign policy.[1] Her movements are routine and subconscious, scripted by her conscious decision to attract the attention of the television cameras but not themselves under conscious control.

---

1. Learning a physical movement in athletics, for example, particularly at intermediate and advanced levels, requires the participant to *feel* what they are doing with a minimal level of conscious semantic intervention. Letting thoughts intrude is often a distraction, especially when the thoughts are concerned with the macrolevel of performance ("Why can't I beat this guy?" or "I can't let myself lose to this woman."). Saying that you're "in the flow" or in a "zone" are ways to describe the heightened attention to body feelings that enhances high quality performances (Csikszentmihalyi 1990).

Suddenly she slips and loses balance. She feels a sudden rush of anxiety as her conscious awareness has been engaged and she now pays a great deal of attention to her bodily movements and the milling crowd. "Forget the cameras," she calculates. "I'll get my fifteen minutes of fame some other time."

This brief scenario illustrates the interaction of two affective subsystems of the brain as they make complex behaviors and rational choice possible. The first of these subsystems, the disposition system, is primarily responsible for managing reliance on habits, previously learned strategies. The other, the surveillance system, is primarily responsible for identifying novel and threatening circumstances, precisely the circumstance in which reliance on habit would be ill advised, and for initiating a shift to reasoned consideration. In this chapter we will examine each subsystem and how they interact with each other and with active conscious thought.

The Disposition System

Located in the limbic region of the brain, the disposition system engages procedural memory and the sensory systems, and has pathways to the areas of the brain where behavioral routines are enacted. It also has input and output connections to the various cortex regions of the brain that are heavily involved in conscious awareness. Its function is essential to the enaction of learned behaviors and to the acquisition of new behavioral routines.

Three broad categories of information are required for successful routine functioning of the disposition system. First, any behavior, like the actions of our sign-waving enthusiast, requires extensive sequences of action and action branching of the already learned habits. Let's call any such sequence a "subconscious script." Every activity we engage in—reading, arguing, shopping, listening, speaking to a friend, answering the question of a stranger on the street—depend on such scripts.

The second requirement is internal feedback from the body—a contemporary report of the physical and psychic demands for successful execution. If, for example, the script demands more energy than we have available, then it must be adjusted to moderate its requirements or be abandoned; otherwise, our persistence will only lead to exhaustion and failure.

The third requirement is external feedback—information of the detailed context so that the anticipated sequence can be matched and adjusted to the specific immediate circumstances. When you wave a sign, there are complex feedback loops between hand and object continually adjusting to changing external conditions. These calculations occur before and outside conscious awareness. Although conscious awareness is a wonderful gift, the responsibility for observing and controlling the flow of habitual behavior lies elsewhere. And that elsewhere is the emotional subsystem we label "disposition."

The disposition system is a comparing system. It obtains somatosensory information (information about the body, its position, and status), sensory data (information about the environment), and plans (from the prefrontal cortex, where procedural memories are located). Integrating these information flows provides the basis for a simple comparison: is the plan being executed in an expected and successful fashion, or is the plan failing? The former circumstance is a "match," the second a "mismatch." As it continuously performs these comparisons, the disposition system influences emotional outputs, in this case the degree of enthusiasm that in turn is related to the conscious mood of enthusiasm, attention to task, and behavior—the completion of the ongoing plan.

Figure 4.1 illustrates the functional process of the disposition system. The characteristic affective reactions that disposition modulates range from depression, for example, feeling gloomy, sad, blue, or frustrated, to increasing levels of enthusiasm, feelings of interest, excitement, joy, and elation. Though this description might suggest a bipolar dimension to the emotions expressed by the disposition system, that would be a misunder standing. We apply semantic labels to many things, including the variety of emotional states we experience. We label very low levels of enthusiasm using such terms as *down, blue, sad, depressed*. Notwithstanding the different

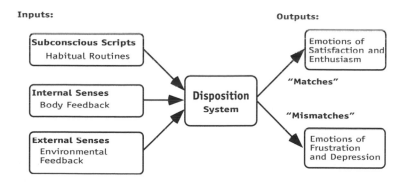

Figure 4.1 The Disposition System

semantic definitions of these terms, the disposition system generates a unipolar dimension of emotional response, responses that range from the absence of enthusiasm to increasingly greater levels of enthusiasm. These gradations of mood form the dimension typically called "positive affect" (Watson and Tellegen 1985). If the disposition system only adjusted our moods, making us feel more excited when things are going well or making us feel gloomy or depressed if plans are going awry, then the role of emotionality would be interesting but not very important, at least with respect to behavior.

Monitoring Subconscious Scripts

The disposition system has pathways to those portions of the brain that manage the execution of previously learned behavior, to procedural memory (that is, feedback), and to the areas of the cortex involved with conscious awareness. First, let's explore the relationship of the disposition system to conscious awareness. Often the proper execution of a task requires full attention to the task itself. Hence, attention must be narrowed to exclude possible distractions. When we find ourselves fully absorbed in a task, perhaps reading a book, making something at a work bench, or taking the controls of a plane for the first time, our attention narrows. Quite literally much of the external world disappears from our awareness.

The state of consciousness is not always the same. Sometimes consciousness widens to attend to the total environment. Sometimes it narrows to focus only on a reduced visual field, as when we get "lost" in a good book or forget that we are sitting in a theater with lots of other people while watching a gripping movie. This widening or narrowing of awareness is one of the tasks that the disposition system manages. Additionally, the mood states and their report of the ongoing success or failure of the plan under execution will prompt appropriate thoughts of success or failure. Moreover, if the ongoing task is going so well that full attention is not demanded, then cognitive resources are freed up so that even as the plan is executed we can do other things, for example, daydream or talk on a cell phone while driving down the road.

Second, the disposition system also influences the enaction of those recurring learned routines that make up our repertoire of habits. Habits, once begun, can be continued with success or abandoned with frustration and despair (each term reflecting a different cause for the absence of enthusiasm). Habits presume familiar contexts. They also depend on sufficient energy to achieve success in confronting the normal array of challenges and difficulties. So long as the usual array of circumstances fall within the range of prior experience and we are reasonably energetic, both with respect to physical and mental resources, reliance on habits will yield good results. Habits may fail us when either the immediate demands confronting that habit are more substantial than expected or when we are more fatigued than usual.

Third, the disposition system receives feedback on the success or failure of the ongoing sequence of actions that make up a habit. The coordination of movements and integration of sensory and somatosensory information enable the disposition system to adjust to the minor variations that any execution of a habit will encounter. As with drawing the capital letter "D," habits are a calibrated series of movements. Feedback on each stage of the sequence enables the disposition system to mark the end of one pen stroke, making whatever minor adjustments are necessary for the success of the next stroke. This is actually a demanding task as each movement in sequence must not only be a success but properly prepare for the next movement in the series.

Finally, the disposition system has important feedback linkages so that what is learned from the execution of *this* plan, *this* time, can be retained in procedural memory. The disposition system, by accessing the detailed abilities to execute simple and complex plans, can also store our general assessment, or inclination, to execute these plans as preferences. Though we normally think of emotions as being distinct from cognitive processes, here we see the interrelatedness of behavioral, emotional, and higher cognitive function.

An important aspect of our attitudes about something or someone is how we feel [2] The more formal definitions in psychology define attitude as having three components: *cognitive*, which is its semantic content; *affective*, the feeling content; and *behavioral disposition*, the action content (Breckler 1984; Osgood, Suci, and Tannenbaum 1957). Our description of the disposition system suggests that the cognitive and affective components can be described as the consciously available semantic representation obtained from declarative memory; the underlying subjective affective state, which conveys the inclination and capacity to execute the linked behaviors, is obtained from procedural memory. But, as we noted above, the former is not always a good guide to the latter.

---

2. We have much more to say about the structure of the feelings we typically associate with people, groups, institutions, activities, ideas, and so forth in appendix B.

The Daily Experience of Enthusiasm

What do we know about subjective mood? Perhaps the person who has studied it the most is psychologist David Watson. He developed what has become one of the standard measurements of subjective mood—the positive affect and negative affect schedules (PANAS) measurement inventory (Watson, Clark, and Tellegen 1988). He has also reported extensive studies of the reliability and validity of these measures (Watson 1988b; Watson and Clark 1991; Watson and Walker 1996). Dr. Watson kindly made available to us a number of sets of data that contain hundreds of subjects' subjective mood assessments. In these studies subjects are asked to rate their mood using the PANAS measures. The PANAS inventory consists of twenty mood terms: ten for positive affect (*enthusiastic, interested, determined, excited, inspired, alert, active, strong, proud,* and *attentive*) and ten for negative affect (*scared, afraid, upset, distressed, jittery, nervous, ashamed, guilty, irritable,* and *hostile*).[3]

What do people report in the way of enthusiasm they experience during their waking hours, the positive affect part of the PANAS inventory? Recall that the disposition system manages the modulation of moods as we succeed or falter in the execution of the many tasks that people undertake over the course of a typical day. We expect, at least for most people, that the moods of enthusiasm vary from high to low and, as with most psychological measures, form a somewhat normal distribution that reflects the relative rarity of stunning success and the more likely result, "I'm doing ok."

In these data, hundreds of subjects were asked to rate how they felt "at the present moment" at various times during each day over the course of a number of days. A minimum of 35 assessments were obtained from each subject. Figure 4.2 displays the frequency distribution of enthusiasm scores for these momentary experiences of mood. Though not a precisely normal distribution, it is clear that, for most people most of the time, their mood of enthusiasm is in the "middle ground," neither very elated nor very frustrated or gloomy.[4]

---

3. Subjects are asked to rate how well these terms describe their mood. A multipoint response format is most often used, which asks subjects to rate how "enthusiastic" they feel (today, at this moment, last week). Subjects then check *very slightly or not at all, a little, moderately, quite a bit,* or *extremely* (Watson, Clark, and Tellegen 1988).

4. Two other large sets of data, each of which, as here, include thousands of assessments, provide essentially identical results (Watson, Clark, and Tellegen 1984; Zevon and Tellegen 1982). Of course, each individual is not likely to have the same "baseline" or characteristic mood. The difference in baseline mood, a facet of personality, is itself a major topic that is concerned with the "trait" aspect of emotion. The dimension of personality held to be the trait facet of positive emotionality, or the disposition system, is typically described as extraversion–introversion (Watson 1988a; Watson and Clark 1992b; Watson et al. 1992).

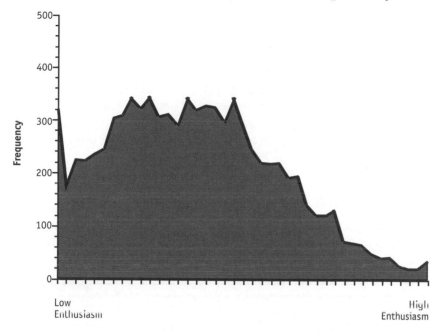

Figure 4.2 The Daily Experience of Enthusiasm

SOURCES: 1985–86 SMU study conducted by David Watson; personal communication.

Learned behaviors are dependent for success on the anticipation of familiar environments. Insofar as familiar environments are consistent and enduring, habits will then behave very much like personality traits. However, to the extent that either the resource demands exceed the specific amounts then available (because, for example, we are more tired than usual) or external circumstances are more problematic or less compliant than normal, the disposition system will operate less like a trait and more like a "state." It can adjust our typical performance by weakening our motivation to continue, accompanied by feelings of frustration and depressive thoughts. Or it can redouble our efforts by increasing our concentration and feelings of engagement and interest. Either departure from a typical performance can lead to new readily available modifications of the plan to be stored in procedural memory. When behavior is executed in a normal fashion, the plan is confirmed, the usual level of enthusiasm associated with that plan is reinforced, and the plan becomes more trait-like, or "habitual."

We are not suggesting that all behaviors are driven by the disposition system specifically or by affective systems generally. Psychologists have suggested that some behaviors are driven by affective systems while others are influenced more by conscious considerations (Edwards 1990; Millar and Millar 1990; Millar and Tesser 1986a, 1986b). Insofar as the behavior in question falls within the realm of learned behaviors, the disposition system is likely to play a major role in the initiation, adaptation, and control of the plan of action. Moreover, reliance on habits, most of which are developed without explicit reasoning, provides efficient and therefore reasonable solutions to the recurring tasks of daily life. Habits offer solutions that, even if not the very best, have nonetheless repeatedly proven their worth.

The Politics of Political Habits

It has been common practice to divide theories of political behavior into two classes—one that asserts the primacy of values and the other that asserts the primacy of interests (Chong 2000; LeVine and Campbell 1972). The former generally holds that early in life people acquire and then persist in relying on deeply entrenched values that determine how they will react and respond in the antagonistic climate characteristic of politics. The principal claim is that habits rule. Theories of identity, theories that argue that sociological factors identify the enduring consequences of early socialization, theories of prejudice and stereotype—all agree that contemporary circumstances and rational considerations of alternatives are largely ignored. Perhaps the most widely known is the theory of symbolic politics (Kinder and Sears 1981; Sears 1990; Sears and Funk 1990; Sears, Hensler, and Spear 1979; Sears et al. 1980). These theories share the view that humans are guided by enduring habits, habits that resist change and resist the explicit consideration of interest that democratic theorists require of citizens.

Let us imagine that the only emotional subsystem available to us is the disposition system. In such a condition, most political behaviors would be driven by the political habits we acquire early in life. What would democratic politics look like if such were the case?

If people were guided only by their political habits then democratic politics would look very much like a truncated version of the normal vote model we briefly discussed in chapter 2. If humans were guided only by the habituated, long-term forces of inculcated partisanship, ideology, and interest-group identity, then the outcome of political elections could be fully explicable by calculating the degree of mobilizations of competing groups. People might vote, or not, based on how enthusiastic they felt about their party, candidate, issue, or group; but little if any political persuasion or appeal to issues or candidate evaluation would be possible without the parallel surveillance subsystem to serve as an interrupt mechanism to engage rational calculation and suspension of habit.

Theories of value recognize the enduring power of political habits. The same can be said of theories of class and cleavage. They recognize how much consequence the mobilization of groups can have (as, for example, in the successful efforts of religious groups and labor unions to get out their "base" in the 1994 and 1998 congressional elections, respectively). Unless a campaign, candidate, group, or interest can effectively communicate auspicious evidence of anticipated success and/or the importance of the collective effort being undertaken, then the "base" is likely to find itself dispirited and apathetic. Of course, the partisan opposition will do their best to induce disinterest and despair among their adversaries. Thus, the disposition system offers each side the twin strategies of energizing their own followers and inducing apathy and gloom among their opponents. We can see much of this in full display in democracies worldwide.

The Surveillance System

We have anticipated the function and character of the surveillance system already in our example of the sign-waving campaign enthusiast who looses her balance and our caricature of disposition-only citizens. The surveillance function monitors the environment for novel and threatening stimuli. It serves to interrupt habitual routine and engage thought. Like disposition, surveillance is a subconscious emotional process, but because of its obvious importance for evolutionary survival, it is very fast-cycling.

It will come as no surprise to anyone familiar with the research in cognitive psychology that people have very limited abilities to consciously classify and interpret stimuli (Kahneman, Slovic, and Tversky 1982; Nisbett and Ross 1982). If our forebears in the jungle had to give a lot of thought to animal classification typologies upon hearing a nearby lion's roar, we might not be here now discussing the dynamics of political judgment. These are indeed primordial emotional processes.

An interesting study by Dennis Jennings, Teresa Amiable, and Lee Ross (1982) provides a good example of the limitations of the conscious apparatus available to humans in calculating the co-occurrence of events and outcomes and thus the probabilities of punishment and reward. The study involved sixty-four college undergraduates who were given "data-based" tasks and were asked to observe and quantify the strength of the association between two classes of symbols and sounds. The tasks presented the subjects with a drastically restricted sensory field: only the two sets of stimuli were presented. In normal mundane environments we are bombarded by rich and diverse sights, sounds, and smells from among which we have to select potential warning signs. Here, the initial problem—discriminating which stimulus warranted greater attention—was already determined by the investigators. Thus the most demanding aspect of securing a reliable warning was not a part of this study; the investigators not only directed attention to the class of stimuli of interest, they removed any competition for their subjects' attention.

So, how did the subjects perform? Not well at all, as shown in a summary of the findings in figure 4.3. The students had considerable difficulty in identifying even robust relationships. Students got it about right when the relationship was essentially nil and when it was near perfect, but in the intermediate range, the students consistently underestimated the true association. Like our typologizing jungle inhabitant, we find that conscious

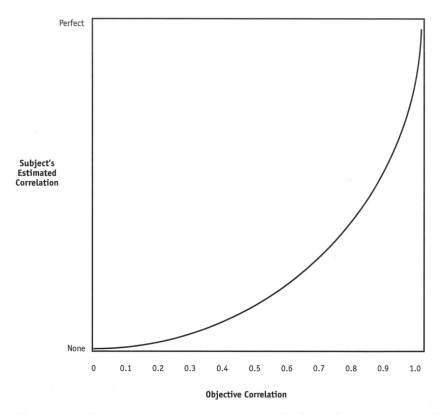

Figure 4.3   Subjective Assessment of Association in Paired Stimuli
SOURCE: Adapted from Jennings, Amabile, and Ross 1982.

calculation of risk and reward is not necessarily a way of engaging the world for which we are well equipped.[5]

Furthermore, before we can estimate the probabilities of potentially punishing events, we first must have the necessary taxonomy to identify what should be classified as threatening or dangerous. But, if threats are often sudden, unexpected, or novel, how is such a class to be defined? Perhaps understanding the evolution of the surveillance system will provide us some help.

Psychologists have found that "negative" events capture our attention far more than do positive outcomes (Derryberry 1991; May, Kane, and Hasher 1995; Pratto and John 1991). The swift identification of unfavorable circumstances has been crucial for our survival and evolution. Such circumstances threaten our security and are identified as being outside the bounds of familiarity handled by the disposition system. Indeed, this is such an important function that we have two different emotional systems, the "fight or flight" and the surveillance systems, to address the problem of threat.[6] The first is a "close in" defensive system; it takes over when we are in dire circumstances that call for immediate and swift action. The "fight or flight" system has powerful and direct control over behavior. As its name suggests, once we find ourselves facing imminent and immediate threat, we are compelled to choose between two behavioral choices: "I'm getting out of here!" or "Put 'em up!"

---

5. Interestingly, the study also had a "theory-based" component in which the subjects were asked to quantify the association between two familiar and well-established classes of events that drew upon prevailing expectations (more on this in a moment). It should come as no surprise that when subjects had some prior expectations they dramatically overestimated the relationship (Jennings, Amabile, and Ross 1982). That humans overvalue their beliefs is not a new observation, but it does again point out why beliefs provide a poor basis for judging whether the immediate circumstance is safe or dangerous.

6. The "fight or flight" system compares the incoming sensory stream for signs of imminent threat. When a threat is identified, the system triggers one of the two possible behavior reactions—fight (especially if no escape is possible) or flight (especially if an avenue of ready escape is available). In addition to triggering the appropriate behavioral reaction, the "fight or flight" system also invokes the appropriate emotional reaction, rage for the fight option and terror or fright for the flight option. Because the amygdala, where this early identification takes place, does not have the sophisticated and complex abilities of the sensory cortexes, we may mistake a crooked stick for a snake or react with fear to someone who, though a stranger to us, is in fact friendly. However, having gained the earliest possible warning, a warning that initiates defensive or aggressive responses often before we have gained conscious recognition of the nature of the threat, we are nonetheless better prepared (De Becker 1997). Because the "fight or flight" system operates in circumstances of direct and imminent danger, circumstances that are not generally political, we shall set it aside and turn to the surveillance system and those circumstances that do have significant political ramifications.

The surveillance system operates in a different fashion. It is a long-distance warning system with the task of providing a "heads up," which is meant more than metaphorically. The surveillance system responds to signals of threat, including precursors, and so is able to identify the possibility of a future threatening situation that is less immediate than those responded to by the "fight or flight" system. The surveillance system identifies novel circumstances as well as those that have previously proven to be destructive or threatening.[7] Though these two different classes of events, novelty and threat, are not often seen as equivalent, they both have the capacity to cause the surveillance system to react with alarm.

The surveillance system does not, by itself, generate a specific defensive reaction. Its function is to stop ongoing action, shift attention to the novel stimuli, uncouple reliance on habit, and foster greater motivation for learning, all of which lead to a greater reliance on "higher cognitive function." Habit is fine in stable and familiarly rewarding environments. The design of the surveillance system, however, enables it to serve as the "front end" for the greater use of conscious faculties such as thoughtfulness, deliberation, and learning. These are precisely those faculties that are the hallmarks of the use of reason. The surveillance system, an emotional system, is therefore a central goad to our greater use of our rational faculties.

The surveillance system enhances cognitive function by surveying the environment to assess its safety. By doing so, it "off-loads" an important strategic assessment: is it safe to devote all my attention, and all the requisite cognitive resources, to the task at hand? If the surveillance system finds nothing amiss, then the answer to that question is safely yes. If, on the other hand, something is found to be amiss, if something is "not quite right," then it interrupts the ongoing task and shifts attention toward the intrusive, threatening, or nonconforming stimuli. Figure 4.4 displays a schematic representation of the surveillance system.

It should be apparent that the principal features of the surveillance system are important to conscious awareness, cognitive functions generally, and behavior, as well as to explaining the modulation of anxiety. The principal affective reactions that are central to the surveillance system are those that range from a sense of tranquility and calm (when the system has observed nothing untoward) to anxiety (when the system has observed either something that signals a threat or, equally importantly, something that is unusual). The disposition system presumes a familiar context for

---

7. The surveillance system accomplishes this task by relying on procedural, not declarative, memory.

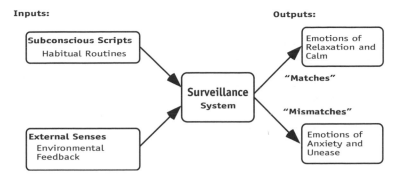

Figure 4.4   The Surveillance System—Affective Apprehension of Novel and Threatening Stimuli

the safe and normal enaction of the various possible behavioral routines. Although it is able to manage normal and expected variations, the disposition system, because it works within the bounds of the familiar, might put us at risk if it persisted in applying habitual routines in novel circumstances. The surveillance system, by identifying those circumstances that are unfamiliar in some strategic sense, by shifting our attention to that novelty, and by inhibiting the continuing execution of the current behavioral plan (that is, the control of habit), invokes greater attentiveness, greater thoughtfulness, and increased motivation for learning in just those situations that demand greater consideration.

We have a considerable array of learned capacities (not surprising with a brain of some 11 billion cells, each with upwards of fifty thousand connections). But using this capacity to make a new plan for each new moment would strain even this capacity. Reliance on previously learned routines obviously makes for greater efficiency, provided that what has previously proved successful is an appropriate template for future success. Reliance on learned capacities presumes that their current execution, as in the past, will yield comparable success in the here and now. But reliance on what has been previously learned may prove neither fruitful nor safe if here and now is not the same as previously.

If the grip of tradition is too great, if we rely solely on the disposition system's ability to manage the deft integration of movement and context, we are bound to those contexts that are least likely to change. Otherwise we will find ourselves in situations where habit's swift routines will either fail or place us in jeopardy. Heightened anxiety is the surveillance system's method of signaling that the moment has come to look for some new solution to novel environmental circumstances. Anxiety identifies those times when we should engage our capacity for learning.

What is most interesting about the surveillance system is that it sheds new light on the use of political judgment. It explains when people rely on previously learned beliefs and habits and when they set these aside. It explains when and why people are motivated to learn. It explains when political decisions are likely to be "up for grabs" and when political leaders have to work hard to get the public's attention. It explains when and why people ignore what some take to be vital information. It explains how people judge the importance of issues, events, and political figures.

The surveillance system is intimately involved with cognitive processes, including some that are often presumed to require the absence of emotion. It is conventionally believed that a calm and tranquil mind is best suited to careful, thoughtful, and deliberate judgment. Yet, the principal hypothesis of the theory of Affective Intelligence is that the surveillance system tells people when they can safely rely on the unreflective abilities of the disposition system to initiate and manage the regular habits of our lives. It also tells people when they should set their habits aside for a more explicit and thoughtful consideration of what is best to do.

When activated, the surveillance system shifts our conscious state away from the task at hand and toward an explicit consideration of what we should choose as the best course of action. Along with the attendant increase in anxiety, people pay greater attention to information about their immediate circumstance. They also demonstrate decreased reliance on habituated decision rules and behaviors and show an increased motivation for learning. In sum, anxious people seem to demonstrate greater compliance than do calm people with the formal requirements of the rational choice model: explicit conscious consideration of the comparative utilities of available choices, investing in the best contemporary information, and diminished motivation to use heuristic or habituated shortcuts.[8]

The Daily Experience of Anxiety

How much is known about the characteristic experience of the moods modulated by the surveillance system? Earlier in this chapter we described

---

8. We should emphasize that little study has been made of the relationship between very high levels of anxiety and political behavior and judgment. There may well be a curvilinear relationship such that anxiety beyond some optimal level degrades performance. This would be consistent with other work on various kinds of arousal that also suggest an inverted "U" relationship between performance and biological system activation (Arnsten 1988).

the data collected by Professor David Watson and we previously presented the distribution of the experience of enthusiasm, the emotion that is modulated by the disposition system. Here we present the distribution of anxiety, the negative affect dimension of the PANAS measurement using the same data. Recall that this measurement comprises an inventory of ten terms (*scared, afraid, upset, distressed, jittery, nervous, ashamed, guilty, irritable,* and *hostile*) used by subjects to assess how "out of sorts" they feel, how much the current context is not normal. As with the "positive" inventory, subjects rated their mood "at the present moment" at various times during each day. What would we expect for this distribution, given the functional role of the surveillance system? Unlike the disposition system, which manages the many recurring tasks of everyday life, the surveillance system is largely unobtrusive except when novel and threatening circumstances arise. Inasmuch as these occasions are likely to be infrequent, rather than the roughly normal distribution displayed by the moods of the disposition system, we expect the moods of the surveillance system to be highly negatively skewed, reflecting the general infrequency of anxiety in daily life. And, indeed, that is what the data reveal, as illustrated in figure 4.5.

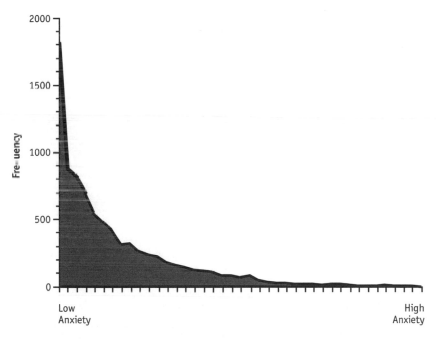

Figure 4.5 The Daily Experience of Anxiety

SOURCES: 1985–86 SMU study conducted by David Watson; personal communication.

Whether by design or chance most people usually find themselves in tranquil environments that are sufficiently safe to be absent much, if any, anxiety. Even moderate levels of anxiety in the mundane experience of daily life seem to be a rather rare occurrence. It is the nature of politics in democratic societies to generate greater levels of anxiety in the domain of politics than shown in figure 4.5.[9] Two factors argue for higher levels of anxiety in the ambit of politics. First, in the United States, our Constitution mandates frequent elections at regular intervals, no matter how satisfactory the electorate finds the state of the country and the state of political leadership. Second, democratic societies offer numerous opportunities for purveyors of anxiety. The various media, interest groups, political parties, elected officials, and their ambitious challengers each will take advantage of whatever circumstances enable them to point to the deficiencies of those in power. So, we may well expect to find political anxiety to be more widely experienced than anxiety in most, but not all, other domains.[10]

The Politics of the Surveillance System

Political habits are best suited to function within some familiar context. Any departures from the normal, especially novel and dangerous ones, require that we shift away from reliance on habits and take on the costs and risks associated with new, untried solutions. Such circumstances warrant investing in learning rather than continued reliance on previously learned habits. But before it makes sense to try something new and untried, people must recognize that the environment is no longer what it has familiarly been in the past. This is one of the principal tasks of the surveillance system. More importantly, the surveillance system and its associated effects makes possible the politics of persuasion.

Just as we did in considering the politics enabled by the disposition system, let's consider how politics would unfold if the circumstances that

9. Authoritarian regimes are likely to try to induce a general mood of tranquility and repose among the citizenry to forestall disquiet and rebellion. If they fail, they may seek to provoke anxiety—strategically targeted at convenient scapegoats, internal and external—so as to safeguard their own position.

10. Health, for some, and job security, for others, may be a recurring source of high anxiety that exceeds the level of anxiety about politics, to give just two examples. In general, however, political anxiety is likely to be for many people a source of worry, in part because democratic politics invites people to reinterpret their worries as public matters, not matters to be quietly and privately borne. We touch on the conversion of social anxiety to political anxiety in the chapters that follow.

generate anxiety were consistently plentiful to invoke the actions of the surveillance system. After all, democratic governments require that the electorate consider the current state of affairs and make a formal declaration whether to endorse or replace political officials.[11] Though it has clearly not been the case that the electorate, in the main, has taken on this task in the formal way that democratic theorists and proponents have wished,[12] let's consider how politics would look if anxiety were sufficiently rampant.

When the electorate is anxious, a condition they find unpleasant and undesirable, politics would nevertheless be very much like that depicted by the rational choice description of making judgments (Downs 1957). First, when anxious, people would no longer rely on their political habits (thus mindless partisanship would no longer figure in the vote equation). Second, anxious voters would experience a heightened motivation to learn, to gather contemporary information, to know more about the issues and where the candidates stand on the issues. Since we know that the public is in general poorly informed about most matters political (Delli Carpini and Keeter 1993), this would seem to be a desirable result. And, third, because the anxious voter is neither committed to prior habits nor inattentive, the way is open for candidates of all political stripes to have a plausible shot at persuasion. Anxious voters are more open minded for having set aside their dispositions. Moreover, unlike the politics of habit, the politics of persuasion is about identifying solutions, interests, and the discussion of goals and the best means to achieve them.

Of course there is a price to be paid for this kind of politics. First, it requires far more work. Coming up with new options (new leaders or new policies) is far more taxing than relying on incumbents and well-established policies. Second, anxiety is an unpleasant experience. People do not look forward to anxious moments, let alone a full campaign period lasting weeks and months. And, third, while making reasonable decisions that weigh all available options may be desirable, there are risks in relying on untried leaders and novel policies. Still, at least in situations that demand novel solutions, these costs seem well worth accepting.

11. To which we can also add, at least at the state and local level, the additional opportunity to respond to substantive policy questions contained in referenda, many of which will have been initiated by citizens and interest groups.

12. Hence the spate of defensive publications arguing that the electorate deserves at least a passing grade (Key and Cummings 1966; Mueller 1992; Page and Shapiro 1992; Popkin 1991).

The Relationship between Political Habits
and Reasoned Consideration

The theory of Affective Intelligence, like the normal vote model discussed earlier in this chapter, also combines its equivalents of long- and short-term forces. However, it does so in ways that lead to substantively different predictions. We hypothesize that people will rely on their political habits so long as the level of anxiety does not rise sufficiently to prompt their taking on the burdens of reasoned choice. Unlike the normal vote model, which draws attention to the nonpartisan and often inattentive independent swing voter, our theory predicts that those who have strong political habits will, when anxious, abandon those habits for reasoned and informed consideration of the alternatives. Consider how this would apply if hard economic times arise late in the first term of a president. It would be the president's partisans who experience anxiety because their leader has become associated with failure. As a result, they would engage in the reasoned considerations that anxiety initiates. The president's partisan opponents, as well as skeptical independents, might well have expected economic trouble and so the bad economic news merely confirms their expectations.

The theory also suggests an important asymmetry between incumbents and challengers. Incumbents, at least for most of the electorate, become invested with more than just the office they hold. They become leaders who bear the responsibility for ensuring good outcomes for all citizens. Incumbents start with the trust of a significant portion of the electorate, those who elected them. Thereafter, their support will depend on political habits (Democrats supporting Democratic office holders) or the support gained by good performance obtained during their term of office ("Are you better off than you were four years ago?"). Challengers have been entrusted, as yet, with little more than the aspirations of their partisan base. Thus, this model suggests that challengers, and the emotions they evoke, will not come much into play unless scandal, crises, or hard times cause sufficient numbers of partisans of the incumbent to become anxious (Marcus and MacKuen 1993).

Anxiety about the challenger is likely to be a less significant factor. Most challengers, being new and less familiar, may generate a modest degree of anxiety. But the anxiety that the incumbent provokes is more serious for it reflects worry not just about the office holder but also reflects concern for the well being of the city, state, or nation. When the office holder and the polity do well, voters will rely on political habits ("Four more years!"). These conditions will produce an election dominated by complacent voters.

Finally, anxious voters, partisans thrown into a state of uncertainty by the unexpected failure, will engage in critical consideration of the alternatives. Unlike weak partisans, and other "floating voters," anxious partisans will learn about the political issues of the day. They will learn where both candidates, or parties, stand on the issues.

While the portrait of the responsible voter is one we might hope to have constantly before us, what we have instead is a dynamic emotional voter able to shift reliance from one conditional strategy to another. In tranquil times the voter will smugly, but reasonably, rely on political habits. But the anxious voter will dramatically and dynamically shift to a far more rational mode of judgment. And all voters are likely to make this shift in just those circumstances that most demand the added effort that reasoned consideration requires.

The implications of Affective Intelligence regarding political habit and reasoned consideration can be summarized as follows:

- Unless anxious, people will rely on their political habits to make voting decisions. Anxiety will undermine the propensity to rely on a political habit.
- The absence of anxiety, however, does not automatically mean that reliance on habits will favor the habitual candidate, party, or program. Unless sufficient enthusiasm is marshaled among the partisan base of supporters, mobilization efforts may well fail to galvanize the partisan base to take the expected political actions (for example, contribute money, vote).
- What makes people anxious depends on the habits they have acquired. For example, concern for the current "decay in moral values" will be more apparent to Christian fundamentalists than to those for whom Christian values play a lesser role. Though some crises may provoke widespread anxiety, for example, fear of nuclear war during the Cuban missile crisis, many other events are likely to be partisan in their effects (for example, Democrats traditionally being more concerned with unemployment and Republicans with inflation).
- Because incumbents carry the responsibility for the well being of the community they lead, anxiety about the state of that community will devolve to them far more than to political challengers.
- When anxious about candidates, issues, or the times they live in, people will rely far less on their political habits to guide contemporary

choices, will be motivated to learn, will pay far more attention to contemporary affairs, and will be far more influenced in the choices they make by the careful consideration of alternative outcomes. Anxious voters will, in most instances, act very much like the rational voters as depicted by theories of public choice. However, when complacent, voters will in most instances look very much like the value protecting voters depicted by theory of symbolic politics.

The principal theme of this chapter is the dynamic and complex nature of the dual brain subsystems each regulating their characteristic emotional processes. It is important to note that the common presumption that being "emotional" has some uniform effect—for example, enhancing memory or degrading cognitive abilities—is almost certainly false. Emotional, behavioral, and judgmental consequences are not uniform across the emotional subsystems. Understanding the effects of emotion requires that one know which emotional system is engaged. Taken together the disposition and surveillance systems have distinct yet interactive roles in enabling us to meet the challenges and choices that life presents.

Chapter 5

Emotion and Political Behavior

In this chapter we turn to some of the empirical evidence available to test the hypotheses and predictions we have put forward thus far. As it happens, we find both encouraging confirmation and some further puzzles. Perhaps these first-cut results establish at least the plausibility of the basic model. Perhaps we have part of it wrong or incomplete. Elaborating the subtleties of the theory of Affective Intelligence and teasing out its genuine political implications will require a great deal additional work. At this point we may exhibit some anxiety and considerable enthusiasm, recalling that these are independent emotional processes.

We are indeed able to establish several key results. First, when people exhibit emotional reactions to politics, these responses make perfect sense from an Affective Intelligence standpoint. We should expect emotions that become attached to politics to have both state and trait characteristics. Several cuts at the evidence show that such emotional responses are dynamic and they incorporate reasonable understandings of the political world. Second, people evince multidimensional emotional reactions. The standard "valence" model, the one that makes so much common sense, turns out to be inadequate for the evidence. We find that the multi-dimensionality of Affective Intelligence provides a much better fit to the data.

We also find that the distinction between enthusiasm and anxiety gives us leverage in understanding how people become engaged in political life. As the theory expects, *both* permanent (trait) dispositions and contemporary (state) facets contribute to the sense of alertness that moves people to pay more attention to politics. But, perhaps most telling, we find that the general disposition, or habit, to engage in politics does little to enhance the extent to which people learn new political information. Instead, it is the surveillance system that not only moves people toward politics but also motivates the acquisition of new knowledge.

The Sources of Affective Intelligence

If people use their affective intelligence to understand the political world, it is critical that emotions be sensitive to changes in the political environment. Affect does little good if these processes operate independently of political events. In this chapter we shall see that people's emotional states do in fact change dynamically to reflect the character of contemporary politics in sensible ways.

The first point to be made is that political emotion is truly dynamic. Changes in political emotion reflect changes in stimuli. At a minimum, we want to establish that political emotion is to some extent a *state* and not solely a *trait*. We do this by examining a set of experiments in which the subjects were artificially stimulated by anxiety-laden messages.

Then we turn to real world conditions to see how people react to the politics they see. We examine data taken from the 1980–96 American National Election Studies (ANES) in which Americans were interviewed during election campaigns.[1] While these data are limited to the emotions elicited by the presidential candidates during political campaigns, they do provide a rich source for people's reactions to the normal politics of American democracy.

Manipulating Emotions

One important way to assess emotional dynamism is to conduct an experiment—to manipulate the environment in order to produce the expected political emotions. If we can elicit specific emotional responses by intentionally altering the sorts of political messages people see and hear, then we increase our confidence that political emotionality is, at least in part, a state. Here we report on two such studies.

The first (Marcus et al. 1995; Marcus, Wood, and Theiss-Morse 1998) studied people's responses to information about fictional political groups in a series of experiments. The investigators matched each experimental

---

1. The ANES have been conducted by the Institute for Social Research at the University of Michigan and serve as a national resource for this type of research. Each presidential year survey (like those used here) includes about two thousand respondents sampled to represent the United States. We thank the staff at the Inter-university Consortium for Political and Social Research for archiving these data and making them available. Of course, it is we and not the principal investigators who are responsible for the analyses in these pages.

subject with political groups that he or she had designated as objection-able and then presented the subject with different messages about the groups' public activities. One message depicted the groups' actions as well behaved and trustworthy while the other described the actions of the group as belligerent and treacherous. In a number of experiments, the subjects either read extensive textual descriptions or watched video presentations derived from network news footage depicting the behavior of actual groups.[2] In different tests, the subjects either filled out mood ratings to express how they felt or they had their physiological responses monitored. As the theory predicts, the belligerent and treacherous depictions made subjects feel more anxious and more threatened than the compliant and trustworthy depictions (Marcus et al. 1995; Marcus, Wood, and Theiss-Morse 1998).

In a second experiment, we manipulated subjects in the context of an actual political campaign. Late in the fall of 1996, during the campaign between Bill Clinton and Bob Dole, we asked a number of college sophomores at Ohio State University to view a set of campaign material.[3] We used actual footage from the real campaigns—selecting from each side "negative" commercials intended to induce anxiety among the viewers. In addition, we showed a few minutes from each candidate's introductory remarks in the first formal presidential debate. These were meant to proxy a "positive" message—one designed to encourage a rise in enthusiasm—although our assumptions about effectiveness were to be disappointed. In addition, some "control condition" subjects watched a nonpolitical short film intended to induce boredom. After watching the short presentations, the subjects then filled out a questionnaire that asked them to select emotional terms that might describe how they felt.

The negative commercials had their intended effect. Students who saw these ads were considerably more likely to describe themselves as "upset" and "distressed" than were those students who watched the positive and nonpolitical film clips. The debate sequences, however, had mixed effects, with the Clinton speech eliciting the expected enthusiasm

2. The investigators also found that manipulating the perceived power of the group, by itself, neither made people more anxious nor altered their tolerance attitudes toward the group. Given our description of the surveillance system as a normatively based system designed to quickly identify immediate and specific departures from familiar routine, this finding, that perceptions of power do not modify the mood of anxiety nor alter attitudes of tolerance, also corroborates our model.

3. This experiment included some 290 undergraduates who were part of the department of psychology's subject pool. We are especially indebted to Joanne Miller for her help in designing and supervising the experiments and for her intellectual contributions to our project. Details are available on request.

(especially among Democrats) but the Dole remarks generating little response at all.[4]

The results from these simple experiments demonstrate that feelings are, indeed, predictably dynamic. In both cases we expected the experimental subjects to have dispositions toward the messages' targets, and they did. But more than habit, or chronic attitude, was at play. In both sets of experiments, those exposed to danger-laden messages were more anxious than the rest. The difference was clearly linked to the nature of the political content of the messages themselves.

Using experiments to establish emotional dynamics is important because we can control the nature of the test. By design, we can be confident that the differences in emotional response are due to the message manipulations rather than to any outside influence that might have occurred without our knowing it. We know that the subjects did see the messages that drove the emotional differences. And we know the sorts of messages that work. By the standard of internal validity, the experimental design serves us well.

However, these experiments do not tell us much about the real world. After all, experimental subjects are forced to pay attention to the stimuli and are invited, by the experimental structure, to develop an appropriate response. In the course of everyday life, on the other hand, people do not pay much attention to political discourse; and, even when they do, they insulate themselves from manipulation by psychological mechanisms such as selective attention and selective perception. That is, many people ignore political news. Further, they see in the news the sorts of messages that are consistent with their own preconceptions. It would be helpful to have real-world data on how politics affects individuals' emotional states to see if the ordinary stuff of mass campaigns actually gets through their inattention and perceptual defenses.

Evidence from within Political Campaigns: Emotional Attentiveness

If people do use their emotions to make sense of politics, then we should see them react to the ebb and flow of ordinary political campaigns. Here we can see the impact of political news as it occurs.

---

4. The students exposed to the positive or neutral clips picked one of the "anxiety" moods only 5 percent of the time while those seeing the negative (anti-Clinton or anti-Dole) messages picked an anxiety mood 22 percent of the time ($p < 0.001$). The experiment had minimal impact on the students' feelings of enthusiasm (marked as "enthusiastic," "hopeful" or "excited"); about 33 percent of students picked such terms regardless of the experimental condition. The only exception was that Bill Clinton's opening debate remarks did seem to engage self-proclaimed Democrats to the point where 51 percent expressed some sense of excitement.

We explore two basic propositions. The first is that we should expect emotional responses to the campaigns to vary over time in meaningful ways. Again, we should see that political emotions have a distinctive state component—one that varies in accord with the changing information environment. Second, and more critically, we should detect *independent* operations of the disposition and surveillance mechanisms.

We begin by studying emotional dynamics during political campaigns. Our focus is on the 1980, 1984, and 1988 presidential elections because we have data that track people's emotional responses over the months of the presidential campaigns during those years. Happily for our purposes, the three histories are different: in 1980 the incumbent Jimmy Carter presided over a year full of political disaster and lost to the challenger Ronald Reagan; in sunny 1984 Reagan held on to win easily as challenger Walter Mondale was never able to stir the electorate; and in 1988 George Bush and Michael Dukakis battled out the campaign with a dramatic change in fortunes from midsummer to the late fall.

The first bit of evidence comes from the full campaign year of 1980, during which the American National Election Studies interviewed people in three waves—January, June, and October. Recall that in January, President Carter was riding (comparatively) high as the dual crises of the Iran hostages and the Soviet invasion of Afghanistan were in the news. Carter's handling of the extraordinary events engendered public sympathy and support. By June, of course, the bubble had burst and Carter was under duress. The hostage rescue attempt failed, underscoring months of painful diplomatic impotence; the economy endured escalating double-digit inflation and credit controls to go along with an oncoming recession; and the president's brother got embroiled in a scandal involving Libya's Muammar Qaddafi. Finally, during the Democratic convention and fall campaign, Carter was noticeably unable to engender much excitement for his failed presidency.

If emotions serve to monitor the environment, we should see movement in people's emotional responses during that year—and we do. The top left panel of figure 5.1 shows the average levels of both enthusiasm and anxiety people had regarding Carter for January, June, and October.[5] First, note the dramatic decline in the enthusiasm people felt for the incumbent

---

5. For this, and the remaining 1980-only analyses, we use seven mood terms for enthusiasm and anxiety: *hope, pride, sympathy, disgust, anger, fear,* and *uneasy.* "Anxiety" is the mean of disgust, anger, fear and uneasy while "enthusiasm" is the mean of hope, pride, and sympathy. For the 1980–96 analyses, where we collapse the annual surveys, we limit our attention to hope, pride, anger, and fear as those items were the only ones tapped through the entire period. See the appendix B for a discussion of measurement issues associated with eliciting emotional states.

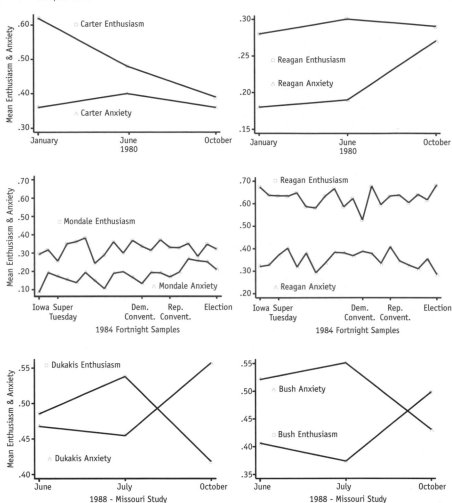

Figure 5.1 Dynamics in Candidate-Evoked Emotion during Political Campaigns
SOURCES: ANES 1980 panel study; ANES 1984 continuous monitoring survey; 1988 Missouri election study.

president from January to October. The public became less and less willing to vest their hopes in Carter's ability to do the job. Presidential failure led to disappointment or, in our terms, depression (i.e., the absence of enthusiasm). For our theoretical test, however, it is important to see that these failures led only modestly to anxiety. People may have sensed presidential incapacity but they did not feel that the president embodied danger. Their willingness to rely on, and identify with, Carter faded away but their surveillance mechanisms were not triggered by the violation of morality or standards of human conduct that we associate with a sense of social alert.[6] This pattern supports the theory of Affective Intelligence and, strikingly, disconfirms the simple valence model. Our disposition and surveillance systems respond differently to the same political environment—they are not mirror images of each other.

The emotional response to the challenger, Ronald Reagan, was more muted—as is typical for nonincumbent candidates.[7] In the top right panel, we see that people were modestly enthusiastic about Reagan, without dramatic changes. However, after the Democratic "scare" campaign in the fall of 1980—designed to induce distress about how Reagan would handle foreign affairs—we see a predictable rise in the public's response on the anxiety dimension. Being the challenger, of course, Reagan did not produce dramatic events that would give people an "objective" sense of his political character. Instead, people's emotional reactions were driven by his and his opponents' media messages. The overall effects were modest, but note that we again observe distinctive responses for the dispositional and surveillance systems.

When we look at the 1984 campaign trends we see similarities. For Reagan, a popular president presiding over an economic boom, the levels of enthusiasm were high and sustained over the year. Equally, he had already produced middling levels of anxiety by the beginning of the year and that level maintained itself. For Mondale, the challenger, the overall levels of emotional response were modest. People were lukewarm about Mondale on the enthusiasm side—a factor that he was never able to overcome. On the anxiety side, however, neither he nor the Republican camp produced much to worry about. At most there was a minor rise during the period after the conventions when it became plausible that the Democrat might want to raise taxes. Overall, though, the year was one of stability.

6. Of course, the ongoing economic failures and their associated worries would have already become factors in the public's emotions toward Carter well before the election year began. Interestingly, note that the public had essentially warm feelings toward Carter as a person, in the sense that they felt that he was well-intentioned. Mirroring the experimental results on political groups, it is the sense of moral disorder that triggers heightened anxiety, not mere incompetence.

7. Presumably, the incumbent president has had a chance to enthuse or disturb citizens by dint of having spent four years performing in the public spotlight. Nonincumbents, of course, are much less visible to most of the public and have hardly had the chance—outside the campaign—to do anything that would elicit a meaningful affective intelligence response. We here make the distinction between political action on the national stage and political campaign messages. Later we will see that the public treats much campaign information as "habitual" news to be interpreted in accord with longstanding partisan leanings.

Given the early strength of Reagan, the lack of anxiety in the air spelled defeat for Mondale. As seems generally the case, unless the challenger can engage the public's surveillance emotions, people will continue to support a successful incumbent. Thus, this apparent quiescence carries meaning for the interactions between affective intelligence, candidate campaigns, and people's ability to make political judgments—a point to which we will return in chapter 6.

The 1988 election did not feature a real incumbent. Bush represented a continuation of the current administration (and in essence ran on Reagan's coattails) but had not actually accomplished much himself—as is the way of vice presidents.[8] Dukakis, on the other hand, generated both modest enthusiasm and minimal anxiety. All this changed, however, following an intensive media campaign during the fall that emphasized the "liberal" Dukakis' support for Willie Horton and his supposed unwillingness to stand up for the American flag. Letting loose convicted murders and neglecting the pledge of allegiance, Dukakis was not merely incompetent but threatened the nation's moral and patriotic order—according to his opponents. This media effort substantially raised the public's anxiety about Dukakis. Equally, the enthusiasm for Bush rose and his anxiety diminished. This all looks like textbook campaigning, where the candidate who is behind in the polls (as Bush was in midyear) takes to negative campaigning to get people to reconsider their original inclinations. While Mondale was unable to get the public to reconsider their support for the frontrunner in 1984, Bush was successful at doing so in 1988. The two campaigns' differences demonstrate one way in which an understanding of the theory of Affective Intelligence enriches our view of American politics.

During these three campaigns, the political messages produced emotional resonance. Dispositions moved in accord with the common perceptions of the campaigns' successes. Surveillance responses, on the other hand, danced to a different beat. The rise in the public's concern about Reagan in 1980 does not seem to have been translated into a reluctance to vote for him. The lack of public concern during the 1984 campaign presaged an easy Reagan victory while the introduction of such worries in 1988 led to a dramatic shift in fortunes and a successful Bush comeback.

8. The data here come from a specially designed survey of Missouri voters who were interviewed during June and July of 1988 (bracketing the Democratic convention) and then again in October. Recall that Dukakis held a substantial lead in the midyear polls—one that Republican strategists took seriously enough to prompt a change in tactics.

Thus we see that the two emotional subsystems operated in distinctive ways during these political campaigns. The level of enthusiasm reflected people's varying support for the candidates as they competed for office. On the other hand, the level of anxiety seems to operate on a different rhythm, reflecting both the nature of the campaigns and the broader scope of political reality.

We get an even sharper picture of how the classes of emotions are distinct when we examine how specific individuals reacted to events. Fortunately, the 1980 study was conducted as a "panel" design—people interviewed in January were interviewed again in June and October. Thus, we can look at how a given citizen processed the news.

The issue we address here is the possibility that enthusiasm and anxiety are merely different sides of the same coin. Again, we want to be able to distinguish our Affective Intelligence theory from the more common "valence" view. The changes in the 1988 campaigns emotions, for example, are consistent with both views: when the electorate became more anxious about Dukakis they also became less enthusiastic. If this were the only pattern observed, then we would feel less comfortable in asserting that candidate-linked emotions do represent the distinctive systems of affective intelligence. However, the broad outlines of the 1980 dynamics suggest something different: the public became less enthusiastic about Carter as his failures mounted and thus less likely to vote for him. But their anxiety did not rise in parallel. And, similarly, the public's level of enthusiasm for Reagan remained roughly similar over time even after their anxiety heightened.

Here we can offer a crisper test. We can look at how *changes* in emotional states are related to each other over time. That is, for cetain individuals we know how their enthusiasm for Carter changed between January and October and we also know how their anxiety changed. The valence approach predicts that when enthusiasm goes up, anxiety should go down (for a sophisticated version of this argument, see Green, Goldman, and Salovey 1993). That is, when people start to "like" a candidate they should simultaneously abandon their "dislikes," or so the valence theory predicts. In contrast, the theory of Affective Intelligence predicts that a person's disposition and surveillance responses are independent.[9]

---

9. In fact, the matter is more complicated. Our perspective suggests that it is the triggering of the surveillance mechanism that encourages people to reconsider their standing dispositions. Thus we should expect to see an empirical relationship when the frightening information also stirs public attention to lower their dispositions toward a candidate—as was apparently the case for Dukakis in 1988. The very same "negative" information may simultaneously dampen enthusiasm.

Empirically, in any given year, there is a modest negative relationship between the levels of enthusiasm and anxiety. While this association between the two is pretty low compared to the "mirror image" prediction of valence theory, the association is not zero. Thus, a test of dynamics is crucial. If we see that an increase in anxiety leads to a decrease in enthusiasm (or vice versa), then we have evidence for the valence view. On the other hand, if we observe that changes in enthusiasm and anxiety are unrelated, then we can reasonably conclude that the two systems operate independently and infer an increased credibility for the theory of Affective Intelligence.

Figure 5.2 plots those changes during campaign year 1980 against one another, with Carter on the left panel and Reagan on the right. In each case, we look at the change in enthusiasm and change in anxiety from January to October. Look at the Carter panel first. The vertical axis displays the changes in anxiety and the horizontal axis changes in enthusiasm. The standard valence expectation is that enthusiasm and anxiety are negatively related: when people move up on the vertical (anxiety) axis they should move to the left on the horizontal (enthusiasm). As is immediately apparent, this expectation is clearly not met. For everyone that became more enthusiastic and less anxious (supporting valence theory) there exists someone else who became more enthusiastic and more anxious (directly contradicting valence theory). If enthusiasm and anxiety were merely different measures of "preference," then the prediction would show as a line running from the upper left corner to the lower right corner: a change in enthusiasm would be associated with an equal and opposite change in anxiety. In fact, the "average" association between changes in enthusiasm and anxiety, depicted by the solid regression line, is almost exactly flat. There is no relationship at all. The political events that diminished anyone's enthusiasm for the president did not, at the same time, increase anxiety. Conversely, anxiety-provoking events did not reduce enthusiasm.

While this was true for Carter—who was on the national stage—we also see it was true for Reagan—who was largely not. This is interesting because the public's assessment of the challenger is more a matter of imagination than perceived events. But even here, where the rise in anxiety may be a function of the fall campaign's mudslinging, people who became concerned about Reagan did not also become less enthusiastic. That is, when the Carter campaign was able to raise doubts in people's minds about Reagan's stability in crises, the campaign did not reduce their enthusiasm and hence their motivation to vote for Reagan. Again, political emotions are not merely a manifestation of overall preference—political affect is much more interesting than that.

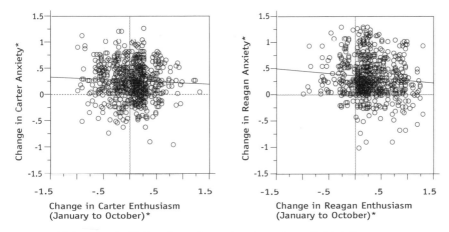

*All data points in this figure have a degree of random variance added to better display the distribution. All analyses in text are conducted on the original data.

Figure 5.2   Concurrent Changes in Candidate-Evoked Anxiety and Enthusiasm
SOURCE: ANES 1980 panel study.

Evidence Comparing Election Years:
The Role of Economic Fortune and Press Coverage

We gain additional leverage for our theory of Affective Intelligence when we compare citizens' reactions to the politics of different years. One central tenet of conventional political wisdom is that it is difficult to defeat an incumbent during years of prosperity. The press refrain for 1996, for example, was that Bob Dole failed to gain the attention of the American people because things were going so well that people were just not sufficiently interested in politics to be engaged by the electoral alternatives. Similarly, Walter Mondale was unable to stir the public during 1984; his attempts to tar Reagan never took hold. Note that such an analysis is exactly what the perspective of Affective Intelligence would envisage.

The question before us is whether the public's emotions fit a reasonable understanding of how political conditions vary over the years. The movement during any given campaign may reflect the ebb and flow of partisan debate. It need not incorporate any "real" information about the external political world. By looking at variation over time, explicitly comparing people's emotional reactions to the candidates under different conditions, can we begin to tell whether affective states indicate intelligence or simply a susceptibility to political manipulation.

The most obvious candidate for translating "reality" into emotional resonance is the state of the economy.[10] Naturally, when the national economy turns sour, when employment is widespread and jobs are likely to be lost, people will become more and more anxious. The question is whether this anxiety about both personal fortunes and national trends translates into a similar anxiety about the presidential candidates. In addition, we can ask whether that feeling of unease focuses on the incumbent (who can at least plausibly be given blame or credit for economic trends) or whether it colors feelings about politics in general.

The easy answer is illustrated in figure 5.3. In the top left panel, we see that the public's anxiety about the incumbent looks to be directly associated with the public's overall sense of economic prosperity. On the horizontal axis is the public's assessment of economic prosperity while on the vertical axis is the level of anxiety about the incumbent president.[11] It is clear that the public was most anxious about Carter and Bush during their reelection bids in 1980 and 1992—times of palpable economic distress. Similarly, they were hardly anxious at all about Reagan in 1984 or Clinton in 1996. Conventional wisdom is sustained here: economic hard times leads to anxiety while economic prosperity yields relative calm. Further, note that these economic bases of emotional response are not at all associated with feelings about the challenger—see the panel at the lower left. There is no good reason for people to condition their feelings about the challenger by their economic experience—and they do not. Here, the public's emotional reaction to the contemporary environment makes good sense.

In contrast to the surveillance pattern, the public's disposition toward the candidates is modestly associated with economic prosperity for both incumbents and challengers (positively for incumbents and negatively for challengers). This is standard stuff: good times lead to an inclination to vote for the incumbent and bad times to a preference for the challenger. But note that we see that anxieties and dispositions react very differently to the environment. The former, as we have seen, represents the surveillance mechanism that signals the need for further attention while the latter stands for a propensity to support.

10. The economy, as measured by people's sense of the nation's economic fortunes, represents a fairly straightforward prediction. Bad times lead to anxiety, good times to calm.

11. Here we ignore 1988 when Bush carried the Reagan legacy. As he had not been in office himself, he had not generated the *level* of enthusiasm and anxiety typical of actual incumbents. Thus his "emotional response" items are not directly comparable in this simple analysis (that is, he had not generated much response at all—more typical of challengers than of incumbents).

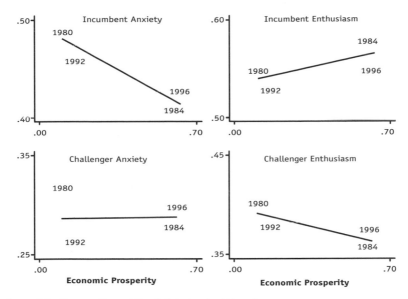

Figure 5.3 Prosperity and Candidate-Evoked Emotion
SOURCE: ANES 1980, 1984, 1992, 1994 election studies.

Partisanship and the Impact of Political News

Our overall argument here is that affective intelligence functions to signal people when they need to reconsider their habitual behavior. If anxiety is to work properly, to signal danger, then it must be able to penetrate the ordinary partisan blinders we find prominent in American political behavior. That is, distressing events should make their mark especially on those whose habitual partisan loyalties need to be reassessed.

In proceeding with this argument, we want to make clear an important theoretical twist. So far we have been careful to show that people's emotional responses are due to their states, not just to their traits. That argument is elaborated a bit by our suggesting that the effects of emotional states will depend on traits as well. We will explore this elaboration as we go forward. Our immediate concern, however, is to explore how the attention mechanism associated with anxiety will operate in the real world where people have very different long-held dispositions toward the political parties. Most Americans have such an enduring disposition, acknowledging themselves to be Democrats or Republicans, which plays a significant role in how they deal with their political world.

In the static sense, as we might expect, partisanship is strongly associated with people's feelings about the candidates. Republicans are more likely than Democrats to be favorably disposed toward Republican presidents. Similarly, though not identically, they are more likely to have been made anxious by Democratic presidents. In part this partisan pattern will be due to the standard psychological defense mechanisms that we know well. However, reality matters too—Democratic presidents *are* likely to say and do things that distress Republican citizens. They give speeches that thump the wrong sorts of values and they push policies that are too liberal. So, in fact, we should expect Republicans to be upset about Democratic presidents, just as Democrats are expected to be about Republican presidents. None of this, however, differs from the conclusions yielded by the conventional understanding about how people make political judgments. We need a prediction that distinguishes the theory of Affective Intelligence from the conventional understanding.

Consider how a major "event" such as an economic recession affects partisans' feelings about the incumbent president. As we have seen (in figure 5.3), bad economic times produce public anxiety—on average. The conventional understanding of how people process news would suggest that the effect of economic distress on their feelings about the president be strongly associated with their individual partisanship. The incumbent's partisans (Democrats for Democratic presidents, Republicans for Republican presidents) should deny the economic danger as posed by their man in office while the incumbent's opponents should be quick to grasp the peril.

The Affective Intelligence understanding, on the other hand, suggests that supporting partisans, perhaps *especially* supporting partisans, should sense the danger. We understand that for affective intelligence to be effective, it needs to inform people relying on routine responses that those routines need reassessment. Supporting partisans should feel uncomfortable because their president's poor performance on the economic front threatens their partisan standing decision. For example, when a Democratic president produces (loosely speaking) a recession, then Democrats should feel uneasy, perhaps even more uneasy than Republicans.

We provide a test of this hypothesis by examining the relationship between national economic conditions and the way that different classes of partisans react. As a first step, consider the simple regression of incumbent anxiety on national economic conditions in the first column of table 5.1.[12] Here we measure the economy with the Michigan Index of Consumer

---

12. In this and the remaining analyses, we use the ANES survey data taken for the five presidential elections during 1980–96. (Though here we do eliminate 1988 due to the nonincumbent status of Bush) The cases are weighted in accord with the ANES sampling weights and also inversely with respect to the size of each national sample to produce a

Table 5.1 Incumbent Anxiety as a Function of National Economic Conditions

	Incumbent Anxiety (Dependent Variable)			
	Total Sample	Pure Independents	Supporting Partisans	Opposing Partisans
National economic conditions	0.47	.086	0.82	0.28
Constant	.17	-0.08^{ns}	-0.17	0.45
Adjusted R^2	.01	.03	.03	.00
RMSE	.38	.37	.33	.36
Total N	6877	738	3079	2933

SOURCE: ANES 1980, 1984, 1992, 1994 election studies.

NOTE: Each column represents a separate regression. All coefficients are statistically discernible from zero unless marked "ns." National economic conditions are measured by the Michigan Index of Consumer Sentiment (the annual average, rescaled to 0–1 and reflected to indicate economic distress). Supporting and opposing partisans are dummy variables for the partisan supporters and partisan opponents of the incumbent party.

Sentiment (and reverse it to indicate economic distress).[13] We expect a positive coefficient and we get it (0.47). This coefficient echos the finding in figure 5.3 that prosperity and recession are associated with complacency and anxiety, respectively, about the incumbent. In terms of our metric, the estimated coefficient suggests that the difference between the worst and best economic years here (1980 and 1984) account for not quite half the difference in incumbent anxiety in those years, a substantial impact.

But what we want to know is whether the incumbent's partisans are less likely to react to economic hardship—as standard psychological theory might anticipate. To assess this, consider the next three columns of table 5.1, which show the impact of national economic conditions controlling for

---

data set that equally represents the United States electorate through time. The total (unweighted) sample size for the five-election composite is 10,682. Given the large number of cases, caution should be exercised with "tests of statistical significance" as an indicator of substantive importance. Accordingly, in order to reduce clutter, we have not explicitly indicated the "significance" of the estimated coefficients in these tables. We do, however, mark as "not significant" ([ns]) those few coefficients that do *not* pass statistical muster.

13. This is the standard Index of Consumer Sentiment (ICS) compiled by the University of Michigan's Institute for Social Research. Here we average the twelve monthly scores for each election year. Note that we use a measure of *national* conditions rather than an individual's personal assessment of either family income or the economy. In work not shown, we understand that personal perceptions or personal conditions are not what drives incumbent anxiety; it is national conditions that drive the system, as ordinary political economic theory suggests. Here we take the standard ICS score and rescale it to the (0–1) interval by dividing by 200. In addition, we subtract it from 1.00 to get a measure that indicates economy misery—properly signed for our modeling incumbent anxiety.

the individual's partisan orientation toward the incumbent. These three columns represent separate models for pure independents and then for supporting partisans and for opposing partisans.

First, look at the column for pure independents (column 2) to establish a baseline. We see that the economy matters a great deal (0.86), indicating that the difference between the best and the worst of economic times accounts for the difference in anxiety during those years. Now note well the numbers for supporting partisans (that is, the partisans of the president's own party). The impact of the economy on anxiety is almost exactly the same for these supporting partisans as it is for the pure independents (0.82 compared with 0.86, a difference that is statistically indiscernible from zero). And then contrast the reactions of the opposing partisans, whose anxiety about the incumbent responded only weakly (0.28) to economic fluctuation.

These results are consistent with the theory of Affective Intelligence and inconsistent with a more conventional understanding of how news is processed by the public. Supporting partisans register economic information and react emotionally just as faithfully as do pure independents. They evince no psychological mechanisms that disable the surveillance system. To the contrary, it is the incumbent's supporters who react with greater emotion (heightened anxiety) compared to the incumbent's opponents. For those opponents, bad economic news registers neither surprise nor threat and their surveillance system rests undisturbed. For supporters, bad news surprises and threatens their habitual partisan views and their surveillance system responds accordingly.

Affective Intelligence and Citizen Participation in Politics

Democracy's deepest challenge lies in getting ordinary citizens to pay attention to public affairs. College professors, schoolmarms, and well-intentioned people everywhere urge citizens to take part in their own self-government, to become informed about what is going on, to consider what is best for themselves and for the country as a whole, to vote, and to engage in politics more generally. Most people, it turns out, successfully resist these entreaties without considerable effort.

Learning about public affairs and then doing something about it takes time and effort. The chances that any single citizen can have influence over matters of policy, especially national policy, are essentially zero. So efforts at self-education are not motivated by classic rational self-interest.

To be sure, many Americans do follow politics and public affairs. For reasons having to do with its intrinsic interest as human drama and, perhaps, with a shared sense of civic duty, news about politics satisfies different appetites. And, depending on how one measures this, anywhere from one-third to one-half of all Americans maintain some frequent attentiveness toward public affairs. Such attentiveness becomes habitual behavior. As such, it constitutes a baseline of democratic participation that undergirds public influence over politicians' decisions.

Other people are more sporadic in their attentiveness to public affairs. From time to time, they pay attention not out of habit but because they are stimulated to do so. It is toward this dynamic that we now turn our empirical focus, asking what are the ways that different people get attracted to public affairs.

Our theory of Affective Intelligence comes to center stage here. People are guided by their emotions in their attentiveness toward many things in life, and we expect that public affairs is not much different. First, the disposition system (feelings of enthusiasm) gives people a sense for whether politics is going to be a rewarding subject for attention. We expect that when they feel enthusiastic about the politics of any given year, they will be much more likely to pay attention to what is going on. When people are depressed, on the other hand, they may choose to ignore politics and turn to other fields of interest. These feelings of enthusiasm will, of course, be partly habitual in the sense that some people get more enjoyment from politics than do others. But there can also be a short-term burst of enthusiasm over a particular period—say when an election campaign is waged between two attractive and engaging candidates as opposed to when the campaign is a matter of having to choose the "lessor of two evils." And, of course, these feelings may be entirely idiosyncratic: a campaign between two liberals or between two conservatives will likely elicit different degrees of enthusiasm from the electorate's liberal and conservative blocs. In this sense, Affective Intelligence's dispositional system will mark both "traits" and "states" in that it reflects both habit and circumstance.

Second, the surveillance system may come into play. Most people are content to ignore politics until something unusual happens. After all, most political contests reflect a repeated game in which politicians from the two parties do battle over much the same ground year after year. Savvy citizens will develop a routine way of handling these ordinary events and feel that they have no need to stop and reflect deeply on what is going on at the moment. So instead of continually monitoring the political environment by paying close attention, they instead rely upon an emotional "alarm" system that signals them when they need to pay attention and when their standard response will likely serve them well.

In this section we examine evidence from five presidential campaigns to see whether the theory of Affective Intelligence has much to say about how people engage in politics. We first examine people's self-reported engagement in terms of their feelings toward the current campaign and their actual voting behavior. Then we turn to a more interesting question: does affective intelligence guide people's information gathering so that they are moved to learn more about the stakes in any given election? And finally, we briefly glance at some data on participation itself.

Political Engagement in Election Campaigns

It matters enormously whether people become engaged in politics. We look first at how citizen traits and emotional states are related to campaign interest. In our election studies, people were asked how much they were "interested in the current campaign." Some of this engagement reflects people's habitual attentiveness to politics while some of it is due to the specific conditions of the current campaign. In order to distinguish between the two, we turn to the evidence from the 1980–96 presidential campaigns.

To begin, we see whether the emotional states that characterize affective intelligence are related at all to campaign interest. We expect that both the disposition system and the surveillance system will motivate interest. In the first case, a positive feeling toward the candidates will signal positive feedback from politics and encourage further involvement. People who like the candidates will enjoy the spirit of politics while those who find the candidates disgusting will turn away. In the second case, when the surveillance system signals novelty or danger, we expect that people will engage to find out what is going on. Bright new politicians are worth watching and dangerous characters demand close scrutiny.

Table 5.2 provides an initial confirmation of our expectations. Here, we break the population into those who are and who are not anxious about the candidates, and those who are and who are not enthusiastic about the candidates. We use anxiety and enthusiasm about the pair rather than about one or the other.[14] Clearly emotions make a difference. Of those who are anxious, 83 percent are interested in the campaign while of those who are calm only 71 percent say they are interested. Similarly, enthusiasm

---

14. For this table, people are scored as "anxious" or "enthusiastic" when they connect two (out of a possible four) anxious or enthusiastic emotions with the candidates.

Table 5.2 Involvement and Affective Intelligence

	Anxiety about Pair of Candidates		Enthusiasm about Pair of Candidates	
	Calm	Anxious	Indifferent	Enthusiastic
Percentage Who:				
Have some campaign interest	71	83	65	83
Care who wins	61	75	54	74
Follow campaign in newspaper	69	82	66	79
Follow campaign in magazine	25	39	24	34
Follow campaign in any medium	82	92	78	90

SOURCE: ANES 1980–96 election studies.

NOTE: Each entry is the percentage of people who have some campaign interest, care who wins, follow the campaign in the newspaper, and so on.

about the candidates evinces increased interest, rising from 65 percent to 83 percent.[15]

These sorts of numbers are reflected in other measures of campaign involvement as well. Those who are either anxious or enthusiastic about the candidates are more likely than not to say that they care who wins the election. And they are more likely to have followed the campaign in the newspapers or in magazines or through other media. Notably, we see that this effect obtains for both anxiety and enthusiasm, that is to say for both the surveillance and the disposition systems.

In general, it seems, different sorts of emotional responses indicate different sorts of motivation that encourage greater political attention. This result is consistent with the theory of Affective Intelligence, but it is not decisive. Moreover, it is surely consistent with a more general notion that people develop long-term habits about political involvement that are independent of the specific emotional signals in the current environment.

We know that many people routinely follow politics out of a sense of personal fascination, a sense of civic obligation, or because they are socially engaged. The danger for our theoretical inference here lies in the fact that people who are habitually attentive to politics will also be more likely to have been emotionally moved by the candidates. For example, people who "follow politics and public affairs most of the time" are considerably more likely to fall into our categories of "anxious" and "enthusiastic." Of

15. The number of cases in these comparisons varies by around eight thousand depending on the specific variables. The standard errors of the estimates run from 1 to 2 percent, so these reported distinctions are all statistically significant.

these habitual attentives, 49 and 70 percent are anxious and enthusiastic, respectively—while of the politically innocent only 20 and 47 percent have been emotionally engaged. If we are to be sure that emotions spark attention, we must be careful not to inadvertently pick up a spurious relationship in which habitual attentiveness completely accounts for both the current emotional state and the current attention to politics.

Thus, we want to hold constant, or control, the long-term impact of habitual attentiveness on both campaign interest and on the emotional responses themselves. That is, we want to wipe out the effect of habit before we measure the effect of emotions. In this way, we tap emotions that reflect the immediate political environment—the emotions of affective intelligence. To proceed, we employ standard multivariate analyses, here regressions, that statistically control for both the immediate and the prior impact of habit.

For the required multivariate analysis, we begin again with campaign interest. In the first column of table 5.3, straightforward regressions show that both candidate-provoked anxiety and enthusiasm are substantially related to campaign interest for the years 1980–96.[16] About one-fourth of the interest range (0.23 and 0.24) is accounted for by each of the affective states. In a different metric, this is the same result as in the percentages of table 5.2.

The multivariate analysis crucially allows us to control for the alternative explanation that it is the long-term trait of attentiveness that dominates our relationship. Here we use habitual political attentiveness, education, and strength of partisanship as traits that will typically lead citizens to become more deeply engaged. Of course, habitual attentiveness is by now a standard measure of political engagement (Zaller and Feldman 1992) and represents citizens' ordinary involvement with political news. Education marks both an increased intellectual skill in dealing with

16. Each variable is scored on the (0–1) interval to make the coefficients roughly comparable. Here we do not collapse the emotional responses, but instead use the full range of measurement. All coefficients are statistically "significant" unless otherwise noted. Caution should be exercised as the large sample sizes make statistical significance tests an unreliable guide to substantive importance. Essentially the same results obtain when we control for the mean for each election year. Only one of these elections stands out in terms of engagement: 1992. Probably due to the Perot campaign, people were somewhat more interested in politics that year than can be explained with conventional theory.

Habitual attentiveness is a four-point scale indicating whether the respondent "follows politics" (the *range of the variable*, here 1–4, is normed to the 0–1 interval). Education is the respondent's formal education (six levels, normed to a 0–1 interval) and strength of partisanship is a range from pure independent, to leaning independent, to weak partisan, to strong partisan (normed to 0–1).

Table 5.3 Campaign Interest as a Function of Affective Intelligence and Citizen Traits

	Dependent Variable		
	Campaign Interest	Campaign Interest	Campaign Interest
Total anxiety	0.23		0.10
Total enthusiasm	0.24		0.13
Habitual political attentiveness		0.49	0.47
Education		0.13	0.11
Strength of partisanship		0.14	0.12
Constant	0.35	0.09	0.03
Adjusted R^2	0.07	0.27	0.29
RMSE	0.35	0.31	0.31
Total N	8313	7077	7061

SOURCE: ANES 1980–96 election studies.

NOTE: Each column represents a separate regression. All coefficients are statistically discernible from zero.

the abstractions of public affairs and also a degree of socialization toward the norms of engagement and participation. Partisanship strength reflects individuals' attachment to the party system and to the players in the political drama. The parameter estimates in the second column of table 5.3 show that the three traits are all positively associated with interest in the campaign—no surprise here.

The test comes when we examine the power of emotional states while we statistically control for the possible confounding effects of trait.[17] In the third column of table 5.3 we put the two components together. Now we see that the independent effects of today's emotional states, once we eliminate the possibility of spuriousness, is only about half the original estimates. And yet, each emotional state has an independent and substantial impact on attentiveness. The difference between being calm and anxious (0.10) or indifferent and enthusiastic (0.13) is just about equal to the difference between a grade school or a college education (0.11) or being a pure independent or a strong partisan (0.12). The impact is not trivial. People who are upset about the candidates or who are enthusiastic about the choices will be noticeably (but not shockingly) more interested in the campaign.

17. The theory of Affective Intelligence predicts, as we have seen above, both a trait effect (embedded in the habits adopted and the personality dispositions characteristic of each individual) as well as a state effect. Here we want to be careful that we can sort out the two components. We give special attention to the state component because the traditional view of emotion is that it interferes with *intelligence*, as that term is conventionally understood.

If this is true about campaign interest, what does it say about engagement more generally? We test the general proposition for three more measures in table 5.4. Column 1 simply repeats the results from table 5.3. In column 2 we see that the same pattern holds for "caring about who wins the election." While similar in nature to campaign interest, this measure of involvement is more clearly linked to a concern about winners and losers—notice the dramatic increase in the strength of partisanship coefficient. And yet, even after holding constant citizens' long-term traits, both emotional systems remain important.

These first two measures of involvement are standard and useful measures, but they are subjective in character. We gain further confidence when we ask about media attentiveness. In the last two columns of table 5.4 we test the significance of emotional signals for newspaper and magazine attentiveness.[18] Again, habit and training are important for both types of attention—as we surely understand. We well know that media attention is a matter of routine. The mystery is not that college-educated political junkies watch PBS or read the front page of the daily newspaper, but instead why others choose to pay closer attention to public affairs at some times rather than others. Crucially, here, we see that the contemporary emotional messages are important as well as habit.

It seems that people who are stimulated by their emotions do become more engaged in politics—at least to the extent that they pay more attention to what is going on. To be sure, most of the variation among individuals is determined by habits of attentiveness. But an important increment seems to be independently driven by how people react emotionally to the politics of the day.[19]

Now consider information. For democracies to work it is not enough for people to get involved. They must also develop a sense of how their and the nation's interests are affected by political choice. We want to see if the emotional systems spur people to learn about the candidates. Again, Affective Intelligence predicts that both emotional systems operate simultaneously. The disposition system moves people to pay attention and, per-

18. The survey question asks whether the individual followed the campaign in the newspaper, and so on. For our purposes, newspaper reading and, more clearly, magazine reading indicates a more substantial interest than does having noticed the campaign on television or radio.

19. Of course, a fuller test would include how people feel about other contemporary aspects of politics, such as significant events, as well as salient policy issues and issue debates. Since we are limited to measures of the emotional reactions to presidential candidates of the day, table 5.4 offers a conservative test of the total impact of emotions generated by contemporary politics.

Table 5.4 Engagement as a Function of Affective Intelligence and Citizen Traits

	Dependent Variable			
	Campaign Interest	Care Who Wins Election	Newspaper Attention	Magazine Attention
Total anxiety	0.10	0.12	0.10	0.12
Total enthusiasm	0.13	0.14	0.12	0.07
Habitual political attentiveness	0.47	0.26	0.36	0.28
Education	0.11	0.04	0.20	0.39
Strength of partisanship	0.12	0.36	0.05	-0.02^{ns}
Constant	0.03	0.18	0.29	-0.18
Adjusted R^2	0.29	0.14	0.15	0.16
RMSE	0.31	0.43	0.40	0.43
Total N	7061	7055	5676	7061

SOURCE: ANES 1980–96 election studies.

NOTE: Each column represents a separate regression. All coefficients are statistically discernible from zero unless marked "ns."

haps only indirectly, to learn. The surveillance system, on the other hand, more directly and powerfully motivates a keen attentiveness because people sense a disturbance in the environment and a need to confront the surprise.

To test this, we develop two different measures of what people know about the candidates. The first represents the "mass" of ideas that people have about the two candidates and the parties. In the ANES surveys, respondents were asked what sorts of things they "liked" and "disliked" about the two candidates and the two parties. We simply add up the discrete mentions to get a sense of "weight." People who have been paying attention to the public affairs of their day and who have learned what is happening politically in any given year will have more considerations in mind when they are asked for their political opinions.

This mass of ideas is one marker of how people see the political world. We naturally expect that people with a large number of facts and ideas will be able to consider the complexities of public life more fully than those who carry only a sparse representation (Neuman 1981). In addition, we know that the sorts of considerations people bring to bear on their decisions will affect the outcome of the vote (Kelley and Mirer 1974; Zaller and Feldman 1992). So measuring how much "stuff" people acquire for political judgment informs us about how they assimilate the information in a political campaign.

As before, we control for people's habitual attentiveness, education, and partisanship strength. All of these factors will lead to greater engagement and, likely, to a greater number of "thoughts" about politics. The results are in column 1 of table 5.5. Here we regress the "information mass" on the emotional responses and the citizen traits, again for the 1980–96 elections. As before, the traits are important. But now we see a difference in the relative impact of the two affective intelligence systems. The surveillance system, marked by anxiety, is roughly twice as important as the dispositional system (compare 0.09 to 0.04). While surely both coefficients are statistically identifiable as nonzero, the disposition system's impact is considerably smaller and almost trivial. The surveillance system's operation produces the same sort of modest but noticeable impact that we have seen previously—roughly comparable to the impact of education.

Finally, we get a sharper picture of the emotional systems' distinctive operations when we push for a "harder" measure of information. The trouble with the simple information mass measure is that much of the respondents' commentary has little to do with the real political choices implicit in the campaign. Further, the simple mass of information may represent incorrect information shaped to correspond with the citizens' already-developed preferences. We want another indicator of information that more decisively depends on information accuracy than on information weight. To accomplish this goal we calculate the percentage of times the respondents can identify the Democratic candidate to be more liberal than the Republican candidate over the set of issues that were important during that election.[20]

Column 2 of table 5.5 gives the results for this more exacting test of information. We see now that the surveillance system stimulates information acquisition while the impact of the disposition system disappears altogether (compare 0.13 with 0.00). For policy-related information, we find that it is danger rather than pleasure that pushes people to learn about politics.

We gain some confidence about this conclusion when we note that, among the traits, it is now education that is most important rather than habitual attentiveness. To do well on this "correct information" scale, it is not enough merely to pick up messages, one must also be able to sort out

20. Here we rely on the ANES staff for the issue selection. We take each of the seven-point policy scales and score the respondent as "correct" if the Democrat is placed to the left of the Republican. We correct for guessing by subtracting as "wrong" answers that place the Republican to the left, and score as zero those in which the candidates are placed identically or in which the respondent says "Don't know." We then take the mean for each respondent over the issue questions in each survey. On average, over our years, 28 percent of the responses are "correct."

Table 5.5 Knowledge as a Function of Affective Intelligence and Citizen Traits

	Dependent Variable	
	Information Mass	Correct Policy Stands
Total anxiety	0.09	0.13
Total enthusiasm	0.04	0.00[ns]
Habitual politcal attentiveness	0.12	0.09
Education	0.14	0.22
Strength of partisanship	0.04	0.06
Constant	−0.02[ns]	0.00[ns]
Adjusted R^2	0.29	0.11
RMSE	0.13	0.27
Total N	7075	5882

SOURCE: ANES 1980–96 election studies.

NOTE: Each column represents a separate regression. All coefficients are statistically discernible from zero unless marked "ns."

correct from incorrect information about both candidates. Voters who are more educated develop the ability to make serious comparisons about the relative policy positions of the candidates.

Thus we see that the two emotional systems are different after all. When it comes to political learning, especially political learning about policy proposals, what is important is not mere engagement but also the sorts of motivations that are associated with, and controlled by, the surveillance system. It is novelty or, more typically, a sense of unease that moves people to think more critically about the political choices before them.

Finally, we turn to participation itself. We want to know not only when people get engaged in the political world and when they begin to learn more about the candidates, but we also want to understand more about what motivates actual participation. What moves people to talk politics with others, display bumper stickers, contribute money, or do campaign work? We first ask whether the emotional systems motivate active participation as well as a special attentiveness.

In table 5.6 we repeat our analytic scheme, examining the two systems in operation when controlling for citizen traits. Here the criterion variable is active participation: whether citizens do anything at all *beyond the voting act* or simply ignore active politics altogether.[21] The evidence is clear that

21. Participation beyond the voting act is a dichotomy that indicates whether the individual did any of the following: try to convince others about the vote, display a bumper sticker or button, contribute to a campaign, attend an election meeting, or work in a campaign. The next column in table 5.6, for amount of participation, measures the number of activities (beyond voting) the individual chose divided by five (the maximum).

Table 5.6 Participation as a Function of Affective Intelligence and Citizen Traits

	Dependent Variable	
	Any Participation beyond Voting Act	Amount of Participation beyond Voting Act
Total anxiety	0.23	0.07
Total enthusiasm	0.10	0.02
Habitual political attentiveness	0.35	0.13
Education	0.18	0.08
Strength of partisanship	0.13	0.07
Constant	−0.10	−0.08
Adjusted R^2	0.14	0.14
RMSE	0.46	0.17
Total N	7076	7076

SOURCE: ANES 1980–96 election studies.

NOTE: Each column represents a separate regression. All coefficients are statistically discernible from zero unless marked "ns." Acts of participation beyond voting include trying to convince others about the vote, displaying a bumper sticker or button, contributing to a campaign, attending an election meeting, or working in a campaign. The amount of participation is the sum of participation acts divided by five (the maximum possible).

both sorts of emotional signals are associated with participation. People's citizenship traits, not surprisingly, are quite powerful. Again, however, we see that the more urgent signals of the surveillance system are about twice as important as positive dispositions (compare 0.23 with 0.10) when we control for the long-term relationship between emotions and traits. And while it works very differently, the surveillance system's trigger is about as important as education in accounting for political activism. Apprehension of novelty and threat can, and does, motivate people to political action.

As a final measure, we examine the amount of participation rather than the simple decision to participate. In the last column of table 5.6 we see that our scheme produces a similar pattern, albeit with smaller numbers (the magnitudes being a function of the participation scale). Again, it is the surveillance system—rather than the good feeling of dispositions—that most clearly prompts increases in participation beyond the ordinary.

All this evidence comes from five presidential elections spanning nearly two decades. These data have the advantage that they represent the characteristic responses of individuals over a number of different political contexts and thus we are unlikely to infer a general pattern from a peculiar election campaign. However, the data are not truly dynamic. For any given respondent in any year, we observe only the level of candidate-evoked emotional response and the politically relevant traits. But we cannot directly separate what was due to the events of the election campaign from the long-term relationships between the Affective Intelligence's contemporary emotional reactions and citizenship traits. Our statistical controls give us intellectual leverage, to be sure, but it would be helpful to be able to observe change directly rather than infer it.

Some Dynamics of Political Engagement

To do this, we return to the 1980 ANES campaign panel study in which individuals were interviewed three times during the year. We can trace how people reacted to the year's events to see whether a change in attention or knowledge is associated with different emotional states. We concentrate on the period between June and October—the period following the primaries that includes the party conventions and the initial month of the campaign. This is the time during which the parties establish their main themes and the candidate campaigns establish their strategic appeals. Simultaneously most voters confirm their judgments about the candidates and parties and they typically harden their voting choices. We want to know whether the emotional signals of this period affect the way that people engage politics.

We begin as before with a subjective measure of campaign interest. We repeat our analytic strategy by regressing interest on our emotional markers as well as on the measures of citizenship traits. The difference now, however, is that we use the *change* in campaign interest, from June to October, as our dependent variable. And the dynamic formulation allows us to control for the individual's previous level of campaign interest (here in June). Thus, our dependent variable more clearly represents the novel *state* of involvement net long-term trait components.[22]

The first column in table 5.7 paints a similar, but not identical, picture to the one that we obtained from the cross-sectional time series data. Change in campaign interest seems mainly a function of habitual attentiveness (compare 0.35 with the rest). But note the clear distinction between the coefficients for anxiety and enthusiasm (0.03 with 0.09, and anxiety is statistically insignificant). We see that the sorts of emotions that we associate with the surveillance system do not play much of a part in people's getting psychologically interested in the campaign. Instead, this seems more nearly a matter of mobilization efforts generated by the candidates and their campaigns, a matter of enthusiasm.

22. In addition, when we control for previous campaign interest in our regressions, we (partially) account for the confounding influences of "regression to the mean" and any positive feedback in which the involved become more involved.

Table 5.7 Dynamics of Engagement as a Function of Affective Intelligence and Citizen Traits

	Dependent Variable		
	Campaign Interest	Care Who Wins Election	Media Attention
Total anxiety	0.03^{ns}	0.02^{ns}	0.14
Total enthusiasm	0.09	0.08	0.04^{ns}
Habitual political attentiveness	0.35	0.26	0.14
Education	0.05	−0.28	0.12
Strength of partisanship	0.07	0.30	0.04
Dependent variable in June	−0.62	−0.61	−0.53
Constant	0.00	0.17	−0.14
Adjusted R^2	0.32	0.31	0.22
RMSE	0.27	0.41	0.20
Total N	712	690	707

SOURCE: ANES June–October 1980 panel study.

NOTE: Each column represents a separate regression. All coefficients are statistically discernible from zero unless marked "ns."

When we shift our attention to caring about the outcome, column 2, we see the same pattern. The extra boost in concern lies among those happy with the candidate set rather than those upset about the choice—though again the numbers for these short-term dynamics are fairly small.

Media attention, however, produces a different result. Now it is anxiety (0.14) rather than enthusiasm (0.04^{ns}) that stands out in stimulating involvement. This pattern holds for increased newspaper, magazine, and radio campaign attentiveness during the fall campaign. But it seems that television attention is different: the emotions associated with the surveillance and disposition systems seem to have little impact on television news watching (not shown). Of course, to the extent that people perceive television as entertainment and print journalism as information, this makes sense. When we shift from a sense of personal commitment to the campaign (in the sense of "interest" or "caring") to one of information monitoring ("media attention"), we begin to see the distinctive operation of the surveillance as opposed to the disposition system.

This pattern should be repeated in our measures of political learning—and it is. For the 1980 panel study we are limited to our more stringent "correct policy stands" measure that depends on the individual's knowing that the Democrat (Carter) is politically to the left of the Republican (Reagan).[23]

23. We thus limit our attention simply because the policy stands questions were repeated in the panel design and the "likes/dislikes" questions were not.

Between June and October the public as a whole increased their "knowledge" by six percentage points, raising the correct placements over the issues of the day from 30 to 36 percent.

We get an initial sense of the different emotions' power by seeing that those who were not particularly stimulated rose by about four points while those who were enthusiastic rose five points—not much difference. Yet people who were anxious about the candidates learned almost "twice" as much, rising nine points to go from 46 to 55 percent correct. But these are just mean values that do not take into account other possible factors. So again, we need to control for citizenship traits. Our dynamic analytic scheme is in table 5.8. When we look at learning (as opposed to personal commitment or attention) we see that it is education that is the most important among those traits. Habitual attentiveness plays a part but strength of partisanship effectively has no role at all. Learning is very different from caring.

And, quite clearly, it is anxiety (0.19) rather than enthusiasm (0.03^{ns}) that provides the emotional stimulus. Once we take out the long-term influence of citizenship traits, positive feelings about the candidates do nothing for learning. But the active operation of the surveillance system is apparent. People who were worried about Carter or Reagan in midsummer of 1980 paid increased attention to the political news and got straight which candidate was the more conservative.

All this makes good theoretical sense. People who find politics emotionally satisfying allow themselves to become emotionally involved. They

Table 5.8 Dynamics of Learning as a Function of Affective Intelligence and Citizen Traits

	Correct Policy Stands
Total anxiety	0.19
Total enthusiasm	-0.03^{ns}
Habitual political attentiveness	0.14
Education	0.32
Strength of partisanship	-0.02^{ns}
Dependent variable in June	-0.47
Constant	-0.18
Adjusted R^2	0.22
RMSE	0.33
Total N	731

SOURCE: ANES June–October 1980 panel study.

NOTE: The column represents a single regression. All coefficients are statistically discernible from zero unless marked "ns."

care about the outcome and pay attention to the daily tournament's progress. And they develop habits of attentiveness and interest that keep them involved over time. People who find nothing engaging in the candidates will not do any of these.

But the sorts of involvement associated with surveillance are quite different. Here it is the sense of lurking danger (or perhaps novelty) that motivates people to pay attention to policy-related information so they can tell what candidates and parties are likely to do. From a narrow sense of rational democratic politics, it is these people who rise up to the challenge of electoral choice and carry the day.

So far so good. The primary claims of the theory of Affective Intelligence are sustained by the results we have examined. We find evidence for two independent emotional subsystems, one responsible for securing the reliance and implementation of habit and one responsible for determining whether the environment is sufficiently safe for reliance on habit. However, our greater interest lies in the further speculation that when the surveillance system finds something amiss, habits are set aside for reasoned consideration. Does anxiety motivate rational choice and considered judgment? We turn to that important question in chapter 6.

Emotion and Political Judgment

Modern democracy depends on citizens' making reasoned judgments about the political world around them. One, perhaps now canonic, view of the typical citizen is that of an individual largely unrewarded for thinking hard about politics and heavily reliant on habit. We have no quarrel with the weight of the evidence that suggests political judgments are largely habitual. Our model of Affective Intelligence suggests, however, that voters have two alternative modes for making political choices. The first and most commonly used mode, as it is in other domains of life, is casual, even thoughtless, reliance on habitual dispositions. The second mode is reasoned consideration. We will show that citizens do indeed deviate from habitual judgments when they are emotionally engaged to do so. We will also demonstrate that reasoned, political judgment is more frequently engaged, and more suitably engaged, than is commonly recognized. In chapter 5 we saw that anxiety can move people to pay more attention to politics and to acquire new and more accurate information about what is going on. But do people apply these antecedent faculties in order to make active political judgments?

The received wisdom is that people who are emotionally engaged are less likely to make rational decisions (Janis 1982; Janis and Mann 1977). Yet, as we have demonstrated in chapter 5, that axiom depends on what we mean by "emotionally engaged." If we mean more anxious, then the theory of Affective Intelligence argues that emotional engagement will motivate people toward making more deeply reasoned decisions about politics than those who remain dispassionate.[1]

---

1. Of course, we mean to limit our discussion to matters of ordinary political affect—the sort experienced by Americans during the past quarter century. We have no evidence for the sorts of deep passion associated with palpable threats to life and self-identity. Whether those sorts of emotional engagements would lead to reasoned choice is a matter for serious investigation. For powerful evidence on threats to self-identity, see Nadeau, Niemi, and Amato 1995.

We offer evidence on three sorts of political stimuli. First, we examine the American public's response to the contemporary debate on free trade and the public's translation of that issue into candidate assessments during the 1996 primary season. Then we consider how people reacted emotionally to the Persian Gulf War in 1991—and how those emotional reactions affected their political judgments. Finally we examine more generally and systematically how emotions associated with the five political campaigns of 1980–96 shaped the quality of people's vote choices.

Affective Intelligence and Free Trade

In American political debate during the second half of the twentieth century, the idea of free trade had been largely a matter of consensus. Intellectual discussion was governed by liberal economic theory that posited the virtues of comparative advantage. Most of the political elites accepted the verdict as the "right thing to do." With occasional exceptions, presidents and leaders from both partisan camps worked together to maintain the dominance of free market principles in trade policy throughout the post–World War II era. However, the coincidence of the agreement for a North American Free Trade Agreement (NAFTA) with the economic restructuring of the 1980s and 1990s provided the sparks to make free trade a matter for political controversy.

The issue produced new coalitions. Opponents included both labor unions and environmentalists who argued that the agreement would allow U.S. industries to shift work to Mexico where labor was cheap and environmental rules lax. The effect, according to presidential aspirant Ross Perot, would be a "giant sucking sound" from the south that would eliminate jobs in the United States and fundamentally threaten the U.S. economy. So when President Bill Clinton and the Democratic party took power in 1993, the issue cut decisively across ordinary partisan lines. Clinton, along with most Democratic and Republican leaders, supported NAFTA and free trade in general. The opposition, however, came from the Democratic party's base—organized labor and environmentalists—and they faced the difficult choice of remaining faithful to their long-standing party loyalties or striking off in a new direction. This choice was made all the more poignant when Pat Buchanan championed the elimination of NAFTA as a signal issue in his run for the 1996 Republican presidential nomination.

The NAFTA issue, thus, proves an interesting case for studying the quality of the public's political judgments. This issue of free trade was relatively new in U.S. politics and for many Americans the constellation of political forces were out of their standard alignment.

In the spring of 1996 we collaborated with Richard Morin, polling editor of the *Washington Post*, to conduct a study of Pat Buchanan's challenge for the Republican nomination for the presidency. Buchanan had just won the New Hampshire primary and looked poised to lead a new populist coalition against the GOP establishment. In a couple of months that effort would fail, but in the spring it looked as though the Buchanan rally might upset the political order. Accordingly, we conducted a nationwide survey in order to assess the sorts of factors that might possibly lead to a Buchanan breakout. Key to that study was an examination of how Buchanan's seizing hold of the NAFTA issue affected the public's potential support for his uprising.

Regarding elections, one strand of conventional wisdom ignores policy matters because, the story goes, most people have only a limited understanding of public policy and they only occasionally translate that understanding into electoral choice. And yet, politicians—especially challenging politicians—are constantly seeking issues, policy questions, that will awaken the electorate. They want to stimulate people to pay attention to politics enough to reconsider their habitual choices. They want people to cross over to the challenger's side. In this case, Pat Buchanan used a traditional "America First" appeal to woo working-class and working-middle-class Americans who traditionally supported the Democratic party.

Our purpose here is to see if the theory of Affective Intelligence tells us something about Buchanan's appeal that an ordinary cognitive account misses. We will see that people's *feelings* about abandoning NAFTA were, in part, driven by their anxiety about job security. More important for the theoretical test, those feelings were of a mixed character—people were both enthusiastic and also anxious about the Buchanan proposal—and had distinctive impacts on people's cognitive support for the idea of abandoning NAFTA and on the way that they evaluated the Buchanan candidacy. In short, those feelings served both the disposition and surveillance functions to empower citizen judgments.

First note that people had mixed emotional reactions to the proposal to leave NAFTA. We asked them three separate questions: whether the United States should drop out of NAFTA and the World Trade Organization; the degree of enthusiasm they felt for this proposal; and the degree of anxiety they felt.[2] Rather than assume that people's feelings about policies, even controversial policies, are unidimensional, we set out to see if they are or are not (for more on the measurement of emotional reactions to proposals and issues, see the appendix B).

And, in fact, they were not. The standard valence model of emotions, which holds that positive and negative feelings are defined as mutually exclusive—that is, as opposite sides of the same coin—predicts that feelings of enthusiasm and anxiety should be almost perfectly negatively correlated. Yet the correlation between being enthusiastic and being anxious is a mere −0.19, hardly what one would expect if the two items were mere mirror images of each other. Figure 6.1 shows the scatterplot of NAFTA feelings, with enthusiasm on the horizontal and anxiety on the vertical axis and a regression line translating one into the other shown across the plot. Valence theory expects a translation that runs from the top left to the bottom right corners. As we can see, the two emotional reactions are weakly related to one another, but are hardly polar opposites.

The question is whether knowing that many people have mixed feelings helps us understand the dynamics of NAFTA. Consider a potential spur for thinking about trade policy—people's fear of losing their jobs. We asked whether people worried about the possibility that they or members of their families might lose their jobs. This economic anxiety, we expect, should lead people to think about the NAFTA proposal and develop an evaluative stand. And in fact the more worried people were about jobs the more they were enthusiastic about Buchanan's proposal to abandon NAFTA.

Of course, this much could easily have been predicted using a standard cognitive model: Buchanan was clearly making an appeal to people's insecurities as he built his populist stance. What might be surprising, though, is that job insecurity was *also* associated with *anxiety* about Buchanan's proposal. That is, the more people worried about jobs the more they also worried about the wisdom of the nation's rejecting the long-accepted principles of free trade.[3]

2. The exact wording was: "Nowadays, people are making proposals to deal with America's problems. People have different feelings about those proposals. I'd like to read you a couple of possibilities and I'd like you to tell me how they make you feel. The first is: In order to protect American jobs, even if it means higher tariffs and a trade war, the United States should drop out of NAFTA and the World Trade Organization. Would you say this proposal makes you feel very enthusiastic, somewhat enthusiastic, or not enthusiastic at all. Would you say this proposal makes you feel very anxious, somewhat anxious, or not anxious at all."

3. We regress both NAFTA enthusiasm and NAFTA anxiety on worry about losing jobs. The coefficients for the two equations are 0.12 and 0.10, respectively—both statistically important. That is, each emotional reaction is modestly driven by the concern over job security. We also used this survey to conduct a survey experiment in which we asked half the

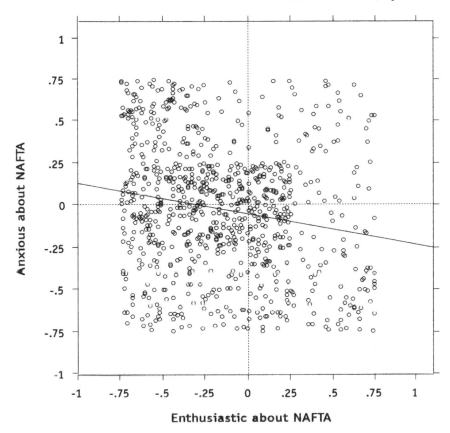

Figure 6.1 Correlation between Anxiety and Enthusiasm toward Abandoning NAFTA and WTO

SOURCE: *Washington Post* spring 1996 survey.

Thus we find that people uneasy about the current state of affairs were both more enthusiastic and more anxious about proposals for radical change. They were more likely to have become engaged in the debate and have developed both sorts of emotional reactions. This complication, of course, does not flow from conventional cognitive theory but it is consonant with Affective Intelligence.

---

sample whether they were worried about losing their jobs and the other half whether it was important that people not lose their jobs. The explicit "worry" prompt produced a response that maps into NAFTA anxiety while the more abstract question about the "importance" of job security did not. On the enthusiasm/disposition side, the "worry" and "importance" prompts had an equal effect. While these results must remain tentative pending further investigation, it seems that eliciting people's anxiety requires explicit attention to how the questions are worded.

Moreover, the two emotions of enthusiasm and anxiety have their characteristically distinctive relationship with verbal support for the policy of abandoning NAFTA. Were the two emotions mere mirror images, then we should expect that each would have an equal and opposite impact on overall support for the policy. However, consistent with years of research on candidate evaluation, we find that enthusiasm is almost directly translated into support and anxiety is almost (but not quite) inconsequential for support. In other words, enthusiasm implements people's dispositions while anxiety does not. In the first column of table 6.1 we regress support for the policy of abandoning NAFTA on people's enthusiasm and anxiety about the policy to assess the relative power of the two emotions over the policy judgments. Compare 0.61, the impact of enthusiasm, with -0.13, the impact of anxiety.

Further, the two emotional responses transfer along separate channels into candidate support. When we measure the extent to which people's feelings about Buchanan were colored by their feelings about the NAFTA proposal, we see that enthusiasm about NAFTA mapped directly into enthusiasm for Buchanan. But anxiety made no such passage. In the second column of table 6.1 we show the regression of Buchanan enthusiasm on respondents' feelings about abandoning NAFTA: compare 0.15 with -0.05^{ns}. Instead, NAFTA anxiety maps into Buchanan anxiety but not into Buchanan enthusiasm (in the third column, compare 0.20 with -0.05^{ns}).

Table 6.1   Feelings about Abandoning NAFTA and Candidate Evaluation

	NAFTA Support	Buchanan Enthusiasm	Buchanan Anxiety	Buchanan Support
NAFTA enthusiasm	0.61	0.15	-0.05^{ns}	
NAFTA anxiety	-0.13	-0.05^{ns}	0.20	
Buchanan enthusiasm				0.55
Buchanan anxiety				-0.06
Constant	0.20	0.20	0.39	0.05
Adjusted R^2	0.23	0.03	0.03	0.26
RMSE	0.42	0.32	0.40	0.31
Total N	868	859	865	840

SOURCE: Data are from a national survey conducted by Rich Morin and the *Washington Post* during the spring of 1996, following the Buchanan victory in the New Hampshire Republican primary.

NOTE: Each column represents a single regression equation, with all variables scaled on the (0–1) interval for comparability. Buchanan Support indicates whether the respondent preferred Buchanan for the Republican presidential nomination.

^{ns}Statistically insignificant at $p < 0.05$.

And consistent with our prior work on emotional reactions and support for candidates (Marcus 1988), we see that it is relative enthusiasm and not anxiety that drives the cognitive support for Buchanan as the Republican nominee. In the last column of table 6.1, we regress Buchanan support on Buchanan enthusiasm and anxiety and it is clearly the former that dominates (0.55 compared with −0.06).

To buttress these conclusions, we can test whether these results are somehow unique to Buchanan and his personal appeal. The NAFTA issue, of course, was not Buchanan's alone. In fact, Ross Perot had articulated the issue well before Buchanan chose to take it up as one of his centerpiece issues. Happily, in this study we also asked people to report their emotional responses to Perot and can thus examine whether there is a parallel translation of NAFTA into Perot feelings. There is. In exactly the same way as with Buchanan, we found that differential enthusiasm for dropping NAFTA translated into differential enthusiasm for Perot—and differential anxiety about NAFTA into anxiety about Perot.[4]

Knowing that enthusiasm and anxiety are distinctive emotions for issues as well as for candidates is helpful. We now know that the phenomenon is not simply a matter of how people deal with personalities. And we know that emotional reactions to issues translate into emotions about candidates in just the way that the theory of Affective Intelligence predicts. Enthusiasm drives the disposition channel—where policy support translates into candidate choice. Anxiety about issues and candidates are linked together, but they are independent of the disposition channel. We want to demonstrate that this is important point.

Consider again our fundamental theoretical apparatus. Because enthusiasm marks the operation of the disposition system, it reflects habitual response. By habit, of course, we mean the sorts of learned repertoires that people bring to bear when they analyze politics. Anxiety, on the other hand, reflects the surveillance system that kicks in when people are confronted with the unusual and with novel threats, when they must consider and reconsider standard ways of thinking about things. In this case, that of free trade and Buchanan's ability to garner support, we expect that people who remain largely undisturbed by the matter will rely on standard ways of evaluating the candidate. On the other hand, we expect that people who find NAFTA and Buchanan unsettling will consider afresh their evaluative

4. As before, enthusiasm for abandonment of NAFTA is related to enthusiasm for Perot (0.10) while anxiety about the proposal is significantly related to anxiety about Perot (0.12), with the "off-diagonals" (NAFTA anxiety related to Perot enthusiasm and NAFTA enthusiasm related to Perot anxiety) proving statistically significant.

frameworks. If anxious, ordinary "liberals" and "conservatives" will weigh their views on trade and be prepared to abandon their long-standing ideological guidelines when assessing the Buchanan candidacy.

We are able to assess the surveillance system's impact by examining how its operation altered how people made judgments about Pat Buchanan. In our survey, we asked respondents to give their preference among the Republican candidates. Of course, many elements go into such a decision. For this theoretical test we concentrate on a comparison of people's liberal–conservative ideology with their views on free trade.

Given Buchanan's long-standing role as spokesman for the conservative cause, we can surely expect that people will line up according to their preferences, conservatives and liberals for and against Buchanan, respectively. And, going just this far, our expectations are confirmed: 23 percent of conservatives picked Buchanan while 13 percent of liberals did so. Further, we expect to see opponents of NAFTA prefer Buchanan and this too turns out to be the case: 23 percent of NAFTA opponents picked Buchanan compared to 12 percent of supporters.[5]

We note, however, that conservatives were modestly more likely to oppose NAFTA than liberals. And, in any case, we want to control for Buchanan's overall ideological appeal before we attribute causal influence to the trade issue. We do so with a spare regression equation by which we predict Buchanan candidate preference as a function of conservative ideology and opposition to NAFTA. The results, presented in the first column of table 6.2, confirm the elementary bivariate analyses: conservatives and "fair traders" preferred Buchanan.[6]

The question is whether these sensible relationships are accentuated or diminished when people have been stimulated to be uneasy about Buchanan. We examine the impact of the surveillance system by estimating the same regression for two different sorts of people. We divide the sample into the "complacent" who reported no or very little anxiety about Buchanan and the "anxious" who say they were "fairly" or "very" anxious about Buchanan. This procedure (actually Buchanan's campaign) divides the public into roughly equal halves.

The theory of Affective Intelligence predicts that when the surveillance

5. In all this, partisanship matters little. All these analyses—and their inferences—hold perfectly well even after controlling for the respondents' partisan loyalties.

6. The dichotomous dependent variable—support for Buchanan or not—calls for a probit or logistic regression. We have echoed all the analyses in logistic form to confirm exactly the same set of inferences. For exposition reasons we keep the regression format, where coefficients make easy sense.

Table 6.2 Buchanan Preference as a Function of Ideology and Trade Policy
That Depends on the Operation of the Surveillance System

	Buchanan Preference		
	Total Sample	Complacent Citizens	Anxious Citizens
Ideology	0.13	0.21	0.08^{ns}
NAFTA opposition	0.10	0.05^{ns}	0.16
Constant	0.05	0.05	0.05
Adjusted R^2	0.02	0.02	0.05
RMSE	0.36	0.38	0.34
Total N	815	395	368

SOURCE: Data are from a national survey conducted by Rich Morin, the *Washington Post*, and ABC *News* during the spring of 1996, following the Buchanan victory in the New Hampshire Republican primary.

NOTE: Each column represents a single regression equation, with all variables scaled on the (0–1) interval for comparability.

^{ns}Statistically insignificant at $p < 0.05$.

system activates conscious consideration, people will rely less on habit and more on new information. In this context, this means that we expect that the half sample who were worried about Buchanan would be less likely to rely on ideology and more likely to make their decision based on new information—here new information about trade policy. And this is exactly what we find in the second and third columns of table 6.2.

Note the dramatic differences. For the complacent, it was ideology rather than the trade debate that governed assessments of Buchanan (compare 0.21 with a statistically insignificant 0.05). The story is reversed for those made anxious about Buchanan. NAFTA opposition was most important (0.16) while ideology mattered hardly at all (0.08 and just short of statistical significance). While the complacent relied on their long-standing ideological disposition to evaluate Buchanan, those whose surveillance system was activated used their assessment of trade policy for judgment.

Thus, emotions do much more than add color to choice. In our example of free trade, we see that enthusiasm (or the lack of enthusiasm) acts as an emotional proxy for policy preference. In the ordinary way, voters who are enthusiastic about aborting NAFTA are similarly enthusiastic about the Buchanan candidacy and are likely to choose him as their favorite. Anxiety works differently, running a parallel course that , while not affecting enthusiasm, drives candidate anxiety instead. And this candidate anxiety serves as an emotional marker that signals people to weigh novel information—here NAFTA policy—in their candidate evaluations and discount habitual inclinations. It is the disturbed, rather than the complacent, who consciously reconsider their candidate preference in the light of novel information, doing the extra work that setting aside habit demands.

The Theory of Affective Intelligence and the Gulf War

Although politics extends well beyond the electoral area, our work provides little evidence on how emotions affect political judgment in nonelectoral settings. This is mostly due, of course, to the relative paucity of data on emotional engagement during times of political quiescence. Thus, we are fortunate to have data from a provocative study conducted by Donald Kinder and Lisa D'Ambrosio (1996) who examined how the U.S. public responded to the Persian Gulf War.[7]

War, of course, presents a very different sort of political stimulus than the typical election campaign. People who routinely tune out politics as being "more of the same" cannot similarly ignore war's drama. The Gulf War proved typical—it commanded the notice of almost everyone, with newspapers, newsmagazines, and television networks giving it round-the-clock coverage. Wanting to understand how emotions affect public judgment, we should surely be interested in the ways that Americans saw and evaluated the war.[8]

Kinder and D'Ambrosio combined two surveys conducted by the American National Election Studies (ANES), marrying the 1991 Gulf War Study (conducted in June, well after war news had settled down) with the prior November's 1990 National Election Study conducted after the United States' initial commitment but before hostilities broke out. The panel design, in which the same people were interviewed before and after the war, allows the investigators to trace the change in people's political judgments that were associated with their emotional engagement in the war's events.

Most Americans, of course, had *some* emotional reaction to the war—being angry at Saddam Hussein, or afraid for American troops, or disgusted

---

7. See Kinder and D'Ambrosio 1996. We rely on the presently unpublished findings of the authors with their permission.

8. Though, of course, one might worry that surveillance emotions are important only when the stimuli are typically low-level in the politics of ordinary democratic decision making. The argument would be that in extraordinary times everyone pays attention so that the extra boost associated with emotional involvement might not matter so much. We see ahead that this is not so.

at the killing, or proud, or upset, or worried that the fighting might spread, or feeling sympathy for the Iraqi people. Between 70 and 90 percent of Americans reported having experienced each of these emotions. (Only one survey respondent of a thousand reported experiencing no emotional reaction!) Kinder and D'Ambrosio showed that these specific feelings were directly associated with people's judgments about the outcome of the war, about several war policies, and about the performance of President Bush. For example, those expressing a sense of anger against Saddam or a more general sense of pride were more supportive and those expressing worry about the war's expansion or who had a more generalized sense of being upset were typically less supportive.

This much is consistent with our overall view of how people process information—and is key to Kinder and D'Ambrosio's main point about how people use specific emotions to generate political views. But many approaches to understanding politics would expect these relationships—and some of these approaches rank emotion as a secondary, derivative phenomenon. We want a more powerful test of our theory, one that distinguishes among the alternative explanatory approaches.

To perform such a test, Kinder and D'Ambrosio combined a sense of being upset, of being afraid for American troops, and of being worried that the fighting might spread into a measure of *anxiety* about the war. If affective intelligence is at work here, such anxiety should motivate people to be more attentive and more willing to engage in considered judgment.

In their analysis, they showed that Americans who judged the war "worth the cost" increased their support for both the general policy of intervention and for President Bush's leadership. This, by itself, is no surprise—after all, it makes sense for those believing the war worthwhile to give credit where credit was due.

A "textbook" view of rational political choice suggests that people who found the war a success should be willing to credit Bush and to credit the particulars of the administration's policies. Any resistance to giving credit would be seen as an irrational intrusion of psychological elements. Think of a liberal Democrat who observed the success of the war effort: that person should be more willing than before to acknowledge the wisdom of intervention and the competence of the Bush presidency. Of course, years of scientific research show that people are pretty good about rationalizing their prior beliefs and and that they are reluctant to change their fundamental political judgments even in the face of contradictory evidence. And it was the case that many liberal Democrats proved reluctant to revise their views of military intervention and the Bush presidency. So it is of interest what sorts of factors might make people more or less willing to reconsider their initial judgments.

The Gulf War data provide a crucial test of the relationship between emotional engagement and reasoned judgment. We expect that people who experienced anxiety during the war—about the troops or about the possible expansion of the war—would think more deeply about policies and about the president's leadership. Those who were unmoved would not do so. And especially intriguing, those who were positively engaged would not necessarily change their political judgments to fit the new evidence.

This is a remarkable prediction. A large percentage of U.S. citizens, of course, did become both psychologically and emotionally engaged in the war's progress. The prediction is that those who became anxious thought more deeply, perhaps discussed more seriously, the sorts of policies and consequences and connections that the war presented. People who then felt that the war was a success were then willing to *change their minds* about both the policy of intervention and about the quality of President Bush's leadership. And, equally, those who experienced mostly conventional "war time" emotions—pride in the efforts of our troops or anger at Saddam—supported the Bush policies and leadership no more (or no less) than they did before the war began.

The evidence lies in table 6.3. The first column tests the proposition that people who recognized the success of the war were indeed willing to ac-

Table 6.3   Persian Gulf War—Anxiety and Political Judgment

	Do the Right Thing?		Bush Presidency	
Variable	Simple Model	Affective Intelligence Model	Simple Model	Affective Intelligence Model
Assessment of war outcome	0.71	0.47	0.14	-0.16^{ns}
Anxiety * assessment of war outcome		0.33		0.39

SOURCE: Adapted from Kinder and D'Ambrosio 1996. Data are from ANES fall 1990 election study and June 1991 Gulf War study.

NOTE: Each entry is the impact of the respondents' assessment of the war outcome on the *change* in their evaluation of Bush's decision to intervene and in their evaluation of Bush's presidency more generally. Each column represents a separate TSLS regression equation with the citizen's assessment of the overall intervention policy and the Bush presidency the dependent variables. The estimation equations also include the direct effects of each emotional response and an evaluation of national economic conditions, and the prior (1990) assessment of policy and Bush. Thus, the coefficients represent different impacts on the *change* in assessment from the prior fall to the subsequent summer.

^{ns}Not statistically significant.

knowledge the wisdom of the initial commitment of troops. This proposition seems a redundancy, but we know better. Encouragingly, the first column suggests that people did give credit to the policy—that is, people who recognized the success were willing to change their minds about the intervention.

Now, note carefully what happens when anxiety is taken into account—as shown in the second column of table 6.3. The first coefficient (0.47) gives—for those who experienced no anxiety—the translation between war success and a change in evaluation. These people did translate success into approval. But more importantly for the theory, those who found the war an uneasy experience were almost twice as likely (0.80 = 0.47 + 0.33) to change their minds. That is to say, original opponents to the war were much more likely to give up their initial beliefs when the war's events elicited an anxious reaction than when it did not.

More telling, perhaps, is how people changed their assessment of the Bush presidency. While it may not take much to concede that intervention was wise in light of its eventual success, giving political support to President Bush for the success should meet stiffer psychological and rational resistance. After all, our liberal Democrat could easily acknowledge the war victory without rewarding Bush. The troops fought valiantly, General Schwartzkopf strategized brilliantly, and the Iraqi forces capitulated without showing much resolve. George Bush merely presided over others' successes and failures. Or, alternatively, our Democrat might credit the Bush team but refuse to support his presidency as doing so might imply support for conservative Republican domestic policies. And beyond such reasoning, of course, is a psychological resistance to identification with a long-standing political opponent.

The coefficients on the right half of table 6.3 (adopted from Kinder and D'Ambrosio) confirm this expectation. In the "simple Model" we see a much weaker conversion of "war victory" to Bush support. These variables are coded to a uniform (0–1) interval to make the coefficients roughly comparable. Understanding this we can see that people were much less likely to translate cognitive understanding into political support for the president than to revise their views about foreign policy. Loosely speaking, 71 percent of initial war opponents changed their views to fit the evidence of its success. But only 14 percent of Bush's opponents changed their support of his presidency in recognition of his leadership.

When anxiety is taken into account, however, the picture changes considerably. Those who were not anxious about the war made no conversion at all (the coefficient of −0.16 has the wrong sign and is statistically insignificant). Only those who were anxious altered their views of the Bush presidency—though such conversion is modest ($0.23 = -0.16 + 0.39$). This change in political support pales in comparison to that for the assessment of the wisdom of the war itself, as one might reasonably expect. However, any change in reassessing President Bush occurred only among those whose surveillance system was activated.

We then ask whether the power of anxiety is merely a shadow of a more generalized emotional arousal. Using the remaining sorts of emotions (anger, pride, disgust, and sympathy) as an alternative index of emotional involvement, Kinder and D'Ambrosio provide for a replication of the analysis (as in table 6.3) and discover that, aside from the anxiety measures, emotional arousal had no discernible impact on Americans' willingness to change their minds. That is, it is not emotions generally but anxiety specifically that encourages people to make rational judgments.

Voting Judgments

We return to the ANES surveys to answer the question whether people change their manner of making decisions when they are anxious about the political leader they are "naturally" inclined to support. We focus on the vote decision both because voting is politically important, of course, and because we have data to test our hypotheses.

We begin with a baseline model of an individual's "standing decision." We know that people develop a habitual response to politics that allows them to deal with elections without committing themselves to deep thought and consideration. Just as in ordinary life, standard routines must dominate because no one can, or need, think through every decision every day. For most people most of the time, electoral politics is a low-stakes matter that asks little and rewards hardly at all. Thus, we understand why making choices about political candidates calls forth only the most modest sort of effort.

This approach is, to be sure, an entirely rational way to deal with politics. For most people, the stakes of elections change little from year to year and, in fact, each contest for political power seems similar to the one that preceded it. Developing a standard repertoire of political issues to support and political party to align oneself with makes good sense—it saves effort and gets good results most of the time. Of course, this approach makes better sense if people develop an additional mechanism that allows them to pay attention and reconsider habits when appropriate.

In the United States, this baseline manifests itself in an individual's *partisanship*—a psychological identification with the Democrats or Republicans.[9] Over the course of their lives, most people develop an attachment toward a political party that incorporates their "standing decision" in the sense that they routinely vote "Democratic" or "Republican" and are typically satisfied with that choice. This partisan orientation typically incorporates a long-standing evaluation component as well as a sense of psychic identification. People routinely vote for the party that they like best—and for the party whose performance seems most worthy of support. The idea of partisanship has received considerable attention in the political science literature. The seminal discussions remain (Campbell et al. 1960; Converse 1966; Key and Cummings 1966; Miller 1991).

This "standing decision" may be understood as an element in the individual's disposition system in that it represents the cumulation of repeated decisions that have been transformed into an emotional representation. Political scientists often discuss partisanship in terms of "rational choice" or "personality psychology"—both to good effect. That is, a person chooses allegiance to a party because that party demonstrates that it governs better. Or an individual develops a deep psychological identification with a political party inasmuch as it provides a reliable reference group—a sense of belonging—within the broader social world. These views are both competing and complementary. For some of the debate about the dynamics of rationality and partisanship, see Converse 1976; Erikson, MacKuen, and Stimson 1998; Fiorina 1981; Green, Palmquist, and Schickler 1998; Green and Palmquist 1995; and MacKuen, Erikson, and Stimson 1989. Our only addition here is to note partisanship's emotional content. People have clear emotional dispositions toward the parties and toward the parties' candidates.

These dispositions carry import for politics. If there is anything that we know about voting choice, it is that partisans will most often adhere to their standing decisions. Democrats will vote for Democrats and Republicans for Republicans. Again, this is not news. While consistent with the theory of Affective Intelligence, the inclination of voters to develop a habitual choice in politics does not distinguish this theory from others.

Instead, in order to test our theory, we focus on what causes people to deviate from their standing decisions. Crucially, we want to know whether people are more (or less) likely to abandon their dispositions when they

9. In other countries, especially in multiparty systems, such habitual support may go to parties associated with social groups (say farmers or Catholics) or to ideological tendencies of the left or right.

are anxious. And even more important, we want to know whether the mechanisms that move people either to adhere to or abandon their dispositions are more or less "rational" in the sense that they produce decisions in accord with people's calculated preferences.

We begin with an overall portrait of emotions and defections. Between 1980 and 1996, the five presidential elections for which we have measures of emotional response, we find that 32 percent of our survey respondents report some sort of anxiety about their party's candidate.[10] That is, of all people with an even mild partisan leaning toward the Democrats or Republicans, 68 percent report no anxiety at all about their "own" candidate—revealing the extent to which the disposition system is secure from outside disturbance.

Of course, most Democrats find the Democratic candidate preferable because, naturally enough, that candidate likely advocates policies and enunciates symbols that are dear to the heart of all Democrats. Similarly, Republicans will charm Republicans. We get some sense of how reasonable all this is when we examine the correspondence of the candidates' issue positions with their supporters' preferences.

We measure "issue advantage" by calculating the relative congruence of the "own" and "opposition" candidates with the stated policy preferences of each voter.[11] Now, to the extent to which dispositions represent sensible standing choices, people will find that their party's candidate advocates policies congruent with their own preferences. Again from 1980 to 1996, we find that only 19 percent of the time does the "opponent" candidate have the issue advantage—the "own party" candidate turns out to be the preferred choice 81 percent of the time.

This does not mean, of course, that those 19 percent and only those 19 percent will defect from their party and vote for the opposing candidate. While people surely pay attention to policy promises, they do not and should not base their votes entirely on such assessments. Many voters will

10. For present purposes, we include independents who "lean" toward one party or the other in their chosen partisan camp. These people are often called "undercover" partisans in that they systematically behave just as self-proclaimed partisans.

11. That is, we take the set of "issue scales" devised by each year's ANES staff to represent each campaign's issue space. We compare the summed absolute distances between the individual's issue preferences (on those scales) and the individual's perceptions of the candidates' issue positions. To be sure, these perceptions represent a fair bit of projection in the sense that citizens must guess the candidates' positions and are likely to guess in ways that are consistent with their vote intentions and their long-term partisan preferences. When we examine the dynamics of "rational" decision making below, it is important to realize that we always control (statistically) for the individual's own partisanship before we attribute importance to these issue scales.

stick with their "own" party even if their party's candidate compares unfa-
vorably with the opposition's—the party carries meaning beyond the
specifics of today's issue debate. Republicans may prefer Republican candidates simply because, when in office, a Republican president is more
likely to advance the general cause of Republicanism in the long run. The
particularities of the current campaign may not dominate the decision. On
a different note, other voters may stick with their "own" candidate because
the personal qualities of that candidate may be more satisfying—a Republican may feel uneasy about the Republican candidate's policy proposals
but feel more comfortable with the leadership capacity or the moral character of the Republican than with that of the Democrat.

We should not expect to see enormously high defection rates, even in
the relatively high-information presidential elections, and we do not. Between 1980 and 1996 our partisans stuck with their candidates and defected only 20 percent of the time.

Of course, policy comparisons *are* important for voting choice. Voters
who prefer the "opposing" party's candidate *are* more likely to defect than
those who do not. The quick summary in table 6.4 shows that 15 percent of
voters who preferred the policy positions of their "own" candidate defected
compared to fully 40 percent of those who preferred the policies of the "opposition." The difference, 25 points, is substantial. Policy matters.

Similarly, we see that anxiety matters as well. When something makes a
voter anxious about the "own" party candidate we expect that the voter will
be more likely to defect. Whatever it was that generated the anxiety will,

Table 6.4 Impact of Anxiety and Policy Preference
on Voting Defection Rates

	Defection Percentages
Issue advantage	
Own candidate	15
Opposing candidate	40
Difference	25
Feeling about own candidate	
Complacent	14
Some anxiety	33
Difference	19

SOURCE: Data are from ANES 1980–96 election studies.

NOTE: The "defection" entries are the percentage of those
defecting from own partisanship—that is, the percentage of
Republicans who vote Democratic and Democrats who vote
Republican. Independents who "lean" toward a party are
counted as partisans of that party.

needless to say, reflect a diminished appeal. That something may, of course, be the policy preferences themselves—a candidate who promises to do the "wrong" things will be seen as threatening (Marcus et al. 1996)—but will likely include other factors such as performance in office or personal qualities. We see in the lower part of table 6.4 that being anxious about one's own candidate raises defection from 14 to 33 percent.

But these data do not provide a test of Affective Intelligence against other theories. It is not enough to note that negative emotions are associated with greater defections from partisanship; the theory does make this prediction but so do other theories about political decision making. Instead, we examine a more specific prediction: that the way people go about making choices will change when their surveillance system has been activated.

The surveillance system, as we have suggested, spurs people to pay closer attention to the outside world and to think a bit harder about the sorts of choices that they make. In chapter 5 we saw that the emotions that trigger the surveillance system do in fact reflect threats to the individual's worldview. Further, these mechanisms produce greater attention to the political world: people do learn more about what is going on and, specifically, they do learn more about policy matters. But do they put this new learning to any use? The standard view is of an electorate largely ignorant and reliant on habit; but if ability and willingness of the electorate to gain new and accurate knowledge has been underestimated, then we might come to consider the standard view overly restrictive.

Here we extend the theory of Affective Intelligence a bit: we expect that the same sorts of emotional signals that spur attentiveness to political campaigns also spur deeper thought and consideration about voting choice. When people sense danger they not only notice more about the external world but they also engage their consciousness to think about what to do. The same mechanisms should apply to politics.

To be sure, we do not want to suggest that people turn into an Aristotle or a Rousseau whenever they encounter negative political news. Rather, we expect that they will engage decision-making processes that lead toward a considered decision. These might include extended reading and deep thought. They are more likely to include conversations with friends and neighbors and family members. At the very least, they will include an increased openness to reconsidered judgment.

Our first glimpse of the data is shown in table 6.5. Here we examine the role of policy preferences, the same policy preferences as in table 6.4. But this time we allow the presence and absence of anxiety, our marker for the surveillance system, to modulate the impact of policy on voting choice. In the column on the left, we see that for "complacent" citizens (those not

Table 6.5 Impact of Anxiety on the Rationality of Defection

	Defection Percentages	
	Level of Anxiety about the Candidates	
Policy Preferences	Complacent	Some Anxiety
Prefer policy of:		
Own candidate	12	24
Opposing candidate	27	58
Difference	15	34

SOURCE: Data are from ANES 1980–96 election studies.

NOTE: Entries are the percentage of those defecting from own partisan-ship. Independents who "lean" toward a party are counted as partisans of that party.

emotionally awakened), policy preferences play a modest role with in-creased defection rates for those who find the "opposing" candidate more attractive. The impact of policy on voting is an important 15 percent. In the column on the right, however, the impact of the surveillance system be-comes dramatically apparent. For those in an uneasy emotional state, a re-alization of the "opponent" issue advantage produces a defection rate of 58 percent. Significantly, the impact of policy matters on voting has more than doubled—rising from 15 to 34 percent.[12]

The activation of the surveillance system goes a long way toward en-abling people to choose rationally. Not only does it stimulate people to ac-quire more, and more accurate, information, but it also motivates them to use that information more decisively. To be sure, all we mean here is a con-sidered choice. That is, when people make their voting decision they take into account their understanding about where the candidates stand on the relevant issues. They make choices that are more nearly consistent with their own preferences. when they understand that the "opposing" candi-date is likely to do better by them, they vote for that candidate.

A Richer Voting Model

The evidence provided by these data is, of course, pretty bare bones stuff. In order to be more confident about the result we need to take into account other powerful explanations of how people make considered choices.

12. Note that the overall levels of defection are higher for the anxious than the compla-cent. This is important but does not supply the crucial bit of evidence for our theoretical test. We find that the impact of policy depends on the level of anxiety, or that the con-sciousness of the policy-vote depends on the operation of the surveillance system.

We do so by generating a richer multivariate model of the vote choice. Begin with an elementary conception: voters weigh the candidates' personal qualities, their policy stands, and then contrast those with their own partisan standing choice. This three-component model represents something of a "classic" standard against which we can then test our theory of Affective Intelligence.

To measure the voters' assessments of the candidates' personal qualities, we take the comments that individuals' volunteered about each candidate when asked what they liked and disliked about each candidate. We then construct a sum of the positive and negative comments about the candidates.[13] We should reasonably expect that people who have much good to say about a candidate and much bad about the opponent will vote for that candidate. Call this measure "personal qualities."

In addition, we construct an index of policy issue advantage as the comparative distance between the individual's ideal point on any issue and his or her perceptions of the candidates' positions. The distances are signed so that a candidate closer to the individual's preferences will get that individual's vote. Then we add up the comparative advantages over all the issues of the day to create an index of "policy preference."[14]

When we use these two components, candidate and policy, to model the vote choice we get table 6.6. Here we also include partisanship so the evident impacts of candidate personal qualities (0.54) and policy preference (0.84) are net of the biasing effects of partisan perception and rationalization.[15] When we estimate the effect of personal qualities and issues on the voting calculus, we eliminate the confounding direct and indirect impacts of partisanship. The resulting model is *vin ordinaire*.[16]

13. In our index, we use only comments about the candidates' personal qualities; we intentionally ignore comments about either partisan orientation or policy stances. We add the sum of the positive comments about the "own" candidate to the negative comments about the "opposing" candidate and then subtract the negative comments about "own" and positive comments about the "opposing." We then norm to a 0–1 interval.

14. Again, these are the ANES staff's selection of issues. The comparative absolute distances are subtracted ("opponent" minus "own") so that a larger number indicates an advantage. Then we norm to a 0–1 interval.

15. This is, of course, the virtue of using multivariate analysis in this manner. The measured impact of any variable is estimated while statistically controlling for the impact of the other variables. Including partisanship on the right hand side of the estimation equation discounts both the direct impact of partisanship on the vote (as though the voter were ignorantly pulling the party lever) *and* the indirect impact in that it biases perceptions and encourages rationalizations of how people rate the candidates. The virtues of this estimation strategy should be apparent for our problem here.

16. We leave aside, but only briefly, other factors often entered into such models such as education.

Table 6.6   A Simple Voting Model

Variable	Simple Model
Partisanship	0.58
Candidate personal qualities	0.54
Policy preference	0.84
Constant	−0.22
Dummies	
1984	−0.08
1988	−0.01
1992	0.06
1996	0.12
Adjusted R^2	0.58
RMSE	0.25
Total N	8888

SOURCE: Data are from ANES 1980–96 election studies.

NOTE: The column represents an OLS regression equation with vote inclination as the dependent variable.

It is clear that both personal qualities and the overall issue calculus matter for choice—as well as does partisanship itself. The influence of each of these three factors on the typical voter is represented in figure 6.2. The figure's pie chart expresses the impact of each component normed to a 100-percent base.[17] This pie chart provides a baseline against which we can compare the effect of adding anxiety into the analysis.

The interesting question is whether the relative weights of the "standing choice" vary when voters are stimulated by their emotions. Our prediction is that when people are emotionally engaged, especially when they feel anxious, they will reconsider their standing choice. Upon this reflection, they may in the end choose to stay with their "own" candidate—normally the "own" candidate will please both personally and on policy matters—but we expect that the surveillant will be more likely than the complacent

17. We sum the three components and then calculate the percentage of the full "modeled" impact that is attributed to each of the three components. From the baseline model in table 6.4 we get three components (0.58 + 0.54 + 0.84 = 1.96) and calculate each proportion accordingly. For example, the part of the pie chart attributed to partisanship is 0.58/1.96 = 0.30), that for personal quality is 0.54/1.96 = 0.28), and that for issues is 0.84/1.96 = 0.42). Note that the raw value of these proportions means little other than as an overall indicator of importance. However, when we examine the change in these proportions as a function of anxiety, we make much more meaningful comparisons—we see when the impact of one component gets much larger or smaller in presence of anxiety.

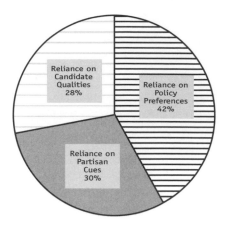

Figure 6.2   Simple Model of Voting—The Comparative Influence of Partisanship, Candidate, and Policy Preference on Vote Choice

SOURCE: ANES 1980–96 election studies.

to defect from that habitual response. At least their reconsideration opens up the possibility of a conscious decision to abandon habit. Such an expectation, as we have argued throughout this book, contrasts with the conventional presumption that emotions cloud judgment and make thoughtful decision making less, rather than more, likely.

Accordingly, we introduce the idea of interaction to our estimation models. The way that people judge candidates will depend on the level of surveillance they are giving politics. Our theory suggests that the surveillance system's response to threatening stimuli results in anxiety, which in turn leads people to abandon reliance on habit and to reconsider their decisions. So we test the theory when we predict, for example, that the presence of anxiety will *diminish* the overall impact of partisanship on the vote.[18] And contrariwise, we expect that the presence of anxiety will *enhance* the impact of candidate quality and policy positioning on the vote. In the first instance, we have something like:

$$\text{Vote} = a \text{ Partisanship} + b \text{ Anxiety} * \text{Partisanship}$$

18. In the analyses that follow we have restricted our test to the anxiety people experience associated with the two presidential candidates. These are not the only sources of anxiety, as we have seen. Anxiety may be introduced, as we have seen, by war, by issues and proposals, and also by circumstances such as a faltering economy. But in the ANES data series, candidate emotion is all we have; so while this is a robust test, given that we have five elections across quite different conditions, we have not exhaustively explored how contemporary anxiety shifts the foundations of judgment.

where *a* Partisanship is the impact of partisanship when anxiety is zero (the second term disappears then). Note that we can obtain the impact of partisanship on the vote for the complacent with the coefficient *a* and the impact of partisanship on the vote for the anxious with the summed coefficients $a + b$. By theory, the coefficient *b* should be *negative*—indicating that anxiety reduces the effects of habit on the vote choice. In parallel, we can estimate the impact of anxiety on judgment by examining the interaction terms for anxiety on personal qualities and policy preference. Here, in contrast to partisanship, the theory of Affective Intelligence predicts *positive b* coefficients as anxiety raises the importance of substance on the vote choice.[19]

The measure of anxiety that we use incorporates a bit of a surprise. We originally had in mind "total anxiety"—the extent to which both candidates made people feel uncomfortable. The expectation was that in a nasty political battle marked by negative campaigning, people would be more apt to stand up and pay attention. However, a closer examination of the data suggests that such an expectation is wrong. Overall anxiety is not related to people's decision-making modes.

We focus instead on "anxiety about one's own candidate." For Democrats this is anxiety about the Democratic candidate and for Republicans it is anxiety about the Republican candidate.[20] As in chapter 5, we now

19. To guard against false inferences, we have replicated this analysis for each election year separately (that is, for 1980, 1984, 1988, 1992, and 1996). The pattern holds consistently across all years with a singular exception. The interaction between candidate anxiety and an increased weight for candidate quality is zero for 1988. In every year, it is clear that candidate anxiety is associated with dramatically decreased reliance on partisanship and increased consideration of policy preferences. In four of the five years the impact is also felt on the weight of candidate qualities.

In addition, for reassurance on the model specification, we have introduced a linear term for candidate anxiety to each of our models. It is plausible that the interaction of anxiety with each of our components serves as a statistical "stalking horse" for a straightforward anxiety–vote connection. In these formulations, the linear anxiety term is statistically significant but modest in magnitude (-0.15). The theoretically critical anxiety * partisanship, anxiety * policy, and anxiety * candidate interactions are robust and hold their magnitudes.

Finally, while all the anxiety interactions in the table are statistically significant, one might worry that the numbers are merely a product of a very large sample size. However, note that the theoretical impact of the interactions is dramatic, effectively eliminating the impact of partisanship and doubling the impact of policy and candidate quality. These are substantively important numbers. Moreover, these interactions carry *t* values of -22.02, 18.27, and 7.52 for partisanship, policy, and candidate quality, respectively. This is not a case of wispy traces of statistical artifact.

20. We include all self-identified independents who "lean" toward the Democrats or Republicans as members of their "undercover" partisan camp. It is only "pure" independents for whom we cannot make a prediction using this measure.

understand that it is *novel* threatening information that is important in capturing people's attention. When Democrats found Ronald Reagan dangerous or Republicans felt uneasy with Bill Clinton, most experienced the emotions of "politics as usual." Their standing decisions were not threatened. On the other hand, when Republicans were disturbed by Reagan or Democrats by Clinton, their emotions signaled a need for closer scrutiny and a more conscious political decision.

Interestingly, what changes here is the reference point for the "threat." That is, the quality of judgment does not depend so much on whether people feel themselves to be threatened but whether they feel their standing decisions are threatened.

The empirical results are in table 6.7. We can see the model for the complacent by simply ignoring the interaction terms (the anxiety interaction is zero) and concentrating on the main effects. Doing so, we see that for the complacent voter partisanship is dominant (0.78) with important but more modest effects of personal quality (0.34) and policy (0.65). More critically, we generate the model for the anxious by adding the interaction terms to the main effects. Now the impact of anxiety nearly eliminates the importance of partisanship (the net effect is reduced to $0.17 = 0.78 - 0.61$) and doubles the impact of both personal quality ($0.78 = 0.34 + 0.44$) and policy ($1.28 = 0.65 + 0.63$).

Table 6.7 Voting Model—Anxiety and Political Judgment

Variable	Affective Intelligence Model
Partisanship	0.78
Anxiety * partisanship	−0.61
Candidate personal qualities	0.34
Anxiety * candidate personal qualities	0.44
Policy preference	0.65
Anxiety * policy preference	0.63
Constant	−0.19
Dummies	
1984	−0.10
1988	−0.02
1992	0.02
1996	0.10
Adjusted R^2	0.63
RMSE	0.24
Total N	7996

SOURCE: Data are from ANES 1980–96 election studies.

NOTE: The column represents a separate OLS regression equation with vote inclination as the dependent variable.

Regression results are common fare in the social sciences. Adding interaction terms, as we have here, is less common. Yet these interactions are central to the theory of Affective Intelligence, and so we want to demonstrate more effectively than with statistical coefficients the impact of these interactions. Figure 6.2, above, suggests that absent any information about anxiety—modeling the voting choice as an average for everyone—we find the standard result: typically, each of the three components (candidate qualities, policy preferences, and partisanship) matters in a substantial way. As we see in figure 6.3, however, the level of anxiety, absent or high, dramatically changes the way in which voters decide whom to support.

Here, in figure 6.3, we can readily see the real payoff in comparing the two pie charts: the one on the left portrays people who are complacent about their "own" candidate and the one on the right shows people who experience some anxiety about their "own" candidate.[21] In the panel for the complacent, it is clear that partisanship plays the major role. Looking at the second panel, however, we see that when the surveillance mechanisms become active, people weight policy much more heavily and almost ignore partisanship altogether. When people are made uneasy about their own candidate, they abandon partisan routines and reconsider their choice. Here, they contrast the candidates' relative appeals on the issues of the day with their own standing preferences—and choose accordingly. This decision-making mode stands in direct contrast to the decision making of the complacent—who rely conveniently on their partisan habits.

This clear result considerably strengthens the case for the theory of Affective Intelligence. Not only do people experience complex emotions about candidates and learn more about politics when they are disturbed, but also they change the way they make decisions when cued by a specific emotional signal that it is worth their while to take care about their judgments. This is exactly what our theory predicts.

Alternative Explanations

We gain greater confidence in our results after testing alternative explanations. Here we explicitly test two theories that might account for our results: (1) that emotions are important only to the extent to which they mark

21. Note that the distinction is between those who experience *no* anxiety about their party's candidate and those who report at least one "anxious" emotional response.

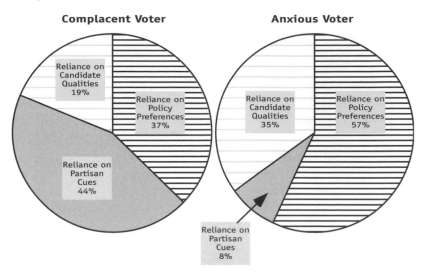

Complacent Voter   **Anxious Voter**

Reliance on Candidate Qualities 19%

Reliance on Policy Preferences 37%

Reliance on Partisan Cues 44%

Reliance on Candidate Qualities 35%

Reliance on Policy Preferences 57%

Reliance on Partisan Cues 8%

***Figure* 6.3**   Anxiety and Its Impact on the Foundations of Vote Choice
SOURCE: ANES 1980–96 election studies.

arousal, and (2) that it is habitual attentiveness, not emotions, that governs decision making.

The first of these alternative explanations stems from the conventional view of how emotions work. In its barest form, it is an extension of the valence model: people experience emotion mainly in a bipolar, positive–negative manner and what matters for the quality of decision making is whether people are stimulated—cognitively and emotionally—to make better judgments. The argument is that the findings represented in table 6.7 and figure 6.3 are due to a spurious relationship we have drawn between anxiety and considered judgment: it is in fact stimulated cognition, not anxiety, that leads to considered judgment. The pattern obtains accidentally because when people get stimulated politically, they also happen to have their emotions stirred up.[22]

As shown in table 6.8, we test whether this alternative explanation makes sense by substituting for "anxiety about own candidate" the remaining emotions people expressed: enthusiasm about own or opposition candidate plus anxiety about the opposition candidate. This measure is the total emotional response *except* that used in table 6.7. If it is simply stimulation that gets reflected in emotional arousal that shapes judgment, then

22. Or, one might possibly argue that emotional arousal itself drives better decisions—though it is hard to think of anyone making such a claim.

Table 6.8 Voting Model—Alternative Operators on Political Judgment

Variable	Arousal (Total Emotional Response except Anxiety about Own Candidate)	Habitual Attentiveness (Follow Politics)	Affective Intelligence (Anxiety about Own Candidate Controlling for Emotional Arousal and Habitual Attentiveness)
Interaction terms			
Modulation of partisanship	0.59	-0.04^{ns}	-0.55
Modulation of personal qualities	-1.67	-0.65	0.71
Modulation of policy preference	-0.68	0.04^{ns}	0.59
Linear Terms			
Partisanship	0.34	0.60	0.68
Candidate personal qualities	1.78	1.55	1.56
Policy preference	1.23	1.02	1.00
Controls			
Total emotions, attentiveness, education, ideological commitment			(Included but not shown here)
Constant	-0.27	-0.33	-0.36
Dummies			
1984	-0.09	-0.08	-0.08
1988	-0.00	0.01	-0.01
1992	0.05	0.07	0.04
1996	0.12	0.14	0.11
Adjusted R2	0.63	0.63	0.69
RMSE	0.26	0.26	0.22
Total N	6293	5807	6611

SOURCE: Data are from ANES 1980–96 election studies.

NOTE: Each column represents a separate OLS regression equation with vote inclination as the dependent variable. The controls in the third column include both the direct and interaction effects of (1) total emotional response except anxiety about own candidate, (2) self-designated habitual attentiveness, (3) extremity of ideological commitment, and (4) formal education. The coefficients are not shown.

^{ns}Not statistically significant.

we should be able to make this substitution and see that this new "arousal" measure reproduces the prior pattern.

In fact, when we examine the results in the first column of table 6.8, we see that "arousal" works in just the *opposite* direction. The first three rows in the column give the modulation effects of emotional arousal—showing how much more or less the aroused weigh partisanship, candidate personal qualities, and candidate issue positions. As people get emotionally charged, they weight partisanship more heavily and they weight candidate qualities and policies less heavily. That is, emotional arousal is associated with reliance on the standing choice rather than a novel reconsideration of the candidates' appeals.[23] The "arousal" explanation fails.

A second and perhaps more compelling explanation is that people have standing dispositions to think about public affairs. This sort of habitual attentiveness (which we saw in the previous chapter) can be expected not only to lead people to gather more information about politics but also to transform their decision-making processes toward weighting more heavily such matters as issue considerations. Habitual followers of politics *do* have stronger emotional reactions to the candidates and *do* think harder about policy than their inattentive neighbors. We might be fooled into thinking that anxiety matters when in fact it is habitual attentiveness that drives both anxiety and thoughtful judgment. We alter our statistical model to see if this competing explanation holds up.

As measures of habitual attentiveness, we examine self-proclaimed attentiveness, strength of ideology, and education. Each captures a different alternative explanation. Self-proclaimed attentiveness (as we saw in chapter 5) is the clearest measure of habit in the sense that it picks up the extent to which individuals feel psychologically rewarded by following politics.[24] Additionally, strength of ideology picks up the tendency of strong ideologues to think about political choice—because they care enough about policy to declare loyalty to the political left or right. And education reflects ingrained habits of public affairs awareness: in the United States those who are better educated develop a stronger attachment to the society as a whole and its cultural norms.

For brevity, we show the results for self-proclaimed attentiveness in the second column of table 6.8.[25] Now we see that the habit of following politics has little impact on the quality of decision making: a statistically insignificant 0.04 impact on partisanship and on policy and a modest

23. We capture the same idea by using either total enthusiasm (about both candidates) or overall total emotions (including everything). Both lead to the same inference: emotional arousal does not produce rational judgment and, if anything, encourages reliance on habitual response.

24. Habit, and its role in sustaining political activities, is itself an important element in the theory of Affective Intelligence. The disposition system provides necessary support to the other neural and biological mechanisms that are central to realizing habit. Here, however, our focus is on the role of the surveillance system.

25. "Self-proclaimed attentiveness" is whether the citizen "follows politics" when there is no election going on. Education is formal education as before. And ideological distinctiveness is the extremity with which the individual adopts a "liberal" or "conservative" position on the ANES seven-point scale.

decrease in reliance on candidate qualities. Similarly, neither education nor strength of ideological commitment has a consistent impact. By themselves, our different measures of habitual attentiveness do not affect the quality of political judgment. Avid political fans, people with advanced degrees, and stalwart liberals and conservatives do pay more attention to politics than the average citizen. But they are no more likely to abandon their standing decisions and consider anew candidate qualities or policy matters.

In fact, the sharpening impact of the surveillance system operates independently of both emotional arousal and habitual attentiveness. In the last column of table 6.8 we repeat the analysis shown in table 6.7 while controlling for linear and interactive effects of all our alternative explanations. The coefficients change a little but the overall pattern is sustained. The alternative explanations do nothing to diminish our confidence in the theory we are proposing: anxiety signals people when they should affirm (one the one hand) or abandon (on the other) their standing decisions.[26]

We now understand that emotions play a critical role in prompting people to pay attention to politics in an efficient and indeed rational way. Confronted with a constant need to make political judgments—not only during election periods but also during the ebb-and-flow of ordinary national

26. We consider another hypothesis: that emotions are entirely endogenous. It is possible that own-candidate anxiety is entirely derivative and that the interactions we observe are spurious. The idea is that own-candidate failure on policy and personal qualities can lead to own-candidate anxiety *and* simultaneously to defections; people satisfied with their own-candidate policies and qualities may vote accordingly but *appear* to vote on party lines alone.

To be sure, this argument is problematic given the empirical results above. We see that own-candidate disappointment matters only when accompanied by own-candidate anxiety. Imagine a cold, calculating accountant who finds shortcomings in the "own" candidate but who experiences no emotional trigger. The "emotion is endogenous" expectation would be that our accountant will defect for substantive reasons despite having no emotional reaction—but the weight of the data suggest that this is not the case. The power of the comparative candidate assessments comes into play only when the surveillance emotions are evident.

Because the primacy of cognition over emotion is so deeply embedded in our conventional way of looking at things, we add a more severe test. To eliminate the possibility that anxiety merely reflects prior cognitive judgment, we purge own-candidate anxiety by an auxiliary regression of anxiety on partisanship, policy, and candidate personal qualities (for Democrats and Republicans separately). We take the residuals as "purged anxiety" and substitute the new measure into the regression analyses of table 6.7 and table 6.8. The exact same pattern of coefficients appears and strongly confirms our original inferences. It is clear that the power of the surveillance system to shape political judgment is not merely an artifact of prior cognitive assessment.

events—people need to find a way to make sense of their world without always having to think hard and long about it. Accordingly, they develop standard repertoires that work well most of the time. And here emotions play a central role for habits have an emotional foundation.

What is especially interesting, though, is how people respond to novelty. It is surely the case that the habitual responses to politics, such as partisanship, will occasionally lead people to make incorrect political judgments. The central role of emotion provides the mechanisms not only to anchor people's "standing decisions" but also, importantly, to signal people when they should abandon those standing decisions and reconsider the character of the political world.

Our evidence supports the proposition of the theory of Affective Intelligence that people use emotions, particularly anxiety, to stimulate active reconsideration of their political views. The tests involve three very different sorts of political judgments. The first, our examination of the NAFTA issue and the emotions it evoked, shows how people can be prompted to abandon efficient reliance on stable ideological dispositions and be led to a reconsideration of free trade policy. The Kinder and D'Ambrosio analysis of reactions to the Gulf War indicates that it is mainly under the stimulus of war-driven anxiety that people reassessed their original views of the war and of the Bush presidency. Similarly, two decades of evidence on American elections indicates that anxiety about leadership drives people to abandon partisanship and reassess the competing candidates' personal qualities and policy proposals. In each of these situations, people who remained emotionally complacent felt no need to reconsider the candidates or their policies.

In the end, we see that emotions enhance citizen rationality because they allow citizens to condition their political judgment to fit the circumstances. We do not expect that citizens will always think deeply about their political judgments. Political choice is, after all, a public good and no single citizen can provide "good choices" by individual action. What makes enhanced citizen rationality possible is the dynamic attentiveness of affective intelligence: people alter the depth of their investment in political judgment in response to the character of the external political world. When the political environment demands real consideration, anxiety spurs the needed reassessment; when the political environment is relatively benign, emotional calm permits the reliance on voters' effective habits, their standing decisions guided by enthusiasm.

Indeed we might well argue that the conventional, normative call for voters to give uniform consideration to each and every issue, each and every candidate for public office, and each and every campaign is naïve and perhaps counterproductive. Our results demonstrate that the electorate does apply itself largely as conventionally expected, but that it does so guided by emotional appraisals when circumstances warrant. While the data we have explored do not demonstrate the central role of the emotions and of affective intelligence in all areas of life, these results do have some interesting implications for both political theory and practical politics.

Chapter 7

Affective Politics

The competence of the mass citizenry has become a central concern in political science and political communication. Even democracy's enthusiasts have called the capacities of the mass citizenry into question. Our investigation of affective dynamics, which started initially in a quite different direction, brings us back to a central theme that has engaged each of our professional careers. It is, as one of us put it, the paradox of mass politics —that the system works as well as it does given the limited attentiveness and knowledge of the average citizen. Seen in light of the traditional Western understanding of emotion, this might seem to be quite an unexpected result indeed. But our findings suggest renewed optimism in the judgmental capacities of the apparently overbusy and frequently distracted citizen-voter.

Principal Findings

The central tenet of the theory of Affective Intelligence is that people accumulate a repertoire of habits to manage the enormous array of tasks that recur throughout the various domains of life—and in the domain of politics no less than any other. As part of the process of evolution, humans have developed two distinct emotional systems—the dispositional and the surveillance systems—to manage the myriad demands on our thoughts and attention, and importantly, to enable our capacity to adapt. The disposition system monitors our everyday interactions with the world, assessing the success and failure of routine behaviors. The surveillance system signals novelty or threat in the environment and indicates the need to reassess routine beliefs and preferences.

In the course of life we naturally accumulate a distinct repertoire of habits to deal with the recurrence of similar demands on our attention. We do not approach each issue anew but instead rely on familiar behavioral patterns and habits successfully enacted in the past. It is the disposition system that monitors the execution of these subconscious behavioral scripts—the activation of learned behavior. Affective intelligence is thus an essential part of our ability to implement what is already learned and to manage the many demands of everyday life without devoting our entire capacity for thought to routine tasks. We find that people carry these useful cognitive-emotional mechanisms over to the political world—relying on learned routines to manage the buzzing and blooming reality of political choice and judgment.

Equally important, however, is the ability to change those routines when confronted with novel circumstances. The theory of Affective Intelligence suggests that certain emotions signal the need to break from routine and pay close attention to the external world. The surveillance system, therefore, acts as a warning system. In politics, the emotions that most clearly drive surveillance dynamics are those associated with anxiety—a sense of uneasiness and fear.

Our theory of Affective Intelligence is rooted in contemporary neurophysiology. A number of neurological functions associated with disposition–surveillance dynamics are centered in the limbic system and are directly and indirectly connected with the cortical regions. Our argument, however, takes a more "macro" perspective insofar as we have yet to fully work out how the neurological specifics translate into political life. Our understanding of how democratic politics works is therefore informed, but not entirely driven, by the implicit neurophysiology. Given the exciting pace of current neurological discoveries, it is likely that our models and hypotheses will change considerably in the years ahead. Our effort, then, attempts to draw on the brain sciences without tying ourselves to a mechanical extrapolation from any particular neurophysiological phenomenon.

The real test of the theory of Affective Intelligence in politics derives most directly from how people deal with political symbols, candidates, and issues. In this book we produce some straightforward empirical tests. We have focussed on how Americans react to presidential elections, partly because these reactions have real political import and partly because we have access to data from the past twenty years with which to test these theories. But we have supplemented the empirical tests, where possible, with experiments and surveys taken outside the presidential context.

The evidence available thus far on the dynamics of attention toward political candidates and issues is consistent with our model of Affective Intelligence. People with a positive disposition toward politics participate in political life as a matter of course—as though politics were a personality trait. This has for years been the received wisdom derived from research in political psychology. But, we argue, more than merely a personal *trait*, political involvement is also a psychological *state*. First, we see that people also modulate their activity in accordance with their enthusiasm about the candidates in a given campaign. Next, and perhaps unexpectedly, people are demonstrably more likely to engage in the political realm when they are anxious about the candidates. Uneasiness about the available political choices leads people to pay closer attention to the political environment. And, also surprisingly, people learn more about the candidates (that is they acquire *new* and *accurate* knowledge) when they are anxious but not when they are enthusiastic about those candidates who dominate the political field.

This evidence of the dual systems' operation extends to the nature of political judgment. Americans paid attention to the Gulf War, of course, and generally believed the outcome to be a success. In a surprise to standard theory, Kinder and D'Ambrosio (1996) showed that the people altered their judgment of President Bush, they gave him credit for victorious leadership, only when they were made anxious by the war's events. People who acknowledged success—but were not anxious about it—did not revise their views of the president. Similarly, conservative Americans favoring protectionism supported the Buchanan insurgency of 1996. But specific policy content, reflected in opposition to NAFTA, played a part in the movement only to the extent that people were anxious about jobs and free trade.

Most clearly, affective intelligence shapes political judgment in presidential elections. Most Americans have some, perhaps weak, attachment to the parties and normally they vote their "standing decision"—Republicans and Democrats coming around to support their "own" candidates. Typically about one-fifth of voters defect from that standing decision, however, and it is in this defection that electoral outcomes are decided. Affect plays a role here. When people feel uneasy about their "own" candidate, they have some tendency to defect—of course. And when they disagree with their candidate's policy proposals they defect as well. But the real significance of defection, which also comes as some surprise, is that it occurs along policy lines mainly when people are anxious. That is, conservative Democrats and liberal Republicans defect from their party mainly when their surveillance systems, marked by anxiety, signal a need to reconsider. Voters who disagree with their candidate, but whose surveillance systems remain quiescent, tend to stick with their standing decision.

All this is important because it means a "rational choice" mechanism is in place. Under normal circumstances, people pay casual attention to political life—some enjoying it for its own sake and others concentrating on other parts of their lives. However, people can and do change their routines. When circumstances merit, people pay more attention to politics, they learn the public policies associated with the candidates, and they vote accordingly. Ordinarily people reenact their standard choices; but, when stimulated by their emotional systems, they think through their decisions and act as relatively well-informed rational voters. That these admirable behaviors are set into motion by an unpleasant experience like anxiety may be one reason why past inquiries into the role emotions play in political behavior have been sidetracked.

Considering the evidence as a whole, the theory of Affective Intelligence "explains" the standard results, extends them a bit, and then produces surprising predictions that the data sustain. This is the sort of theory–hypothesis–empirical test pattern that normally accompanies theoretical advance. To be sure, we are not certain that we have all the dynamics right. But the overall weight of the available evidence indicates that the scientific community might fruitfully devote more attention to the idea that emotions are centrally important to political behavior. For that we have no reason to apologize. We need not avert our eyes. It is an important and central element of how mass politics works.

The Sometimes Return of Political Judgment— Reconsidering Rational Choice

We began this book with a review of the curious tensions between research on emotion and on rational choice modeling of political judgment. The flourishing trade in polemics about citizen competence, declining social and political engagement, and electronic democracy draws our attention

In our view the Affective Intelligence perspective is fundamentally complementary to and commensurate with rational choice approaches. We find problematic, however, the very thing that rational choice modeling usually finds it useful to hold constant. In the real world political attention is a variable not a constant. The theory of Affective Intelligence models those conditions under which engagement of rational choice is more or less likely. Do conditions sufficiently differ from the familiar to warrant abandoning efficient reliance on established cognitive routine? Only if the answer to that question is "yes" does the burden of rational consideration become relevant.

One element of the rational choice literature that merits further attention was highlighted in a collection edited by Ferejohn and Kuklinski (1990). A theme that spans several of the contributed chapters and that is highlighted in the chapter by Converse (1990) is the signal-and-noise metaphor. Briefly summarized, the rational choice perspective includes the view that human judgment is indeed influenced by numerous psychological distractions and distortions. But these micro effects tend to be random "noise," in effect, canceling each other out. Some may vote for a distinguished candidate because he reminds them of their wise father while others vote against that same candidate because he reminds them of an evil uncle. The meaningful political signal is the cumulative and common calculation of individual or group self-interest, the appropriate focus for research. The self-canceling noise of psychological distortions in the perception and calculation of self-interest may be of interest to psychologists but can be safely ignored by political scientists.[1]

What merits further attention is the assumption of self-cancellation. If, as we suggest, the dynamics of political attention are dependent on hardwired mechanisms in the human brain, the dynamics of attention and inattention would tend to be cumulative and convergent in collective choice. Rather than "noise" we should expect to observe political behavior that will be, in the aggregate, an admixture of anxious and rational voters and complacent voters relying on standing decisions.

A central theme in this book is the transition from cognitive autopilot to alert attention. In the political gamesmanship of spin doctoring, the strategic cueing and framing of issues reflects a deep appreciation of that process of transition. If the political challengers and their spin doctors proclaim a crisis and make the case that we have moved beyond politics as usual, citizens should feel threatened and should pay attention. Sometimes noise is just noise and the strident claims of the challenger are indeed politics as usual. But sometimes a warning warrants considered judgment.

The politics of attack and defend is not self-canceling noise; it lies at the heart of the political communication process. Is a political threat or

---

1. Page and Shapiro (1992) adopt this stance. Though not rational at the individual level, the "miracle of aggregation," presumably the random introduction of noise that is filtered out, results in rational decisions at the collective level.

promise real? Perhaps the public could have been convinced that Watergate was just a third-rate burglary, a nonissue rather than an unprecedented constitutional crisis. Perhaps Reagan might have failed in assuring the public that it was morning again in America had the savings and loan and the Iran–Contra debacles come to attention earlier. These are the dynamic political challenges that the public regularly confronts. They are real, politically important, and invisible to rational choice modeling narrowly defined.

But these approaches also differ in other more precise respects. Here we return to the three models of political judgment we have discussed earlier: the Normal Vote model, Rational Choice, and, the theory of Affective Intelligence. Table 7.1 summarizes the array of differences among these three models. We have not placed all of the possible issues on which the empirical claims might be compared. For example, the Normal Vote and Rational Choice models are rather inattentive to the question of motivation for learning and the circumstances that lead voters to gather accurate information. These are important crucial precursors to capable rational consideration. In a large, diverse, and dynamic society many of the candidates for national office, initially at least, will be unfamiliar to much of the electorate, which will also be presented with foreign and dometic issues with which it is largely unfamiliar. The demands of making an informed judgment requires, in such extended republics, heavy reliance on learning about the abilities of those who seek leadership roles as well as where they stand on the leading issues of the day. In chapter 5 we outlined how learning may be understood from the perspective of the theory of Affective Intelligence. Here we consider just the characteristics of judgment in the array of comparisons in table 7.1 suggesting that the theory of Affective Intelligence offers a new perspective on some enduring issues.

One important corollary of our approach is the rehabilitation of habit. Habituated behavior receives surprisingly little attention in the theories of mass politics and communication. When habitual patterns enter theory— for example, in models of prejudice, stereotyping, and partisan voting—it often confirms our worst fears that political behavior inevitably is characterized by inattentiveness to contemporary circumstances and habitual reliance on previous decisions.

Yet, as we saw in chapter 6, voters are quick to abandon reliance on habit when circumstances warrant. Moreover, reliance on habit interacts with the capacity for learning and reasoned consideration. These two approaches to life decisions are dynamically paired and thus enrich the range of ways people can respond to the challenges they face.

Table 7.1 Comparing Models of the Normal Vote, Rational Choice, and Affective Intelligence

	Normal Vote Model	**Rational Choice**	**Affective Intelligence**
Who is attentive?	Partisans	Everyone	The habituated attentive and the anxious voter
Who is receptive to new information?	Independents and weak partisans	Everyone	Those for whom new information generates anxiety
View of partisanship	Ingrained commitment to historical learning	Not particularly relevant	Provides reliable cues to guide recurring political choices
View of issues and policies	Effective to mobilize supporters and to seduce the inattentive and weakly informed	Always relevant	Important when anxious voters seek information and also to articulate habituated commitments
Views of information levels in electorate	Curvilinear relationship between partisanship and knowledge gathering	Information readily available though "costs" may limit the number of people who are well informed	Information levels highly dynamic and responsive to the strategic importance of information
Voting decision	Dependent on partisanship and especially for independents "short-term" forces	A self-interested comparison among salient issue positions, with the candidate choice reflecting the candidate who takes the position closest to the voter	Either reliance on habituated cues or reasoned considerations when unfamiliar or threatening situations preclude routine reliance on habit

Other Implications for Politics

Political Participation, Civic Culture, and Social Capital Theory

The classic argument about civic culture developed by Almond and Verba (1965) and developed in a new vein recently by Putnam (1993, 1995) under the heading of social capital is that cultural norms are centrally important to public life. This research renews attention to the distribution of feelings of trust and civic responsibility and faith in public institutions. Other more specialized research on political development in the Third World and on political alienation and disaffection has also emphasized this theme (Finifter 1972; Huntington and Dominquez 1975). How does the the theory of Affective Intelligence engage these literatures?

First of all, it gives us a fresh perspective on the nature of civic culture and its relationship to individual behavior. Rather than a high-level abstraction, civic culture may be seen as the collective summation of individual-level "habitual politics." Citizens develop a comfortable set of standing decisions about political life—including their enduring views about the rewards of personal involvement, about the responsiveness and legitimacy of central political institutions and actors, and more specifically, about which political party is to be trusted with power. The standing decision may be based on disaffection and distrust and result in routine nonparticipation or protest voting. Or it may result in acquiescent support for incumbents. The civic culture for a given polity at a given time is, in fact, a distribution of individual beliefs along such dimensions.[2] Almond and Verba's classic comparison (1965) across five nations may be remembered as differences of means with Italy and Mexico the most cynical and the United States the least; but the data they reported, appropriately, were the comparative distributions on any given dimension across political cultures. Moreover, such comparisons may well yield different results as times change. Indeed, in the ensuing years a central theme of the study of American mass politics has been the dramatic growth in political cynicism in the United States.

We see political culture as a dynamic, cumulative process comprising individual-level calculations of the relative benefits and costs of the political regime and its policies viewed in the aggregate as a civic culture. America's traditionally exceptional civic culture, it appears, still bears a substantial burden of cynicism resulting from the recent historical traumas of Vietnam and Watergate (Nye, Zelikow, and King 1997). How history is reflected in individual calculations of political trustworthiness is a complex process tied to how people interpret political symbols and how they calculate individual and collective benefit. This represents an active and fruitful area of current research.

There is another telling connection between the theory of Affective Intelligence and the notion of civic culture. We have in mind the "eat-your-

---

2. Though, as we argue in appendix B, we may well achieve a richer description of civic culture if we regularly collected data on people's feelings about various public and civic activities.

spinach school" of civic culture. Central to much of democratic theory, also strongly reflected in the handwringing by those concerned with insufficient civility, inadequate thoughtfulness, and mass political indifference and ignorance, is the notion that politics requires strenuous civic virtue. The voter should study candidate policy white papers, track congressional votes, study foreign policy options, and sit through *Face the Nation* whenever possible. Such expectations reflect a norm of citizenship as obligation. Those individuals who see things otherwise are uncultured or slothful and certainly not living up to their civic responsibilities.

We contrast this "normative" approach with one that deals more realistically with the fact that, despite its nutritive benefits, political spinach is not always, well, appetizing. As spinach aficionados, political junkies often observe with some puzzlement that citizens seem to pay more attention to political debates than to routine stump speeches. But the debates have the character of tournaments—with winners and losers; and because they are broadcast live on television, there is always the prospect that unrehearsed emotions may be expressed to reveal the character of otherwise very well-coached speechmakers. Some of the most memorable campaign moments are such dramatic exchanges as Lloyd Bentsen's comment to Dan Quayle that "You're no Jack Kennedy" and Bernard Shaw's interrogation of Michael Dukakis about rape and capital punishment. Such moments were emotionally charged and revealing. Three-minute exhortations on policy positions from those same debates are perhaps not so easily recalled. Insight into the hard-wired narrative structure of human memory and the compelling horse-race character of political contests drive successful reporting, advertising, and campaigning (Neuman, Just, and Crigler 1992). To reject these psychologically important elements of political culture merely because they violate normative political behavior is not likely to lead to the successful building of civic institutions.

Sociotropic and Symbolic Politics

When citizens exercise their electoral calculus and select one candidate over another or consider alternative referenda, do they try to ensure their own personal optimal benefit or do they optimize the collective benefit with respect to a perceived public good? The presumption that citizens are driven by self-interest is part of the conventional rational choice model; that citizens are oriented to maximizing the collective benefit, on the other hand, reflects some very intriguing findings generally associated with the terms *sociotropic* and *symbolic politics* (Kinder and Kiewiet 1981; Sears 1993b). Our view is that there is evidence to support both views and, in fact, most citizens, depending on how questions are framed and political values are cued, exercise a rather sophisticated calculus engaging their sense of both individual and collective benefit (Mutz 1998).

One way to inform our understanding of the interaction of self-interested and symbolic perceptions is to explore how each is constructed from the perspective of Affective Intelligence. The surveillance system responds to immediate signs of novelty and threat without distinguishing between individual and collective interests. Because it is a learning system certain individuals, catchwords, or political symbols can come to elicit an attention-cueing response, just as fire alarms and ringing doorbells and telephones engage our attention. And in that manner we may find evidence of a two-way communication between the disposition system and the surveillance system. Again, we expect that the normal state is inattention to the political world punctuated by moments of attention driven by surveillance processes. Symbolic politics engages the individual when novelty or threat is deemed relevant and then through the calculation of possible response whether framed in individual or collective terms.

Issue Framing, Schema, and Constructionist Perspectives

In the mid-1980s there was a distinct surge of research interest in the schematic organization of political ideas and the active construction of political interpretation (Conover and Feldman 1984; Hastie 1986; Lau 1986; Lodge and Hamill 1986). Like many other trends in research literature, it represented a reaction to the dominant paradigm that characterized the citizen as a relatively passive recipient of political communication and that characterized issue preferences as distinct and free-standing phenomena. Research on political schema took pains to demonstrate how various political symbols, factual premises, beliefs, and issues preferences were differentially organized among different individuals and in predictable patterns in contrasting the belief systems of liberals and conservatives. Constructionist research drew on qualitative and depth interview methodologies to demonstrate both different schema and how such schema resulted from a natural, proactive cognitive process in which individuals struggle to make sense of the symbolic and informational stimuli that bombard them.

Our sense is that currently schema theory and constructionist theory get a respectful nod from researchers in the broader field of political behavior acknowledging their contributions to a deeper understanding of political cognition. The work is cited in passing but has not yet made a definitive mark on the broader field. The reason for this may hearken back to the discussion of signal and noise in the rational choice debate. Schema and cognitive construction draw attention to individual variance, in that sense random noise rather than accumulating signal, in broader theories of elections and collective outcomes (Converse 1990). Thus, although one might demonstrate that schema exist, what systematic difference do they make? This is where we would hope the theory of Affective Intelligence might be helpful. We will posit two connecting links.

The first is the linkage between construction and attention. As we have noted, the theory of Affective Intelligence posits inattention rather than attention as the norm. It turns the usual refrain of democratic theory on its head. Ask not why people pay so little attention to politics, ask why they pay any attention at all. We propose that most of the time the average individual does not struggle to understand the complex political world but rather ignores or shrugs off most such information as largely irrelevant. When, however, individuals do pay attention and feel compelled to construct a meaningful interpretation with some effort, the telling question asks what cued them to do so: what connections between symbols and ideas in a political presentation resonate with the existing beliefs and opinions of a listener? No doubt further research will reveal a variety of such cues, but we suggest one important candidate to be the perception of threat and novelty—the surveillance system's cue. Understanding how individuals, and the polity, focus attention should prove central for democratic theory (Jones 1994).

The second link deals with how particular symbols and ideas become emotionally charged. This notion is closely akin to the concepts of "hot cognition" (Marcus 1991) and symbolic politics (Sears 1993b; Sears, Hensler, and Speer 1979; Sears et al. 1980). Think for a moment of the premise of lie detector technology. Various relatively autonomous bodily functions such as breathing, heart rate, sweating, and facial muscle contractions are monitored as they involuntarily respond to emotional cues, in this case the guilt and fear associated with telling a lie, especially the prospect that doing so might be revealed. Some patriotic Americans find themselves emotionally charged, sometimes to the edge of tears, by the mere sight of the American flag. Others are much more casual about the flag as a political symbol, but find their blood pressure rising involuntarily in response to a threat to freedom of speech. Most of us have a political symbol, or perhaps several, to which we respond like the bull to the red cape. Sometimes these result from significant life experiences, at other times from deep and abiding but abstract political values. To the extent that a community's experiences and values are coherent, we would expect these attentional effects to be cumulative and systematically important rather than individual-level noise.

Campaign Coverage, Negative Ads, and the Spiral of Cynicism

Political scientists pay a great deal of attention to campaign coverage in the mass media, coverage that is more apt to treat the political campaign as a horse race rather than focus on the issues (Patterson 1991, 1993). They mull over the visceral negativity of much of the advertising and the alienation, cynicism, and low participation levels that appear to result (Ansolabehere and Iyengar 1995). An idealized conception of democratic practice drives much of the analysis of political scientists. Why can't journalists and candidates be more issue-oriented, less negative. Why don't voters care? Again, there is a preachy, eat-your-spinach character to much of this literature within political science.

The theory of Affective Intelligence suggests that journalists cover campaigns as a horse race, political operatives use negative ads, and citizens respond cynically for good and proper reasons rooted in the fundamental psychology of public attention and cognition. If democratic practice is to be improved, we need to understand these causal dynamics more fully.

Journalists have discovered that a narrative form that emphasizes winners and losers, heroes and villains, attracts an audience. The narrative form tends to interpret abstract issues in personal, concrete terms designed to win audiences. Broadcasters get instant feedback in terms of ratings on how well their coverage does against the competition. Broadcast and print executives conduct extensive research on what grabs attention and sells products. The applied science of advertising and marketing is indeed relevant here (Ansolabehere and Iyengar 1995; Grunert 1996). Those critics who proudly criticize today's campaign specialists for selling candidates much as they would sell soap flakes need to understand why such practices have evolved. Research into human psychology reveals similar dynamics at work in the realm of politics as in commercial advertising. We may wish that the threat of bad breath or ring around the collar were somehow in a different category from the threat of Willie Horton or tax-and-spend excesses. And it may prove to be that they are indeed different in important ways. But the psychological dynamics of the human response to a perceived threat is deeply ingrained.

Our primary argument here is that simple regulation imposed to limit or constrain negative advertising, for example, is unlikely to succeed. Negative advertising works under some conditions because the threat/novelty message succeeds in stimulating public attention. We need to explore procedures and institutional practices that both account for the incentive structure of the political combatants and the innate psychology of the generally inattentive mass audience.

But even more importantly, this research has the ability to more sharply redefine some of the key terms in the debate about the effects of negative campaigning. One of the most important is unpacking the different meanings now conflated in the term *negative*. People experience the absence of enthusiasm, anxiety, and aversion as unpleasant (Rusting and Larsen 1995). Thus it is tempting to treat these experiences as equivalent expressions of a general feeling of negativity. Yet, as we have seen in chapter 5, the effects of anxiety are quite different from those of depression (the absence of enthusiasm). In recent events, the persistent GOP attacks on President Clinton during 1994 led to depression among the Democratic base and reduced turnout while equally persistent attacks in 1998 frightened the Democratic base and stimulated turnout—in both cases the "negative" campaign affected the course of national politics but in opposite directions. So, it is true that the failure of campaigns to sustain enthusiasm among their supporters will depress turnout, but increased anxiety enhances turnout. Thus, the current discussion about negative campaigning must abandon its current presumption that all things negative have uniform effects (Brader 1999; Krosnick, Lowe, and Miller 1997; Lau et al. 1999; Wattenberg and Brians 1999).

Additionally, the perspective we are proposing can be useful in addressing why so much negative campaigning fuels fund raising. The surveillance system, we recall, is a normative system. Anxiety is generated when norms are violated; the more they are violated, and the more strategically central those norms are to people, then the greater the anxiety. Thus, under some conditions the most effective way of capturing attention and mobilizing political action is to play up the violation of deeply held norms.

What Remains to Be Done

The theory of Affective Intelligence has ramifications for methodological design. The affective component of political thought and judgment has tended to be ignored not only by the American National Election Studies series in particular but also, more generally, in the traditional design of questionnaires for political survey research. We are all constrained by the limits of current methodological traditions. These are well-worn data sets. A thorough examination with new item batteries in survey and systematic and complementary research in the experimental domain represents an important next step (see appendices A and B for a discussion of our suggestions).

The authors of this book have their roots in the study of American politics and political communication. An issue of critical importance we have chosen not to address is the question of emotion, national identity, ethnic identity, and international political conflict. In appendix B, for example, there is an extended discussion of stable negative dispositions we term *aversion*. Although throughout much of our analysis we have remarked on the "positive" cognitive consequences of "negative" feelings, the phenomena of stable aversion, more plainly hatred, surely produces less admirable consequences. Popular accounts, as well as theory, suggest that the mobilization of citizens to participate in ethnic cleansing or genocide or mass warfare stems from the engagement of emotions of this sort. It represents a particularly important area for further investigation in both domestic and international settings (Volkan 1988; Lanzetta and Englis 1989; Jervis 1997; Rosenau 1997; Sniderman et al. 1996).

Finally, much of the literature we have reviewed is modeled on a static representation of the issue-linkage between the mass public and the political establishment. This is in part an unintended outcome of the historical dependence of behavioral political science on single-interview survey designs. The theory of Affective Intelligence, drawing on surveys and experimental and quasi-experimental designs, models the dynamic of attention and perception over time and over changing environmental situations. As a result the interactive linkages between events, issues, and political outcomes become a pivotal point of focus.

Rethinking Models of Political Behavior

We have explored four areas of current research in political communication and behavior and found some resonance in each with our ongoing work. We are led to conclude this chapter, therefore, with a brief overview of how the theory of Affective Intelligence might contribute generally to the development and refinement of theory in political science.

First, there is a consistent tension between the normative and the behavioral. Citizens, candidates, and journalists do not always behave in ways that are consistent with the prerequisites of democratic theory. Western political values tend to vilify emotion and sanctify reason in the public sphere. While we share an enthusiasm for sound democratic practice, we find ourselves skeptical of those who would ignore or restrict the interaction of affect and reasoned judgment.

Second, we continue to marvel at the paradox of mass politics. It is part of our ongoing effort to identify those conditions under which citizens attend, learn, and participate in political life and to understand how they fit in the broader context of a realistic theory of human judgment.

Third, threat and novelty have been studied indirectly and at times implicitly in the literature of political behavior. We find significant theoretical leverage in bringing them front and center as part of an analysis of the surveillance system of affective intelligence.

Finally, our line of research defines emotional processes as essentially complementary to rational choice. Rational calculation would lead average voters to compute that the likelihood that their individual votes can affect election outcomes is infinitesimal. Yet millions take time to study the issues and trudge to the polls. Rational calculation would dictate that a vote for a protest-oriented, third-party candidate is a "wasted" vote. Yet millions vote in protest. In part, the theory of Affective Intelligence picks up where rational choice theory leaves off. It models the conditions and constraints of real-world choice.

Affective Intelligence and the Dual Model of Emotional Systems

We have put forward several arguments in this book in relatively brief compass. The three appendices are designed for those who continue to find the dual model of emotional systems particularly counterintuitive (appendix A), for those interested in measurement issues and further research (appendix B), and for those wishing to read further in this evolving literature (appendix C).

The dual systems approach is counterintuitive. As we described in chapter 2, most languages, and certainly English, reinforce a notion of emotion as valence—a single bipolar dimension of approach and avoidance. Further, most languages, often elaborately, distinguish between emotional states such as guilt, shame, and anger. The dual systems approach, however, accommodates both the valence and discrete-states conceptions of human emotion.[1] While the function of evaluation that underlies the understanding of discrete emotions as valence is important, the dual model asserts that emotional processes do more than evaluate.

The key here is the existence of preconscious emotional processes that precede the more familiar and accessible emotional states expressed in conscious awareness. This conception does not dictate that affective assessments will produce two, and only two independent factors, one measuring the level of anxiety and one the level of enthusiasm. As Cacioppo (1999) has recently argued, form follows function. The number of emotional

---

1. David Watson offers one such synthesis by positing that the structure of emotion is organized hierarchically with two broad dimensions of emotion, one positive and one negative, but that negative affect has a number of facets that discriminate among themselves (Watson and Clark 1992a). We draw on that work and our own research to posit that stable disapproval, a facet of negative affect, will be discriminated from anxiety, which Watson and we understand to be the broad dimension of negative affect.

dimensions generated by the dual systems depends upon contextual and motivational circumstances. Here we consider the history of measurement of emotional response in political science and its early findings.

Evolving Models of Political Judgment

The principal claim of the theory of Affective Intelligence is that two emotional processes arise before conscious awareness, one reflecting variation in enthusiasm and one reflecting variation in anxiety. This claim has been widely endorsed in recent studies of human emotional response.

Renewed attention to the structure of emotion in psychology can be dated to the early 1980s when analysis of mood terms and facial expressions revealed a two-dimensional space, sometimes called a "circumplex." The initial analyses of these data were interpreted in terms of two axes, a valence and an arousal dimension (Larsen and Diener 1992; Plutchik 1980; Russell 1980; Russell, Lewicka, and Niit 1989). Subsequently others argued for a 45° rotation of these axes that have been most commonly defined as positive, depicting differences in enthusiasm, and negative, depicting differences in anxiety (Watson, Clark, and Tellegen 1984; Watson and Tellegen 1985). In both cases, the thinking was that these dimensions were each bipolar (for example, for the valence dimension, running from dislike to like, and for Watson's conception at that time, running from sad to happy, defining the positive dimension). More recently still, these dimensions are now conceived as two unipolar dimensions (Watson 1988b; Watson and Clark 1992a; Watson et al. 1992; Watson, Clark, and Tellegen 1988).[2]

In political science the study of emotional response to candidates and issues predated this important work in psychology and drew heavily on the older notions of bipolar valence and discrete emotional responses. In 1979, for example, a group from Yale University proposed a new set of emotional measures to be tested in the American National Election Studies (ANES) pilot experiments. The measures were retained for the 1980 and

---

2. Green, Goldman, and Salovey (1993) recently seemed to argue that only one affect dimension can be identified in mood data. This has led to further controversy and analysis in the literature over the sample of mood terms Green and his colleagues analyzed. More recently, Green, Salovey, and Truax (1999) have expanded the earlier analysis and concluded that two dimensions are indeed necessary to account for the full range of mood variables. Much of the problem with these debates stems from a confusion in semantic labeling, a point to which we return later in this appendix. These are important questions of empirical consequence, as we demonstrate in appendix B (see also Watson and Tellegen 1999).

subsequent election studies. The theoretical foundation of these new instruments was explicitly derived from Roseman's discrete model of emotional response (Abelson et al. 1982; Kinder, Abelson, and Fiske 1979).

The discrete emotional concepts included seven mood terms: *hope, pride, sympathy, disgust, anger, fear,* and *uneasy.* These terms reflect the "cognitive" appraisals that were thought to be central to identifying and differentiating the basic emotions. For example, the basic emotion elicited by being uncertain about a politician was *unease.* Those who saw a politician as conflicting with their basic values or beliefs would experience *anger.* Those who perceived a politician taking positive action would experience *pride,* and so on. The standard format for questions used in these studies was "Has [political figure]—because of the kind of person he is, or because of something he has done—ever made you feel [basic emotion term]?" This reflects a clinical focus on the enduring power of a single emotional experience rather than attention to affective intensity or frequency.

A New Angle on Old Data

A reconsideration of this early work on the structure of political emotion reveals important clues to the evolving understanding of affective intelligence, particularly the notion of dual unipolar measures. Recall that in the bipolar valence all emotional reactions are taken as indicating liking (approach) or disliking (avoidance). Thus in that model it would not much matter whether we ask whether some political figure makes you feel proud or hopeful. In either case, it is the same fundamental dimension—do you like this person? *Proud* or *hopeful* reflect the positive side of the dimension, *unease* or *anger* the negative. Statistically, if the valence model provides the better fit, we would find high positive correlations between all of the negative terms, high positive correlations between all of the positive terms, and high negative correlations between the cross-valenced pairs of terms, one negative and one positive. If all positive mood terms and all negative mood terms have the same common content, as the valence model would here presume, then the correlation coefficient between any two of the items can be used to check whether this is supported by the data. The conventional method would be to square the correlation coefficient. The resulting number is the measure of the shared variance and thus measures the common meaning of any two items.

For our purposes, however, another way of considering the data proves especially revealing. How might we check two different items to see if they suitably define one dimension or whether they are two different measures, each measuring a different dimension?

The correlation coefficient defines the angular relationship between two measures. If people gave exactly the same answer to any two questions posed with respect to a specific politician, let's say anger and fear as an example, then the correlation would be r = + 1.00. This correlation converted to the appropriate angle would be 0°.[3] That means the two lines (actually vectors) would lie exactly on top of each other, just as the valence model would predict (there being only one dimension). What would we expect to find for two items, when one is positive and one is negative? Well, each would be a good measure of the respective ends of the bipolar dimension of valence. Thus we would find, for example, pride and anger for any political figure to be very highly negatively correlated (e.g., r ≈ −1.00), which would yield two lines that would lie in opposing directions, close or identical to 180° (←→). The valence model, then, anticipates that any mood measure will be highly correlated with any other mood term. Terms of approbation would be highly positively correlated with each other, as would terms of disparagement.

Before we turn to the findings of Abelson et al. 1982, consider what we would find if the expected discrete model provided an optimal account of these emotional responses to political candidates. People are expected to apply a series of discriminating appraisals that differentiate one emotion from another. As a result we would expect that people would report either *anger* or *fear* or *unease*, and so on. To support the discrete model approach to emotional experience, the results should indicate relatively low correlations between all nonsynonymous mood terms.

Abelson and his colleagues, however, discovered a relatively robust pattern that fits neither the discrete nor even the valence model very well. They found a pattern of noncorrelation between "positive" and "negative" mood items where one might expect strong negative correlation.[4] What does such a low or noncorrelation mean? Following our previous discussion about a geometric approach to correlation, a near zero correlation coefficient is equivalent to 90°, a right angle. Substantively, this means that people are reporting that they are experiencing two different emotions

---

3. The cosine is the key trigonometric function for transforming the correlation coefficient to degrees. The transformation is not linear, so while r = 1.00 = 0°, r = 0.00 = 90°, and r = − 1.00 = 180°, r = 0.45 does not equal 45°.

4. Actually, Abelson et al. (1982) report correlations that range from near 0 to −0.6. Thus, the correlation between two dimensions of affective response, a positive and negative dimension, is dynamic, a topic of their consideration and, shortly, ours.

when they are asked about politicians, a positive reaction, which could be strong or weak, *and* a negative reaction, which can also be strong or weak. The near zero correlation means, technically, that the relationship between these two reactions is *orthogonal* and, more directly, that knowing how much of a positive emotional reaction we feel about a politician is not the inverse of how much of a negative reaction we feel.[5] Thus assessing only how "positive" a respondent feels about a politician represents only part of the empirical reality, masking or ignoring much in the complexity of the affective dynamics of political judgment.

This finding of two orthogonal dimensions turns out to be one of the most frequently replicated findings in the psychology of emotional response (Cacioppo et al. 1993; Carver and Scheier 1990; Davidson 1995; Derryberry 1991; Derryberry and Reed 1994; Gray 1987a; Heath 1986; McHugo et al. 1985; Robinson 1995; Tellegen 1985; Thayer 1989; Watson 1988a). Abelson and colleagues thus actually set the foundation for a major tenet of the theory of Affective Intelligence, the dual systems model of emotional response.

The dual systems model holds that two different appraisals are executed in repeating cycles of approximately one-tenth of a second in duration. This enables emotional appraisals to be fully and repeatedly completed during that one-half second gap in time that it takes for sensory information to be represented in consciousness.[6] The dual model holds

5. There has been some controversy about how to analyze the data obtained by asking people, as in the 1982 study by Abelson et al., how they feel. Some have argued that since such data is inherently bivalent—likes and dislikes—an unfolding model is the appropriate statistical model (van Schuur and Kiers 1994). Still others have asserted that such data is inherently subject to methodological bias and therefore recommend fitting a "methods" factor (Green and Citrin 1994; Green, Goldman, and Salovey 1993). We have more to say about this later in this and the appendix to follow. Here we claim, as do Fabrigar, Visser, and Browne (1997), that assessments of emotion describe vectors in a multidimensional space. The relationship of these vectors can be best described by transforming the correlations into the angle that depicts the location of any two vectors (for example, $r = 0 = 90°$; $r = -1.00 = 180°$, etc.).

6. Conscious awareness is the product of a biological system. Though we have the subjective sense of instantaneously experiencing events in our immediate world as they take place, that is impossible for it would require a biological system—the brain—to begin and complete its work with no passage of time. It is also an important point to make that consciousness is a variable condition. That is to say, we are not always conscious (as when we sleep, enabling our biological systems to rest and be restored). And even when awake we are not always fully attentive to the outside world (as when we daydream—an activity that comprises a rather high percentage of our waking moments). The estimate of one-tenth of a second is a generally accepted value, though there are individual differences. Some emotional appraisals have a longer gap, others a briefer one, and the gap can shrink or expand depending on circumstances (Gray 1984, 1985, 1987a, 1990; Gray and McNaughton 1996).

that two independent emotional systems process the incoming stream of sensory information and manifest these appraisals subjectively by variations in mood.

What does it mean to say that there are two independent emotional systems? The conventional understanding of the term *independent* suggests that the two systems would be unrelated, expected to always produce a zero correlation between the moods of each system. As is often the case, however, things are not so simple. For while many of the correlations that Abelson et al. (1982) report are close to zero, some of the correlations between positive and negative reactions for some of the political figures are very highly negatively correlated (some reaching negative correlations of more than r = −0.60). This pattern of correlations ranging from r = + 0.20 to r = −0.60 for political figures has been confirmed in our most recent work with the Annenberg 2000 election study and has been widely replicated in other years and with different political figures in the ANES since 1980 (Bruce 1991, 1994; Marcus 1988). However, using nonpolitical stimuli, the range in correlations between the positive dimension and the negative dimension has generally been reported to be between r ≈ − 0.1 and r ≈ −0.3 (Berry and Hansen 1996; Watson 1988b). Figure A.1 shows how the characteristic ranges appear for nonpolitical stimuli (part A) and for political figures (part B).

The patterns displayed in figure A.1 confirm that the valence model does not fit these data very well, even when the correlation between the two dimensions rises to r ≈ −0.60. Even this angle between the positive and negative dimensions is just not close enough to 180° to support the conclusion that such political judgments are unidimensional.

Abelson et al. (1982) interestingly argued that the correlation between the two dimensions may be dynamic rather than static based on the varying familiarity of political objects. The more familiar the stimulus, the more feelings will be organized into the single bipolar valence dimension. On further analysis, we find that familiarity is a necessary but perhaps not sufficient condition to generate a single valence dimension. The crucial factor turns out to be the substantive significance of the stimulus. When politicians are unfamiliar, people generally experience two concurrent reactions, one positive and one negative. As people get to know a politician better they integrate these two distinct reactions into a harmonized like or dislike.[7]

7. That repeated exposure is sufficient to generate liking is a long-standing hypothesis (Titchener 1910).

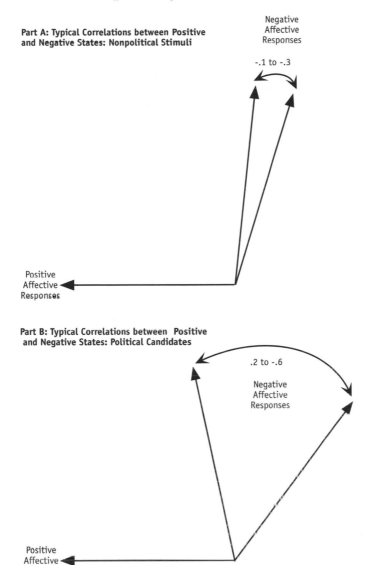

Part A: Typical Correlations between Positive and Negative States: Nonpolitical Stimuli

Negative Affective Responses

-.1 to -.3

Positive Affective Responses

Part B: Typical Correlations between Positive and Negative States: Political Candidates

.2 to -.6

Negative Affective Responses

Positive Affective Responses

Figure A.1   The Change of Mood Structure—Nonpolitical and Political Stimuli

Replications of the Dual Unipolar Model in Social Psychology

Data recently reported and generously made available to us by Cheryl Rusting and Randy Larson (Rusting and Larsen 1995) suggest why familiarity is not, by itself, the primary explanation for this phenomenon. The data that were gathered concerned which moods people experienced over the course of a day. They used a wide array of mood terms, some forty-eight different terms in all. Having such a large array of different terms would enable them to discern which terms were merely synonyms and which terms discriminated among different emotional experiences. Recall that the 1982 study by Abelson et al. suggests that, in the realm of assessing politicians, many mood terms thought to be distinct prove to be equivalent. Expanding the array from the seven mood terms then used in the ANES studies to forty-eight provides a fuller exploration of whether reducing all emotional reactions to just two, one positive and one negative, is warranted.

The subjects, 232 University of Michigan psychology undergraduates, were asked to rate—from 0 (extremely rare) to 8 (extremely often)—how frequently they experienced, on average, each of the listed moods during the course of a day. If two terms depicted the same emotional experience then each would have the same precise rating as the other. Similarly any two terms that described different experiences would be given different ratings. The correlations between these ratings were then evaluated in the usual manner by subjecting them to a factor analysis, which yielded the now familiar two-factor plot (Clark and Watson 1988; Plutchik 1980; Plutchik and Kellerman 1989; Watson and Tellegen 1985). The results, displayed in figure A.2, reveal a two-dimensional pattern that replicates Abelson's and now many other descriptions of emotional response.

As confirmed by their statistical analysis (Rusting and Larsen 1995), the experience of actual moods during the course of a day is indeed two-dimensional (Thayer 1989; Watson 1988a, 1988b). However, a closer examination of figure A.2 reveals additional findings of relevance. If you examine the plot you can readily see that the variation in these terms is fairly described as variation along two axes each of which ranges from the absence of emotion to greater emotionality. Along the horizontal axis one moves from *relaxed, at ease,* and *calm* (the absence of anxiety), to *nervous* and *jittery* (increasing levels of anxiety). Similarly, along the vertical axis, one moves from the absence of enthusiasm and elation, in other words depression, to increasing levels of elation. Rather than a space created by two bipolar dimensions, we have a space defined by two unipolar dimensions of emotionality.[8] Thus, rather than modeling these two factors as positive and negative valences, the common terms in social psychology, we under-

---

8. Of course this interpretation fits the clinical as well as the research literature. Depression is not the abundance of emotion but that state of chronic absence of emotion, the emotion of enthusiasm that energizes and mobilizes behavior.

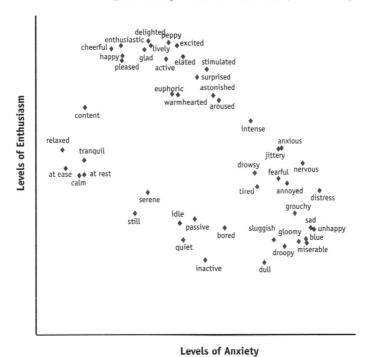

Levels of Anxiety

Figure A.2 The Experience of Actual Moods
SOURCE: Adapted from Rusting and Larsen 1995.

stand them to be dimensions of enthusiasm and anxiety, conceptions drawn from the neurosciences (Derryberry and Reed 1994; Derryberry and Tucker 1991; Gray 1987b; Gray 1990).

The Enduring Measurement Paradox:
Emotions Experienced versus Emotions Described

If such a pattern is so easily replicated, why has it taken so long for it to become reported in the literature? Again, the Rusting and Larsen 1995 study suggests an answer. The same 232 subjects were also asked to rate the identical forty-eight moods as before but now on a different rating scale. In this second task the subjects were asked to rate how desirable—from 0 (extremely undesirably) to 8 (extremely desirable)—they felt each term to be. As you can see in figure A.3, the forty-eight terms fall along a single dimension with the more desirable feelings at one end and the undesirable

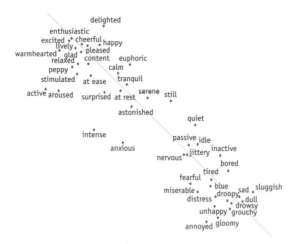

Figure A.3   The Description of Ideal Moods

SOURCE: Adapted from Rusting and Larsen 1995.

feelings at the other end. The two-dimensional character of emotion displayed in figure A.2 has disappeared.

This is a result that is quite close to that which the valence model might predict. More importantly, it is a pattern that reveals our natural inclination to simplify the world into clear normative oppositions—good guys versus bad guys. This is a powerful impulse, one that masks the underlying complexity of emotional experience. It is deeply embedded in language and culture, so much so that when Osgood and his associates (1957) assessed the primary dimensions of meaning across cultures they found the natural opposition of good versus bad to be the dominant analytic dimension in their data. Their subjects readily accepted the semantic differential oppositions as an appropriate tool of evaluation. But such a method, by its nature, precludes any findings of the character displayed in figure A.2.

People, both lay and scientific, reflect their common culture and cleave to unambiguous and unconflicted preferences along a single dimension of approach and avoidance. Although such a pattern may accurately reflect our cultural heritage, it may distort the nature of what we actually experience. This is particularly important inasmuch as emotional ambivalence—an admixture of anxiety and enthusiasm—may in fact be a common experience but one that, as a result of our culturally inherited understanding of emotion, is most often simply ignored or confused with indifference.

Numerous studies have shown that a simple instruction to "pay attention to your thoughts" (or some variant) weakens the influence of affective appraisals (Marcus et al. 1995; Millar and Tesser 1986a, 1986b; Tesser and Clary 1978; Wilson 1979). This is consistent with a principal tenet of Affective Intelligence: affective appraisals arise before consciousness. The instruction to pay attention to your thoughts does not inhibit the affective appraisals themselves; rather, it reduces attention to the feelings and enhances attention to thoughts (Marcus et al. 1995).

The evidence we present in chapters 5 and 6 offers, we hope, an auspicious beginning for addressing these intertwined issues of measurement and theory. In a recent review of measurement controversies in this field, Abraham Tesser and Leonard Martin (1996, 409) conclude:

> Should positive and negative evaluations be measured separately? Measuring evaluations as a single dimension has a variety of advantages. It is consistent with tradition; many standard approaches to attitude measurement assume a single bivalent evaluative dimension. Therefore, unidimensional measurement makes findings comparable to past work. The unidimensional score is easy to interpret and understand. It is parsimonious. One score is easier to deal with than two scores and the multitude of ways in which two scores can be combined. Finally, unidimensional evaluative measures appear to work well in most contexts. All of these are valid arguments for using unidimensional measures; however, we recommend that separate measures of positive and negative evaluation should be taken as standard practice. The potential increase in information yield, over the long term, will more than repay the cost associated with combining the measures if they turn out simply to reflect a single underlying dimension in a particular context.

We find their conclusion most persuasive.

Toward a Measurement Theory
of Political Affect

The array of methods available to neuroscientists to study the brain is not as yet generally suitable for political science research. As a result, political scientists interested in emotional response will have to rely largely on self-report in surveys and experiments. The core data of political science is self-reported recollections of what people think, what they do, and how they feel.[1] Naturally, what people report will be influenced by the character of the particular research stimulus as well as the question format. As reported in appendix A, when respondents are asked to describe their actual feelings a very different structure of emotion emerges than when they are asked to describe what they would like to feel: self-reports of actual feeling fit the expected orthogonal two-dimensional solution while ideal feelings fit a single bipolar solution.

Broadly speaking, there are two approaches to self-report measurement. The first tries to avoid providing explicit direction to the respondent by asking, "How do you feel about X?" This approach has merit but poses some analytic problems. Some repondents may report that a political stimulus makes them feel anxious while others say the same object makes them feel worried. Are these different or equivalent responses? The second approach avoids this problem by providing an explicit rating battery. This approach allows comparisons to be made more readily but may complicate the issue of external validity. We need to work toward a measurement

---

1. There are, of course, other means of assessing emotional reactions. It is possible to observe people surreptitiously or overtly and have judges rate their body posture or facial expressions for emotional content and intensity. Additionally, skin conductance and facial electromyographic measurements provide a more intrusive form of measurement (Cacioppo et al. 1993; Cacioppo and Tassinary 1990; Cuthbert, Bradley, and Lang 1996; Fowles et al. 1981; George et al. 1995; Lang 1994; Plutchik and Kellerman 1989; Robinson 1995).

theory to help clarify the interaction of measurement effects and behavioral effects in this delicate domain of behavioral subtlety and lability.

We demonstrate that question design can, by itself, produce results that suggest that the structure of emotional responses is best described as a single bipolar dimension, as two orthogonal unipolar dimensions, or three largely orthogonal unipolar dimensions. Thus, what appear to be substantive differences in the outcomes of different studies may be due to different choices in methodology made by investigators.

Measuring Emotion with Self-Report in the Psychological Tradition

Here we briefly explore one of the most widely used and exhaustively tested measures of emotion, the PANAS measures (Positive and Negative Affect Schedule) developed by David Watson (1988b; Watson, Clark, and Tellegen 1988). We examined some of his data on the distribution of positive and negative emotion in chapter 2. Watson has evaluated a wide array of emotion terms, a variety of question formats, and a variety of response formats. His results demonstrate that his chosen affect terms consistently reproduce two independent dimensions of mood whether ascertained by measures of intensity or by measures of frequency. He finds that the structure of emotional reaction is invariant across the temporal framing of the response format (Watson 1988b).

In psychology it has been common practice to label these two dimensions of emotion as "positive" and "negative." As we make clear in our exposition of the dual model of emotional response in chapter 3, we prefer to use the terms *enthusiasm* instead of *positive*, and *anxiety* instead of *negative*. In the present discussion of Watson's work, however, we carry over his terminology. In tables B.1—B.3, two sets of labels are provided: the conventional psychological terms, *positive* and *negative*, and in parentheses the corresponding terms we have proposed, *enthusiasm* and *anxiety*. We think the latter pair of terms more precisely identifies the emotional content of the reactions associated with each factor.

Reproduced in table B.1 are the median varimax-rotated factor loadings of the twenty emotion terms used by Watson (1988b, table 5) to define the positive and negative affect dimensions.[2] We present these results to

2. The median result is obtained from six administrations that asked subjects to rate their mood states (the scale points were labeled *not at all* or *very slightly, moderately, quite a bit,* and *very much*) in six different temporal frames of reference (today; during the past few days; during the past week; during the past few weeks; during the past year; in general, that is on average).

Table B.1 Median Varimax-Rotated Factor Loadings of the Positive and Negative Affect Schedule (PANAS) Descriptors across the Six Solutions

PANAS Mood Term	Factor I Positive Affect (Enthusiasm)	Factor II Negative Affect (Anxiety)
Enthusiastic	.75	−.12
Interested	.73	−.07
Determined	.70	−.01
Excited	.68	.00
Inspired	.67	−.02
Alert	.63	−.10
Active	.61	−.07
Strong	.60	−.15
Proud	.57	−.10
Attentive	.52	−.05
Scared	.01	.74
Afraid	.01	.70
Upset	−.12	.67
Distressed	−.16	.67
Jittery	.00	.60
Nervous	−.04	.60
Ashamed	−.12	.59
Guilty	−.06	.55
Irritable	−.14	.55
Hostile	−.07	.52

SOURCE: Watson, Clark, and Tellegen 1988.

represent the typical solution obtained for most nonpolitical stimulus as well as to draw particular attention to the emotion terms that best anchor the high end of each unipolar dimension of emotional response.

Notice that the emotion terms Watson uses are generally descriptive rather than normative. Relatively absent are terms that suggest or imply expressly normative attributions, such as *contempt* or *disgust* or *love*. Using descriptive rather than normative terms is appropriate for a measurement model attempting to ascertain the variation in emotional arousal that results from emotional systems that operate in the time interval *prior to* conscious awareness and the appraisal process that lies at the heart of discrete models. It is worth noting that the terms that are more expressly normative—such as *ashamed, guilty, proud,* and *hostile*—are less reliable than those terms that are less confounded with conscious appraisals. Relying on Watson's research base we have concluded thus far that the best markers for the positive affect dimension are the terms *enthusiastic, interested, determined,* and *excited* and, for the negative affect dimension, the terms *scared, afraid, upset,* and *distressed*.

Because there are over seven hundred mood terms in the English lexicon (Storm and Storm 1987), we have an overabundance of prospective markers. Moreover, the semantic rules for the use of the term *feeling* barely constrain its use in normal conversation. For example, we might say either "I feel smart today," or "I feel today's going to be a nasty day." It is likely that many other terms from the everyday lexicon of emotion response will similarly complicate theory building insofar as many such terms may be confounded, may be an amalgam of different mood states, or may be an admixture of cognitive assessments and moods. *Sympathetic*, for example, is a frequently used mood term that is a demonstrably confounded and complex mixture of anxiety and enthusiasm (Marcus 1988).

Measuring Emotional Response Evoked by Politicians

In 1995 the American National Election Studies research team decided to give the measurement of emotional response special, and as it turns out, much needed attention in the pilot study of that year. This study is especially useful in exploring the consequences of the different measurement choices that flow from different theoretical conceptions because these different choices were embedded in a split-half experimental design allowing us to contrast directly the consequences of these alternative measures.

Since the original 1980 study of emotion and electoral politics, competition for space in the questionnaire reduced the standard emotion items to four, two positive terms (*pride* and *hope*) and two negative terms (*angry* and *afraid*).[3] In the special 1995 pilot study one additional positive term (*enthusiastic*) and seven negative terms (*anxious, worried, bitter, resentful, disgusted, hatred,* and *contempt*) were added for a total of twelve items. Among these additions are some items that duplicate or are synonymous with those used in the PANAS schedule (*enthusiastic, anxious, worried*) and some that are expressly normative (*bitter, resentful, disgusted, hatred,* and *contempt*).

A methodological extension added a follow-up query to the traditional dichotomous response option. Form A added the follow-up query: "How often would you say you felt [anxious]—very often, fairly often, occasionally, or rarely" to each emotional term. Those indicating "No, never felt" in response to the initial question, were coded as "Never," yielding five levels to discriminate the frequency of experience of that emotion associated

3. This reduction was no doubt influenced by the principal findings that only two factors emerged (Abelson et al. 1982). This might have led those in charge of the design of the ANES studies that followed to conclude that retaining the additional items would be a waste of valuable survey time.

with the named politician.[4] The design of Form A, by providing additional discrete emotion terms as referents, including terms with expressly distinctive normative content, was intended to reveal the discriminations anticipated by discrete models of emotion.

We are now able to examine how these specific measurement choices affect conclusions about the structure of emotional response. We look first at the results obtained when the designated politician is Senator Robert Dole. Table B.2 shows the results of two factor analyses: the first, a truncated set of six emotion terms, three "positive" and three "negative," the items closest to those used by Watson; and, the second, the full set of twelve terms including the added expressly negative normative disapproval terms.[5] Do we get different results in these two analyses?[6] For if we did we would draw different conclusions merely as a result of a decision as to which emotion words we chose for people to use in their ratings. Does it make a difference when we add the normatively explicit terms most suited to discrete models and their concern for conscious prior appraisal? As shown in table B.2, our results suggest that as long as the mood terms we select are diverse, the structure of emotion is essentially the same.

The results in table B.2 demonstrate that the truncated set duplicates the pattern obtained by the full PANAS schedule—two essentially orthogonal dimensions, one labeled positive (level of enthusiasm) and the other labeled negative (level of anxiety) (compare with table B.1). The three negative items (measures of anxiety) define a dimension that is very weakly correlated with a dimension marked by the three positive items (measures of enthusiasm). The correlation between the two factors, $r = -0.10$, represents a 96° angle between the two vectors, dimensions, a solution that is

4. One obvious benefit of using either frequency or intensity response options is that one can, with more confidence, use conventional multivariate statistical techniques such as factor analysis, multiple regression, and the like (Bollen and Barb 1981). However, this two-question branching format inflates the number of "No, never felt" responses as against those elicited by single unipolar formats such as those used by Watson (see the respective distributions in chapter 4).

5. We apply a principal components analysis, orthogonal solution, with varimax rotation. Factors with eigenvalues near or greater than one are retained for analysis (also informed by examination of the scree plot of eigenvalues). We then obtain an oblique solution to assess the independence of the extracted factors.

6. An alternative mode of analysis is to use structural equation model statistical analysis. The results are essentially the same, though on balance over a wide array of analyses the correlation between factors tends to be somewhat higher than that found with the oblique solutions derived from factor analyses. Since the substantive conclusion is no different, and inasmuch as exploratory factor analysis is more widely understood, we present our work using that mode of statistical analysis.

Table B.2   Factor Analyses of Emotion Terms Used to Describe Senator Robert Dole

A. Orthogonal Solutions

	Truncated Set			Full Set	
Emotion Term	Factor I Negative Affect (Anxiety)	Factor II Positive Affect (Enthusiasm)	Emotion Term	Factor I Negative Affect (Anxiety)	Factor II Positive Affect (Enthusiasm)
Hope	−.04	.90	Hope	−.05	.90
Enthusiastic	−.04	.87	Enthusiastic	−.08	.86
Proud	−.11	.86	Proud	−.10	.86
Worried	.91	−.06	Worried	.86	−.06
Afraid	.89	.15	Afraid	.82	−.15
Anxious	.86	.00	Anxious	.70	.01
			Resentful	.83	−.07
			Disgusted	.80	−.25
			Angry	.78	−.18
			Bitter	.73	−.05
			Hatred	.63	−.03
			Contempt	.61	.03
Eigenvalues	2.70	1.98		5.36	2.19
B. Correlation between factors (oblique solution)		$r_{FI \cdot FII} = -.10$	$r_{FI \cdot FII} = -.16$		

SOURCE: ANES 1995 pilot study, Form A.

essentially orthogonal. Thus the oblique factor solution is essentially identical to the orthogonal solution.

What is the consequence of the addition of six expressly normative emotion terms, terms such as *bitter*, *disgusted*, and *hatred*? When we factor analyze the full set, the initial six items plus the six additional negative normatively explicit mood terms, we obtain the same two-dimensional structure as with the truncated set, the same structure shown by Abelson et al. (1982) and replicated many times since. Moreover, while adding an additional question to assess the frequency of the emotional response provides the ability to discriminate more finely the frequency of emotional experience, it does not alter our conclusions about the structure of emotional responses. This analysis also raises an issue of meaning. What does the equivalence of the words *disgusted* and *hatred*, on the one hand, and *anxious* and *worried*, on the other hand, mean? Does it mean that people are actually feeling a set of discrete emotions, labeled by these semantic referents, and then find them all to be associated with a common target, in this case Senator Dole? Or does it mean that people are using any negative semantic label to define a sense of apprehension about the target? We think the latter is more likely,[7] and examine some of the relevant evidence for that view below. Finally, the correlation between the two factors, r = −0.16, is equivalent to a 99° angle between the two vectors, or factors, again essentially orthogonal and identical to the result obtained from the truncated set.

Here, even when the political object is a long-known and familiar partisan figure, and a presidential candidate, the nine "negative" items clearly define a single dimension, what we have labeled the "anxiety" dimension, much as the dual model anticipates. The three "positive" items define the second (enthusiasm) dimension of the dual model of emotion. At this point, the two-dimensional solution not only undermines the discrete model, by virtue of the clean fit of the two-dimensional solution to such a rich array of discrete emotion terms, but also the valence model as well.

This conclusion, however, is premature, as will be apparent when we turn to an equally familiar, though in 1995 more strategically salient politician, President Clinton. It has been a consistent feature of Clinton's political persona, even when he was a politician successfully running for statewide office in Arkansas, that he provokes a deep dislike and distrust among some people. Thus, President Clinton is an excellent "stimulus" to use in exploring whether, as we propose below, at least for some highly polarizing leaders, we obtain a third emotional response—aversion. The conventional approach to emotional reactions in psychology anticipates two distinct reactions, one positive and one negative. We offer an extension of this conventional approach to account for this occasional third dimension of emotion. We argue that the disposition system also manages our learned associations to deal with recurring punishing or nonrewarding intrusions. This will be revealed by a third dimension marking strong normative disapproval, which we term *aversion*, a reaction that is distinguished from that generated by the surveillance system because who and what we loathe is part of the familiar world, which is the domain of emotional response that is managed by the disposition system.[8] If President Clinton is such a politician, then, unlike the case with Senator Dole, we will find that the nine "negative" mood terms divide into two distinct groups: one group

7. There is an alternative view, developed by David Watson and Lee Anna Clark (1992a), that negative affects are organized hierarchically with a general overarching dimension, negative affect, and subordinate and more specific variants such as we find below.

8. This requires further research to corroborate what is now merely a speculation. Panksepp (1998) argues that there is a distinct emotional system to handle rage; it is possible that what we have assigned to the disposition system is really under the control of either a "rage" system or the "fight or flight" response system.

to mark the general dimension of anxiety, reflecting appraisal by the surveillance system; and one group to mark aversion resulting from appraisal by the disposition system. Moreover, we can predict which mood terms will gravitate to each group. We again use Form A from the 1995 ANES pilot study. Table B.3 presents these results again as two-factor analyses.

If, as before, we rely on just the truncated set of six mood terms—*proud, hopeful, enthusiastic, anxious, afraid* and *worried*—what would we conclude? The truncated set of mood terms does a fine job of differentiating the familiar two dimensions, one positive dimension that marks the inclination to support and identify with the politician (that is, the disposition to work with, to support and identify with, to enthuse) and one negative dimension that marks the degree of uncertainty and threat evoked by that politician (that is, anxiety).

There is one interesting difference in the comparison of the results of the truncated sets, the items best suited to measure enthusiasm and anxiety. For Dole the first factor, accounting for a higher proportion of the total variance in the six items, is the anxiety dimension. For Clinton, however, the opposite is the case: the first factor, accounting for more of the variance in the emotion measures, is the positive dimension. Apart from this difference, the truncated sets of emotional terms for Senator Dole and President Clinton yield identical results with respect to the structure of emotional response. Had this or any study used only these six measures, we would have concluded that the dual model and its expectation of two dimensions, one of anxiety and one of enthusiasm, had been yet again replicated and confirmed.

However, when we turn to the full array of twelve emotional measures available in Form A to assay the emotions elicited by President Clinton, we obtain a different result. Adding the six expressly negative normative items produces a three-dimensional solution. The first factor appears to be a negative evaluative dimension, appropriate for identifying the stimuli that have become associated with stable negative dispositions. In the realm of the familiar, there will be familiar enemies and deep dislikes of proposals, terrain, and activities. This factor identifies that for at least some people, here Clinton haters, President Clinton had become just such a figure. The second and third factors replicate the dual model's two dimensions of enthusiasm and anxiety as revealed in the truncated set analysis for Clinton and in both the truncated and full sets for Senator Dole. It is worth noting that the aversion factor is remarkably distinct from the anxiety factor (using the oblique solution, the correlation of $r = 0.26$ translates into a 75° angle between these factors, hardly similar). This is not surprising given that

Table B.3 Factor Analyses of Emotion Terms Used to Describe President Bill Clinton

A. Orthogonal Solutions

	Truncated Set			Full Set		
Emotion Term	Factor I Positive Affect (Enthusiasm)	Factor II Negative Affect (Anxiety)	Emotion Term	Factor I Stable Disapproval (Aversion)	Factor II Positive Affect (Enthusiasm)	Factor III Negative Affect (Anxiety)
Proud	.88	−.06	Proud	−.10	.86	−.04
Hope	.85	−.21	Hope	−.16	.84	−.18
Enthusiastic	.85	−.06	Enthusiastic	−.01	.85	−.06
Anxious	−.02	.81	Anxious	−.10	−.22	.75
Afraid	−.06	.80	Afraid	−.05	−.03	.80
Worried	−.25	.80	Worried	−.08	−.01	.76
			Hatred	.78	.03	−.05
			Contempt	.71	−.06	.09
			Bitter	.68	−.11	.36
			Angry	.58	−.27	.50
			Resentful	.64	−.21	.35
			Disgusted	.43	−.40	.47
Eigenvalues	2.70	1.57		4.61	1.82	1.24
B. Correlation between factors (oblique solution)	rFI · FII = −.15			rFI · FII = −.16	rFII · FIII = −.24 rFI · FIII = .26	

SOURCE: ANES 1995 pilot study, Form A.

the surveillance system is looking to identify novelty and threat, not those familiar domesticated stimuli that we intensely dislike. What should we make about the low correlation, in the oblique solution, between aversion and enthusiasm? If they are each a result of the disposition system, should they not be more strongly related? The short answer is "no." Those who feel Clinton to be "punishing" experience aversion for him. Enthusiasm for Clinton is limited to those for whom he is a rewarding stimulus. Had we included a series of proposals about what to do about President Clinton, such as to raise money to support his opponents or to sign petitions for impeachment, we would have likely found a strong positive correlation between aversion to President Clinton and enthusiasm for these actions. Certainly, political fundraisers have found that presenting aversive targets in their appeals is a good way to motivate people to take actions directed against those targets. Enthusiasm about actions to deal with recurring threatening targets will be correlated, we expect, with aversion toward those targets.

It is also worth noting that although Senator Dole had long been on the national scene as a partisan politician, no evidence of a distinct emotional reaction of aversion could be identified in this study. This suggests that even in as combative a domain as democratic politics, most politicians do not have to worry that many people will respond to them with aversion.

The appearance of a three-dimensional solution for Clinton and a two-dimensional solution for Dole suggests a lesson for measurement strategy. Because the Dole analysis produces only the two dual model emotions, the analytic technique does not seem to produce a third dimension when there is none. And because the truncated set (missing the expressly negative normative, evaluative, emotion items) produced the two-dimensional solution for Clinton, we now understand that we will fail to see an important affective dynamic when our measures preclude identifying it.

The 1995 ANES pilot study included a second measurement approach for assessing the emotional reactions elicited by politicians. Form B measures turned out to be a failure. But, while we did not anticipate the results when we designed these items, as is often the case we learned more from that failure than we could have anticipated. Form B included a total of five emotion terms: two intended to measure the operation of the disposition system (levels of enthusiasm) and three to measure the operation of the surveillance system (levels of anxiety). Form B used an explicit bipolar response format, presenting the subject with labeled Likert format emotions terms to anchor each end of the specified emotion opposition. Two of the emotion terms, *enthusiastic—indifferent* and *hopeful—discouraged* were intended to define the enthusiasm dimension of the dual model. Three of the emotion terms, *anxious—calm, upset—relaxed*, and *angry—comfortable*, were intended to define the anxiety response of the dual model. An example of a Form B question is: "Does X make you feel very enthusiastic, somewhat enthusiastic, neither enthusiastic nor indifferent, somewhat indifferent, or very indifferent?"

Thus, Form B mimics two bipolar dimensions of emotion, one that ranges from lack of enthusiasm (indifferent and discouraged) to enthusiastic, and a second that ranges from lack of anxiety or threat (calm and relaxed) to anxious. We have argued that the dual model is better understood as having two orthogonal unipolar dimensions. What consequence does selecting an explicitly labeled bipolar response set have on subjects' assessments of emotion?

The analysis of the 1995 pilot data for Form B demonstrates unambiguously that we obtain a single dimensional solution with these five items. Table B.4 shows this in the factor analyses for the Form B emotional response items used for Clinton and Dole.[9] This is the case both for the items used to measure emotional response evoked by Clinton and for the items used to measure emotional response evoked by Dole.

Unlike the results we obtain using Form A, Form B items collapse the apparent underlying structure to a single bipolar valence dimension.[10] By making the response options explicitly bipolar, subjects are led in their self-report to collapse the otherwise dual character of emotional response to a single valence dimension. Thus, if we rely on measures that present opposing terms, as in the Likert format or as in feeling thermometers, the structure of emotional response will appear to be a single bipolar factor. Because people try to organize their feelings along a simple valenced dimension, we must rely on an appropriately sensitive measurement strategy to recover the underlying multidimensional structure.

Because of the split-half experimental design of the 1995 ANES pilot study we can safely conclude that the collapse to a single bipolar dimension is a measurement artifact. When unipolar response options are provided, as in Form A, then the two largely orthogonal dimensions of the dual model are uniformly extracted from the variance of candidate feeling mea-

9. The second eigenvalue is well below the value needed to warrant extracting a second factor. For the Dole items, the second eigenvalue is 0.63, for Clinton, 0.51.

10. Confirmatory factor analyses, not shown, confirm that a single dimension, with all positive items defining one end and all negative items defining the other end, essentially exhausts the variance in these items.

***Table* B.4** Factor Analyses of Emotion Terms Used to Describe Senator Dole and President Clinton

Senator Dole		President Clinton	
Emotion Term	Factor I	Emotion Term	Factor I
Hopeful–discouraged	−.88	Hopeful–discouraged	−.87
Enthusiastic–indifferent	.75	Enthusiastic–indifferent	−.82
Upset–relaxed	.86	Upset–relaxed	.81
Angry–comfortable	.85	Angry–comfortable	.88
Anxious–calm	.70	Anxious–calm	.79
Eigenvalues	3.29		3.49

SOURCE: ANES 1995 pilot study, Form B.

sures. However, when explicitly bipolar response formats are offered, as in Form B, then only a single valenced dimension can be identified. Since subjects in the 1995 ANES pilot were randomly assigned, the differences between Form A and Form B can be attributed solely to the differences in the question design.

These issues resonate closely with the controversy following Green's proposal of a "method" factor in the assessment of political affect (Green, Goldman, and Salovey 1993). However, because Green's analyses did not include an array of mood terms sufficiently diverse to discriminate between a single dimensional solution and a dual model (the work relies heavily on cognates of *happy* and *sad*), the implication that affect can be parsimoniously understood as a single bipolar valence dimension remains untested.[11]

There may be two reasons for declining adherence to the methods factor approach. First, studies of the brain have found that instead of a single site for emotional activity, for "positive" and "negative" stimuli, the brain processes these different stimuli in different regions of the brain (Davidson

11. Green's finding may be little more than a rediscovery of the initial conception of the structure of emotion as proposed by Plutchik (1980), Russell (1980), and others in the early 1980s. In this earlier view, two dimensions, a bipolar valence dimension and a second "arousal" dimension, best describe the structure of emotion. What Green then identified as a "response bias" factor had earlier been identified as an arousal dimension. Green now accepts the need for two dimensions to account for emotional response, and he prefers this earlier valence and arousal placement of axes (Green and Salovey 1999). Thus, Green has come to adopt the Plutchik and Russell view that there are two dimensions in emotional response measures, one measuring valence and one measuring arousal. Though this conception of emotional response is still adhered to by some (Diener and Emmons 1985; Lang, Bradley, and Cuthbert 1990; Larsen and Diener 1992) and perhaps continues to yield some reliable results, the general view of emotion as valence and arousal is apparently losing adherents.

and Tomarken 1994; Davidson 1992; Davidson 1995; Davidson and Fox 1989; Tomarken, Davidson, and Henriques 1990; Tomarken et al. 1992). This is consistent with the more widely held view that appetitive and surveillance functions are differentiated into separate evaluative systems. For those interested in a recent review of the treatment of emotion from a neuroscience perspective, see Bradley forthcoming. Second, valence and arousal models are generally restricted to describing the "structure of emotion" and have yet to develop surprising hypotheses about the behavioral and thoughtful consequences that might follow from different emotional responses.

Aversion and the Disposition System

As we noted above, many if not most of us have dispositions to manage those situations in which we encounter those we have grown to despise or fear (Devine 1989). Moreover, we will have learned how to manage those situations. This is the domain of prejudice. We have, after all, strong feelings about our enemies as well as our friends. We rely on these feelings not only to successfully guide the implementation of our plans but also to avoid or, if necessary, confront those we fear or dislike.

Although we may imagine an ideal world without malice, aversion is a powerful and important psychological and cultural phenomenon. We are often quick to label others as untrustworthy or evil (Lanzetta and Englis 1989; LeVine and Campbell 1972). Even in the most homogenous of societies, people will likely be confronted at some time by ideas that upset them and subgroups that annoy them, which results from the instinctive seeking out of the invidious differences among a society's members.

Implicit memory retains these negative associations as readily as it does the more positive associations. And procedural memory stores the plans we have secured to deal with these negative symbols as well as the plans to achieve positive goals. Aversion in its various guises—feelings of disgust, loathing, ire, bother, scorn, disdain, contempt, hatred, annoyance, and wrath—is functionally similar to the emotion of enthusiasm. Both report on the state of the current plan of action. The moods of aversion, however, identify those instances when we need to achieve a measure of success against something or someone that affronts. Enthusiasm marks the importance of executing a plan to achieve something that benefits us as well as the success of a plan to foil some foe. It provides the rapid continuous feedback on the success of that course of action.

While the antecedents of enthusiasm and of aversion are quite distinct, the principal cognitive and behavioral outputs are quite the same. Aversion and enthusiasm both highlight and and strengthen reliance on previously learned understandings and stereotypes. Both also strengthen the link between attitude and behavior. Indeed, once an aversive stimulus is identified, we will likely feel a substantial measure of enthusiasm when we undertake action to deflect, undermine, or destroy the aversive target.

Although it is premature to assert that the issue is settled, we believe that it may be the disposition system that animates those available actions we need to take when we are confronted with negative symbols. Thus enthusiasm is associated with a plan of action for achievement and aversion is associated with a plan of avoidance or conflict. We see below that familiar issues and structures such as the economy bring forth aversion as well as anxiety and enthusiasm more often than do politicians.

Measuring Emotional Reactions to Other Political Stimuli

What about the emotions people experience when something other than a politician is the focus of attention, say, issues of the day or, more generally, how they feel about the state of the economy or the state of the nation?

Professor Don Kinder of the University of Michigan has been exploring the role of emotion for over two decades.[12] He was involved in the very first effort to include measures of emotion in the ANES (Abelson et al. 1982) and has been active in trying to widen the interest in emotion ever since. The 1985 ANES pilot study included questions initially proposed by Kinder to explore the emotional reactions that people experienced when considering the policy of affirmative action. Although Kinder's theoretical focus has been associated with the discrete model (Kinder 1994; Kinder, Abelson, and Fiske 1979), these data are particularly useful for our purposes, in this case to see if these measures offer some evidence that the dual model holds when the focus turns away from politicians and towards issues.

Some four hundred adults, a subsample of subjects who had previously participated in the 1984 ANES survey, were reinterviewed in 1985 (Kinder

---

12. We do not mean to say that only Don Kinder has been interested in the role of emotion and political issues. Certainly others have been as well (Conover and Feldman 1986); but for the work with the most enduring interest, Kinder looms large. In addition one might cite David Sears' extended work on symbolic politics as another extended consideration of emotion and issues related to public affairs (Sears 1990, 1993a, 1993b; Sears, Hensler, and Speer 1979).

1994). Using a split-half design, two issues of affirmative action were presented to these subjects, each in two different articulations. One policy articulation focused on affirmative action with respect to hiring and promotions. The second dealt with college admissions and affirmative action. For each policy on affirmative action, two "frames" were paired: one of the frames focused on reverse discrimination and the other on unfair advantage (Kinder and Sanders 1990). We confine our analysis here to the hiring and promotion questions. We thus have two different positions statements, though on the same topic of affirmative action. The reverse discrimination frame was given as follows:

> Some people say that because of past discrimination against blacks, preference in hiring and promotion should be given to blacks. Others say preferential hiring and promotion of blacks is wrong *because it discriminates against whites*. What about your opinion—are you for or against hiring and promotion of blacks?

The unfair advantage frame was given as follows:

> Some people say that because of past discrimination against blacks, preference in hiring and promotion should be given to blacks. Others say preferential hiring and promotion is wrong *because it gives blacks advantages they haven't earned*. What about your opinion—are you for or against preferential hiring and promotion of blacks?

In either formulation, most whites were strongly opposed to affirmative action: 67 percent opposed the first formulation and 63percent opposed the second (Kinder and Sanders 1990). Following established ANES practice, a series of ten emotion terms were presented. Subjects were asked if they had ever felt *angry, afraid, uneasy, disgusted, infuriated, bitter, hopeful, proud, sympathetic,* or *happy* in response to "preferential treatment of blacks." The same dichotomous yes-or-no format used for measuring feelings about politicians was again used here.

What can we expect about the structure of emotion as revealed by these measures? As we have noted previously, the inclusion of explicitly normative terms, such as *infuriated* and *disgusted,* is capable of revealing a second "negative" dimension, one defined by feelings of stable disapproval in addition to primary "negative" dimension of anxiety. Moreover, affirmative action is just the kind of political issue likely to elicit, at least among some people, a powerful feeling of disapproval in as much as affirmative action was then, as it is now, a heavily politicized issue that has generated substantial and deeply felt opposition. Further, convenient for our exploration, this list includes some emotion terms likely to reveal just such a response if one obtains. Finally, the list also includes emotion terms that have generally worked well to elicit the two dimensions of anxiety (*uneasy*, *afraid*) and enthusiasm (*happy*, *proud*).

Thus, as we did with President Clinton (see table B.3), we might find three dimensions—a dimension of aversion in addition to anxiety and enthusiasm. Because these variables are coded as dichotomies, we must use special methods suitable for such restricted items. We rely on structural equation modeling to estimate the structure of emotional response in these items, calculating polychoric correlations to estimate the item-item covariation (the appropriate measure of covariance when the variables, as they are here, are categorical) prior to estimation.[13] Figure B.1 displays the results of our analysis. We find that the phrase *preferential treatment for blacks* does elicit three distinct emotional reactions.[14] After some preliminary analysis, we define the aversion dimension with the terms *angry* and *disgusted*.[15] The terms *afraid* and *uneasy* define the anxiety dimension and *proud*, *happy*, and *hopeful* the enthusiasm dimension.

As we found with the 1995 pilot study measuring feeling related to President Clinton, the aversion dimension is largely defined by the normatively explicit terms while the remaining terms define the expected dimensions of anxiety (*afraid*, *uneasy*) and enthusiasm (*happy*, *proud*, *hopeful*), the two general dimensions of the dual model.[16] The dual model factors have a near

13. Because the number of cases is limited, only about four hundred, and because analysis requires dropping cases with missing values, we do not divide the sample further into halves, according to the different definition of affirmative action policy presented prior to the "How do you feel about preferential treatment" question. Since the overarching reaction to affirmative action was strongly and almost equally opposed to each framing of the policy, we do not expect a major impact on the structure of emotional response. Whether different framing of issues affects the structure as well as the distribution of emotional response remains, then, an open question that is likely to be a fruitful one for future research.

14. The fit parameters, though based on polychoric correlations, are quite acceptable. The comparative fit index (CFI) is .90, the Bentler Bonnett Normed Fit Index is .90, and the chi-square statistic is 184.74 with 11 degrees of freedom (with p less than .001). The average residual is .03, another indicator of goodness of fit. We made no effort to improve this model beyond this level of fit by allowing for correlated error terms or other model adjustments. We estimated other models, including models that fit all terms as defining a single, valence, factor, another fitting all "negative" terms to a single factor. In each case, the models can be safely discarded because of their very poor fit to the data.

15. The emotion term, *bitter*, proved to be a poor measure for this dimension and so was dropped. The term *infuriated* works well to define this dimension and could be added without great detriment to model fit.

16. It is noteworthy that *sympathy* seems, for the Form B version of affirmative action, to be a confounded term, a result we have previously found when that term is applied to politicians (Marcus 1988). As such, it is an emotion term that we think is best avoided.

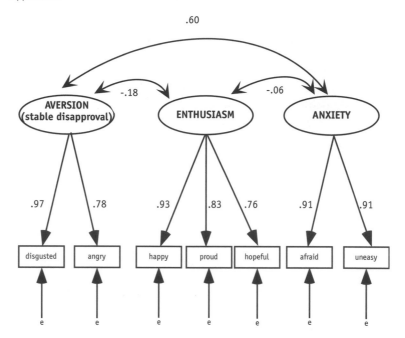

Figure B.1 Structural Equation Model of Emotion Terms Used to Describe Emotional Reactions to "Preferential Treatment of Blacks"

SOURCE: ANES 1985 pilot study.

zero structural parameter, −0.06. We might expect enthusiasm and aversion to be opposite conditions—that is, negatively correlated. But the structural parameter estimated between stable disapproval factor enthusiasm factor is −0.18, which is negative but hardly suggestive of an either/or relationship. There is a strongly positive structural parameter between the aversion factor and the surveillance factor, 0.60, suggesting a not surprising relationship: those who already hold a strongly held aversion toward a long-familiar policy are likely to be more alert and reactive to new and novel information relating to that policy.[17] Those who intensely dislike a policy position are more likely to feel anxious when it is put forward. It is worth remarking that here the relationship between aversion and anxiety is higher than we found it to be with President Clinton. We have argued that crystalization becomes more pronounced for those strategically salient re-

17. As we have noted before, if we treat these factors as vectors in evaluative space, then a correlation of .60 is equivalent to an angle of 53°—greater than 45°, which is the halfway point between two vectors sharing the same angle (a correlation of 1.00) and vectors that are orthogonal (a correlation of 0.00).

curring stimuli as a function of their recurring familiarity and salience.[18] Further, inasmuch as feelings toward minority groups like black Americans are, in the United States, learned early in life (Aboud 1988), they readily translate into specific policy issues (Carmines and Stimson 1989).

Consider another example. In 1982, Pamela Conover (now at the University of North Carolina, Chapel Hill) and Stanley Feldman (now at the State University of New York at Stony Brook), began a large three-wave panel study, interviewing a sample of adults from Lexington, Kentucky (Conover and Feldman 1986). This is, to our knowledge, the first study that sought to extend the research on the relation between emotion and political leaders to other stimuli. Conover and Feldman were interested in how people felt about the national economy and how they felt about their own personal circumstances. They posed the following questions to the respondents:

> I'd like to ask you about some of the feelings that you have when you think about the *nation's* economy—not your *own* personal economic situation. In the last six months, has the nation's economy made you feel . . . ?

Then they listed ten affect terms, five positive and five negative. Each provided for only a simple yes or no response. Happily, the ten affect terms listed provided an excellent array of mood terms. The five negative terms used were *angry, afraid, disgusted, frustrated,* and *uneasy* (notice here that we have items that should define the aversion dimension as well as the anxiety dimension); the five positive items included *hopeful, proud, happy, sympathetic,* and *confident* (again an excellent selection, though they found, as we have since repeatedly discovered, that the term *sympathetic* does not well define any dimension of emotional response). Later in the interview period, respondents were also asked:

> Just like we did a few moments ago for the nation's economy, I'd like to ask you about some of the feelings you have when you think about your *own personal economic situation*. In the last six months, has your own economic situation made you feel . . . ?

As before, the ten affect terms were listed, with yes or no responses being recorded.

Let us first consider their results for how people feel about the nation's economy. Using structural equation modeling, LISREL, they report three factors: one "positive" factor, defined by *hopeful, proud, happy,* and *confident*

---

18. This expectation is confirmed in a recent study (Nelson 1998).

(we note they also excluded *sympathetic*) and two "negative" factors. The first "negative" factor, defined by *angry*, *disgusted*, and *frustrated*, is essentially the same dimension we have identified as aversion. The second "negative" dimension is defined by *afraid*, *uneasy*, and, *frustrated*; this is the anxiety dimension. So, the structure of emotional response associated with the "nation's economy" mirrors what we anticipated: two general dimensions of emotional response, enthusiasm and anxiety, and one specific dimension, that of aversion, for those recurring political stimuli that are, for some people, matters of intense dislike. These results, then, corroborate what we find with other salient political stimuli—that we will generally encounter reactions of *enthusiasm* and *anxiety*. Furthermore, we will also often find on the part of some people, particularly when confronted by such stimuli as polarizing issues and polarizing leaders, an emotional reaction of aversion, reflecting a history of bad experiences and inability to fully control such sources of bad outcomes.

Now we turn to what the study's subjects feel about "their personal economic situation." The same model as described above provides a comparable set of results. However, Conover and Feldman (1986) report that for the "personal economic situation" a simpler model is all that is required for a good fit, a model in which all the negative terms define just one dimension. Thus, as we found with the 1995 ANES pilot data on President Clinton and Senator Dole, when subjects are presented with a full array of negative emotion terms from which to choose, including explicitly normative terms, we find that some stimuli generate aversion and anxiety (Clinton, affirmative action, and the nation's economy) while other stimuli generate only anxiety (Senator Dole and one's personal economic situation). This result also confirms our claim that anxiety and enthusiasm are general emotional reactions, always present, while aversion is a more restricted emotional response, arising only in certain contexts and in response to certain stimuli.

What about other political stimuli? Professor Wendy Rahn of the University of Minnesota has extended the dual model of emotion to what she calls "public mood"—how people feel about their country (Rahn forthcoming a,b; Rahn, Kroeger, and Kite 1998). Through her efforts the 1996 General Social Survey included a new set of questions, seven in all, that asked 705 of the 2,199 respondents to report how they felt about "this country, the United States." The respondents were asked to state how frequently they felt worried, satisfied, frustrated, enthusiastic, angry, hopeful, and upset.

Six of the seven mood terms are frequently used to elicit a subject's self-report. These terms—*frustrated, angry, upset, worried, enthusiastic,* and *hopeful*—

fit well with Watson's choice of emotion terms and the other terms we have found that work well to identify *enthusiasm* and *anxiety*. However, we have previously found the term *satisfied*, as well as the term *sympathetic*, to be a complex and confounded term that argues against its use as a measure of mood (Marcus 1988).

What makes some mood terms confounded? Consider why people might report that they feel satisfied. If, as we have argued, emotional systems evaluate the immediate environment for signs of unexpected intrusion and threat, they might report feeling satisfied because things are as they should be, safe and routine. On the other hand they might report feeling satisfied because their activities as well as the activities of those they feel identified with are going well. That is, "feeling satisfied" applies equally well to the favorable outputs of the surveillance system as well as of the disposition system. When either is "going well" we can equally adopt the language of satisfaction. Thus, we can expect that the mood term *satisfied* will "load" on both dimensions when included in factor analyses. This is an excellent example of what confounded means: a term that has multiple meanings that does not differentiate properly between different emotional reactions.

The response options in the General Social Survey provided for five levels of frequency: *always, most of the time, some of the time, rarely,* and *never*. As we previously noted, Watson's work demonstrates that asking people to report frequency of an emotion does not distinguish their responses from the responses they give when asked to report the intensity of emotional feeling. The analyses of these data again fit the dual model of emotion quite well (see table B.5 below). We should note that Rahn did not include any of the negative normative mood terms, such as *frustrated, contempt,* or *disgust,* that we have found to define the aversion dimension of emotional response. There may be some people who feel that way when considering the United States (certainly, we can imagine some people who would be most likely to report such feelings). However, we can explore whether all people feel, as we expect, *enthusiasm* to varying degrees and *anxiety* to varying degrees.

As expected, the mood descriptor *satisfied* is a confounded term that does not differentiate between the two dimensions of emotion. The other six terms do an admirable job of differentiating the two dimensions of the dual model. Four of the emotion terms—*frustrated, angry, upset,* and *worried*—define the anxiety dimension. Two terms—*enthusiastic* and *hopeful*—define the enthusiasm dimension. We might expect that because feelings about the United States are among the most salient and familiar to most Americans, that the most likely solution would be a single valence dimension.

Table B.5   Factor Analysis of Seven Emotion Mood Terms
Used to Describe Public Mood

A. Orthogonal Solution

Public Mood Emotion Term	Factor I (Anxiety)	Factor II (Enthusiasm)
Frustrated	.82	−.16
Angry	.80	−.15
Upset	.79	−.13
Worried	.70	−.03
Enthusiastic	−.06	.86
Hopeful	−.06	.83
Satisfied	−.44	.60
Eigenvalues	3.06	1.41
B. Correlation between factors (oblique solution)	$r_{FI \cdot FII} = -.13$	

SOURCE: 1996 General Social Survey.

Yet when we examine the oblique solution, we find, again, a near zero correlation (r = −0.13) between the two dimensions in table B.5. Though we could impose a single valence framework on feelings about the United States, much as we can about anything else, once again we find that providing for multiple mood reports will generally show, at a minimum, a surveillance assessment as well as a disposition assessment.[19]

Strategies for Measurement

We have applied the dual model of emotion to a wide array of political stimuli and responses: political leaders, both incumbents and challengers; political issues; and feelings about the United States. This hardly exhausts the possible applications of the dual model. How do people feel about political parties, about referenda, about political institutions such as Congress, the Supreme Court and its various rulings, social groups, interest groups? We expect that most people will feel, as with issues and can-

19. We also ran a structural equation model of these data. The appropriate structural equation model to test is a two-factor model that has "satisfied" as a confounded measure. As noted before, the principal difference when such a model is tested is that there is a somewhat higher correlation between the anxiety and enthusiasm dimensions, in an EQS model, r = −.31, than is found with standard factor analysis. The difference between estimates of the covariation between factors of −.13 and −.31 may sound substantial. However, when converted to the angles between vectors, the differences are quite modest (97° and 108° respectively). Our analysis is available on request.

didates, some mixture of anxiety and enthusiasm. But we know less about these matters because, by and large, the usual way to elicit people's feelings about them is to use feeling thermometers or the even more general request for a favorable versus unfavorable assessment. Because most conventional measures, such as the feeling thermometer measures, impose a single bipolar dimension of likes opposing dislikes; the bivariate evaluative space is masked.

There is a strong tradition from Osgood onward that has tended toward using juxtaposed bipolar terms in attitude measurement. Respondents are presented with forced choices or feeling thermometers and they quickly accept this unidimensional evaluation as a comfortable and familiar task. An unfortunate characteristic of this approach is that the measurement strategy itself may encourage people to harmonize their self-reports of feelings in ways that obscure the feelings that they actually experience (Cacioppo and Berntson 1994; Cacioppo, Gardner, and Berntson 1997).

Depending on one's theoretical purpose, then, items used to describe the emotional reactions people experience can be designed to implement any of the three measurement theories—discrete, valence, or the dual model. Our review of the ANES candidate feeling items suggests that the traditional array of ANES items are well suited to measure the dual model dimensions of emotional response. Further, the evidence suggests these measures are directly comparable to equivalent measures of emotional response obtained using the PANAS measures. We can conclude that the two orthogonal dimensions of emotional response in the ANES series define the degree of anxiety and the degree of enthusiasm elicited by politicians.

When the politician is a highly polarized figure, as was President Clinton in 1995, a distinct emotional dimension of aversion may be identified, provided that expressly negative normative emotional terms are included in the response options augmenting the existing items. The dual model posits two ongoing contemporary continuous evaluations. Inasmuch the surveillance system is dedicated to scanning for sudden strategic interventions of novelty and threat, its operation is revealed by fluctuations in anxiety and unease. However, some prior assessments will have crystallized into deeply felt dislikes in the realm of the familiar, which is to say, the realm of the disposition system. Sometimes familiarity does breed contempt. Such stimuli will generate deep dislike, the emotion we label "aversion." Thus, when a powerful and polarized stimulus is the subject of study, a distinct negative emotional factor of stable disapproval is likely to emerge, provided, of course, we have included the appropriate emotion terms for subjects to use to rate their emotional reactions.

We earlier noted our discontent with the general practice in psychology to classify emotions as either "positive" or "negative." The work we have reviewed should make clear why the term *negative*, in particular, should be avoided. We have identified three distinct dimensions of "negative" emotion: depression (the absence of enthusiasm), anxiety, and aversion. Each has different antecedents and each is associated with different cognitive and behavioral consequences. Continued use of the term *negative* to label emotional response will create not only confusion as to what is being identified but considerable confounding if measures of each of these distinct dimensions are haphazardly combined into an index or scale.

In summary, when putting together the questions to elicit a self-report of emotional responses, one might consider the following:

- The focus, or target, should be clearly identified when the goal is to define the emotional response evoked by particular stimuli (for example, "How do you feel about politician X?" or "How do you feel about situation Y?"). It is, of course, possible to define broader classes of stimuli, even the most general, and we do not mean to suggest that one should always use the narrowest field of focus. We recommend being precise in defining the specific target of interest, whether narrow or broad.

- The emotional term, as marker or referent, must be clearly specified (for example, "Would you say you feel *upset*?" "Would you say you feel *enthusiastic*?"). We recommend the Watson items for measures of the levels of anxiety and enthusiasm and those we review in tables B.3 and B.5 for aversion.

- A time frame for evaluation should be explicitly provided, choosing from the past (for example, "Have you ever felt . . . ?"), the present (for example, "How do you feel about . . . ?"), or the future (for example, "How worried would you feel if you were to hear that Saddam Hussein had obtained nuclear weapons?"). The significance of locating the emotional reaction in the past or present or in an anticipated future has yet to be explored in political science.

- We recommend the use of multiple measures for each dimension of emotional response.

- In designing response options, we recommend that they be clearly formulated as unipolar (for example, "How angry would you say X makes you feel: *very angry, somewhat angry, a little angry, not very angry at all*?"). We advise against using bipolar emotional terms (for example, "Would you say you feel *very upset, somewhat upset, neither upset nor calm, somewhat calm, very calm*?") as these evoke the inclination to idealize and harmonize self-reports of emotional response.

Suggestions for Further Reading

We have compiled a list of suggested readings for those who might wish to further pursue the topic of emotion and politics. The list is organized into three sections—general readings on neuroscience and emotion, on current thinking about the structure of emotional response, and on the measurement of emotional response. While these references do not constitute a thorough course of study on emotion and politics, they at least provide a good place to begin.

General Readings on Neuroscience and Emotion

Damasio, Antonio R. *Descartes' Error: Emotion, Reason, and the Human Brain.* New York: Putnam's Sons, 1994.

Gazzaniga, Michael S. *Nature's Mind: The Biological Roots of Thinking, Emotions, Sexuality, Language, and Intelligence.* New York: Basic Books, 1992.

Gazzaniga, Michael S. *The Mind's Past.* Berkeley: University of California Press, 1998.

Gray, Jeffrey A. *The Psychology of Fear and Stress.* 2d ed. Cambridge: Cambridge University Press, 1987.

LeDoux, Joseph. *The Emotional Brain: The Mysterious Underpinnings of Emotional Life.* New York: Simon & Schuster, 1996.

Nørretranders, Tor. *The User Illusion.* Translated by Jonathan Sydenham. New York: Viking, 1998.

Zuckerman, Marvin. *Psychobiology of Personality.* Problems in Behavioral Sciences, ed. Jeffrey A. Gray. Cambridge, England: Cambridge University Press, 1991.

Readings Related to the Dual Model Theory of Emotion

Broadbent, Donald, and Margaret Broadbent. "Anxiety and Attentional Bias: State and Trait." *Cognition and Emotion* 2, no. 3 (1988): 165–83.

Cacioppo, John T., and Wendi L. Gardner. "Emotion." *Annual Review of Psychology* 50 (1999): 191–214.

Carver, Charles S., and Michael F. Scheier. "Origins and Functions of Positive and Negative Affect: A Control-Process View." *Psychological Review* 97, no. 1 (1990): 19–35.

Carver, Charles S., and Teri L. White. "Behavioral Inhibition, Behavioral Activation, and Affective Response to Impending Reward and Punishment: The BIS/BAS Scales." *Journal of Personality and Social Psychology* 67, no. 2 (1994): 319–33.

Derryberry, Douglas. "The Immediate Effects of Positive and Negative Feedback Signals." *Journal of Personality and Social Psychology* 61, no. 2 (1991): 267–78.

Eysenck, Michael W., and Angela Byrne. "Anxiety and Susceptibility to Distraction." *Personality and Individual Differences* 13, no. 7 (1992): 793–98.

Gray, Jeffrey A. "Brain Systems That Mediate Both Emotion and Cognition." *Cognition and Emotion* 4, no. 3 (1990): 269–88.

MacLeod, Colin, and Andrew Mathews. "Anxiety and the Allocation of Attention to Threat." *Quarterly Journal of Experimental Psychology* 40A, no. 4 (1988): 653–70.

Marcus, George E., John L. Sullivan, Elizabeth Theiss-Morse, and Sandra Wood. *With Malice toward Some: How People Make Civil Liberties Judgments.*Political Psychology, ed. James Kuklinski. New York: Cambridge University Press, 1995.

Pratto, Felicia, and Oliver P. John. "Automatic Vigilance: The Attention-Grabbing Power of Negative Social Information." *Journal of Personality and Social Psychology* 61, no. 3 (1991): 380–91.

Watson, David, and Auke Tellegen. "Toward a Consensual Structure of Mood." *Psychological Bulletin* 98 (1985): 219–35.

Zajonc, Robert B. "Feeling and Thinking: Preferences Need No Inferences." *American Psychologist*, 39 (1980): 151–75.

Zajonc, Robert B. "On the Primacy of Affect." *American Psychologist* 39 (1982): 117–23.

Readings on the Measurement of Emotion

Bagozzi, Richard P. "An Examination of the Psychometric Properties of Measures of Negative Affect in the PANAS-X Scales." *Journal of Personality and Social Psychology* 65, no. 4 (1993): 836–51.

Cacioppo, John T., Wendi L. Gardner, and Gary G. Berntson. "Beyond Bipolar Conceptualizations and Measures: The Case of Attitudes and Evaluative Space." *Personality and Social Psychology Review* 1, no. 1 (1997): 3–25.

Green, Donald Philip, Susan Lee Goldman, and Peter Salovey. "Measurement Error Masks Bipolarity in Affect Ratings." *Journal of Personality and Social Psychology* 64, no. 6 (1993): 1029–41.

Ingram, Rick E. "Affective Confounds in Social-Cognitive Research." *Journal of Personality and Social Psychology* 57, no. 4 (1989): 715–22.

Lang, Peter J. "The Emotion Probe: Studies of Motivation and Attention." *American Psychologist* 50, no. 5 (1995): 372–85.

Russell, James A., and James M. Carroll. "On the Bipolarity of Positive and Negative Affect." *Psychological Bulletin* 125, no. 1 (1999): 3–30.

Russell, James A., and Lisa Feldman Barrett. "Core Affect, Prototypical Emotional Episodes, and Other Things Called *Emotion*: Dissecting the Elephant." *Journal of Personality and Social Psychology* 76, no. 5 (1999): 805–19.

Russell, James A., Anna Weiss, and Gerald A. Mendelsohn. "Affect Grid: A Single-Item Scale of Pleasure and Arousal." *Journal of Personality and Social Psychology* 57, no. 3 (1989): 493–502.

Tellegen, Auke, David Watson, and Lee Anna Clark. "Further Support for a Hierarchical Model of Affect." *Psychological Science* 10, no. 4 (1999): 307–09.

Tellegen, Auke, David Watson, and Lee Anna Clark. "On the Dimensional and Hierarchical Structure of Affect." *Psychological Science* 10, no. 4 (1999): 297–303.

Tomarken, Andrew J., Richard J. Davidson, and Jeffrey B. Henriques. "Resting Frontal Brain Asymmetry Predicts Affective Response to Films." *Journal of Personality and Social Psychology* 59, no. 4 (1990): 791–801.

Tomarken, Andrew J., Richard J. Davidson, Robert E. Wheeler, and Robert C. Doss. "Individual Differences in Anterior Brain Asymmetry and Fundamental Dimensions of Emotion." *Journal of Personality and Social Psychology* 62, no. 4 (1992): 676–87.

Watson, David. "The Vicissitudes of Mood Measurement: Effects of Varying Descriptors, Time Frames, and Response Formats on Measures of Positive and Negative Affect." *Journal of Personality and Social Psychology* 55, no. 1 (1988): 128–41.

Watson, David, and Auke Tellegen. "Issues in the Dimensional Structure of Affect—Effects of Descriptors, Measurement Error, and Response Formats: Comment on Russell and Carroll." *Psychological Bulletin* 125, no. 5 (1999): 601–10.

Watson, David, and Lee Anna Clark. *The PANAS-X: Manual for the Positive and Negative Affect Schedule—Expanded Form.* Unpublished manuscript. Iowa City: University of Iowa, 1994.

Watson, David, and Lee Anna Clark. "Measurement and Mismeasurement of Mood: Recurrent and Emergent Issues." *Journal of Personality Assessment* 68 (1997): 267–96.

Watson, David, Lee Anna Clark, and Auke Tellegen. "Development and Validation of Brief Measures of Positive and Negative Affect: The PANAS Scales." *Journal of Personality and Social Psychology* 54, no. 6 (1988): 1063–70.

Watson, David, David Wiese, Jatin Vaidya, and Auke Tellegen. "The Two General Activation Systems of Affect: Structural Findings, Evolutionary Considerations, and Psychobiological Evidence." *Journal of Personality and Social Psychology* 76, no. 5 (1999): 820–38.

References

Abelson, Robert P. 1996. "The Secret Existence of Expressive Behavior." Pp. 25–36 in *Rational Choice Theory: Economic Models of Politics Reconsidered*, ed. Jeffrey Friedman. New Haven: Yale University Press.

Abelson, Robert P., Donald R. Kinder, Mark D. Peters, and Susan T. Fiske. 1982. "Affective and Semantic Components in Political Personal Perception." *Journal of Personality and Social Psychology* 42 (4): 619–630.

Aboud, Frances. 1988. *Children and Prejudice*. Social Psychology and Society, ed. Howard Giles and Miles Hewstone. Oxford: Basil Blackwell.

Almond, Gabriel, and Sydney Verba. 1965. *Civic Culture*. Boston: Little, Brown.

Ansolabehere, Stephen, and Shanto Iyengar. 1995. *Going Negative: How Political Advertisements Shrink and Polarize the Electorate*. New York: Free Press.

Arkes, Hadley. 1993. "Can Emotion Supply the Place of Reason?" Pp. 287–305 in *Reconsidering the Democratic Public*, ed. George E. Marcus and Russell L. Hanson. University Park: Pennsylvania State University Press.

Arnsten, Amy F. T. 1998. "The Biology of Being Frazzled." *Science*, 12 June, 1711–12.

Arrow, Kenneth J. 1987. "Rationality of Self and Others in an Economic System." Pp. 201–15 in *Rational Choice: The Contrast between Economics and Psychology*, ed. Robin M. Hogarth and Melvin W. Reder. San Diego: Academic Press.

Bagozzi, Richard P. 1993. "An Examination of the Psychometric Properties of Measures of Negative Affect in the PANAS-X Scales." *Journal of Personality and Social Psychology* 65 (4) 836–51.

Bechara, Antoine, Hanna Damasio, Daniel Tranel, and Antonio R. Damasio. 1997. "Deciding Advantageously before Knowing the Advantageous Strategy." *Science*, 28 February, 1293–95.

Becker, Gary S. 1976. *The Economic Approach to Human Behavior*. Chicago: University of Chicago Press.

Berntson, Gary G., Sarah T. Boysen, and John T. Cacioppo. 1993. "Neurobehavioral Organization and the Cardinal Principle of Evaluative Ambivalence." *Annals of the New York Academy of Science* 702:75–102.

Berry, Diane S., and Jane Sherman Hansen. 1996. "Positive Affect, Negative Affect, and Social Interaction." *Journal of Personality and Social Psychology* 71 (4): 796–809.

Bessette, Joseph M. 1994. *The Mild Voice of Reason: Deliberative Democracy and American National Government*. Chicago: University of Chicago Press.

Bollen, Kenneth, and Kenney Barb. 1981. "Pearson's R and Coarsely Categorized Measures." *American Sociological Review* 46:232–39.

Brader, Ted. 1999. "Campaigning for Hearts and Minds: How Campaign Ads Use Emotion and Information to Sway the Electorate." Ph.D. diss., Harvard University.

Bradley, Margaret M. Forthcoming. "Motivation and Emotion." In *Handbook of Psychophysiology*, ed. John T. Cacioppo, L. G. Tassinary, and G. G. Berntson. 2d ed. New York: Cambridge University Press.

Breckler, Steven J. 1984. "Empirical Validation of Affect, Behavior, and Cognition as Distinct Components of Attitude." *Journal of Personality and Social Psychology* 47:1191–1205.

Broadbent, Donald, and Margaret Broadbent. 1988. "Anxiety and Attentional Bias: State and Trait." *Cognition and Emotion* 2 (3): 165–83.

Bruce, John. 1991. "Emotion and Evaluation in Nomination Politics." Paper presented at the annual meeting of the American Political Science Association, Washington Hilton, 29 August–1 September, Washington, D.C.

———. 1994. "The Question of Emotional Response." Paper presented at the annual meeting of the Midwest Political Science Association, Palmer House, 14–16 April, Chicago.

Buchanan, James M., and Gordon Tullock. 1962. *The Calculus of Consent.* Ann Arbor: University of Michigan Press.

Cacioppo, John T., and Gary G. Berntson. 1994. "Relationship between Attitudes and Evaluative Space: A Critical Review, with Emphasis on the Separability of Positive and Negative Substrates." *Psychological Bulletin* 115:401–23.

Cacioppo, John T., and Louis G. Tassinary, eds. 1990. *Principles of Psychophysiology: Physical, Social and Inferential Elements.* Cambridge: Cambridge University Press.

Cacioppo, John T., and Wendi L. Gardner. 1999. "Emotion." *Annual Review of Psychology* 50:191–214.

Cacioppo, John T., J. T. Bush, and Larry G. Tassinary. 1992. "Microexpressive Facial Actions as a Function of Affective Stimuli: Replication and Extension." *Personality and Social Psychology Bulletin* 18:515–26.

Cacioppo, John T., Wendi L. Gardner, and Gary G. Berntson. 1997. "Beyond Bipolar Conceptualizations and Measures: The Case of Attitudes and Evaluative Space." *Personality and Social Psychology Review* 1 (1): 3–25.

———. 1999. "The Affect System Has Parallel and Integrative Processing Components: Form Follows Function." *Journal of Personality and Social Psychology* 76 (5): 839–55.

Cacioppo, John T., David J. Klein, Gary G. Berntson, and Elaine Hatfield. 1993. "The Psychophysiology of Emotion." Pp. 119–42 in *The Handbook of Emotion,* ed. R. Lewis and J. M. Haviland. New York: Guilford.

Cacioppo, John T., Jeffrey S. Martzke, Richard E. Petty, and Louis G. Tassinary. 1988. "Specific Forms of Facial EMG Response Index Emotions during an Interview: From Darwin to the Continuous Flow Hypothesis of Affect-Laden Information Processing." *Journal of Personality and Social Psychology* 54 (4): 592–604.

Cacioppo, John T., Richard E. Petty, Mary E. Losch, and Hai Sook Kim. 1986. "Electromyographic Activity over Facial Muscle Regions Can Differentiate the Valence and Intensity of Affective Reactions." *Journal of Personality and Social Psychology* 50 (2): 260–68.

Campbell, Angus, Philip E. Converse, Warren E. Miller, and Donald E. Stokes. 1960. *The American Voter.* New York: Wiley.

Cappella, Joseph N., and Kathleen Hall Jamieson. 1997. *Spiral of Cynicism: The Press and the Public Good.* New York: Oxford University Press.

Carmines, Edward G., and James A. Stimson. 1989. *Issue Evolution: Race and the Transformation of American Politics.* Princeton: Princeton University Press.

Carver, Charles S., and Michael F. Scheier. 1990. "Origins and Functions of Positive and Negative Affect: A Control-Process View." *Psychological Review* 97 (1): 19–35.

Carver, Charles S., and Teri L. White. 1994. "Behavioral Inhibition, Behavioral Activation, and Affective Response to Impending Reward and Punishment: The BIS/BAS Scales." *Journal of Personality and Social Psychology* 67 (2): 319–33.

Chong, Dennis. 1996. "Rational Choice Theory's Mysterious Rivals." Pp. 37–57 in *Rational Choice Theory: Economic Models of Politics Reconsidered,* ed. Jeffrey Friedman. New Haven: Yale University Press.

———. 2000. *Rational Lives: Norms and Values in Politics and Society.* Chicago: University of Chicago Press.

Clark, L. A., and David Watson. 1988. "Mood and the Mundane: Relations between Daily Life Events and Self-Reported Mood." *Journal of Personality and Social Psychology* 52:296–308.

Cloninger, C. Robert. 1986. "A Unified Biosocial Theory of Personality and Its Role in the Development of Anxiety States." *Psychiatric Developments* 3:167–226.

Conover, Pamela, and Stanley Feldman. 1984. "How People Organize the Political World: A Schematic Model." *American Journal of Political Science* 28:95–126.

———. 1986. "Emotional Reactions to the Economy: I'm Mad as Hell and I'm Not Going to Take It Any More." *American Journal of Political Science* 30:30–78.

Converse, Philip E. 1964. "The Nature of Belief Systems in Mass Publics." In *Ideology and Discontent*, ed. David Apter. New York: Free Press.

———. 1966. "The Concept of the Normal Vote." In *Elections and the Political Order*, ed. Angus Campbell, Philip E. Converse, Warren E. Miller, and Donald E. Stokes. New York: Wiley.

———. 1976. *The Dynamics of Party Support: Cohort-Analyzing Party Identification*. Beverly Hills: Sage.

———. 1990. "Popular Representation and the Distribution of Information." Pp. 369–88 in *Information and the Democratic Process*, ed. John A. Ferejohn and James H. Kuklinski. Urbana: University of Illinois Press.

Csikszentmihalyi, Mihaly. 1990. *Flow: The Pyschology of Optimal Experience*. New York: Harper and Row.

Cuthbert, Bruce N., Margaret B. Bradley, and Peter J. Lang. 1996. "Probing Picture Perception: Activation and Emotion." *Psychophysiology* 33:103–11.

Damasio, Antonio R. 1994. *Descartes' Error: Emotion, Reason, and the Human Brain*. New York: G. P. Putnam's Sons.

Davidson, Richard J. 1992. "Prolegomenon to the Structure of Emotion: Gleanings from Neuropsychology." *Cognition and Emotion* 6.245–68.

———. "Cerebral Asymmetry, Emotion and Affective Style." 1995. Pp. 361–87 in *Brain Asymmetry*, ed. Richard J. Davidson and Kenneth Hugdahl. Cambridge: MIT Press.

Davidson, Richard J., and Andrew Tomarken. 1994. "Frontal Brain Activation in Repressors and Nonrepressors." *Journal of Abnormal Psychology* 103:339–49.

Davidson, Richard J., and N. Fox. 1989. "Frontal Brain Asymmetry Predicts Infants' Response to Maternal Separation." *Journal of Abnormal Psychology* 98:127–31.

Davies, A. F. 1980. *Skills, Outlooks and Passions: A Psychoanalytic Contribution to the Study of Politics*. Cambridge, England: Cambridge University Press.

De Becker, Gavin. 1997. *The Gift of Fear: Survival Signals That Protect Us from Violence*. Boston: Little, Brown.

Delli Carpini, Michael X., and Scott Keeter. 1993. "Measuring Political Knowledge: Putting First Things First." *American Journal of Political Science* 37 (4): 1179–1206.

Derryberry, Douglas. 1991. "The Immediate Effects of Positive and Negative Feedback Signals. *Journal of Personality and Social Psychology* 61 (2): 267–78.

Derryberry, Douglas, and D. M. Tucker. 1991. "The Adaptive Base of the Neural Hierarchy: Elementary Motivational Controls on Network Function." Pp. 289–342 in *Nebraska Symposium on Motivation*, ed. R. Dienstbier. Lincoln: University of Nebraska Press.

Derryberry, Douglas, and Marjorie Reed. 1994. "Temperament and Attention: Orienting towards and away from Positive and Negative Signals." *Journal of Personality and Social Psychology* 66 (6): 1128–39.

Devine, Patricia G. 1989. "Stereotypes and Prejudice: Their Automatic and Controlled Components." *Journal of Personality and Social Psychology* 56 (1): 5–18.

Diener, Ed. 1999. "Introduction to the Special Issue on the Structure of Emotion." *Journal of Personality and Social Psychology* 76 (5): 803–04.

Diener, Ed, and Robert A. Emmons. 1985. "The Independence of Positive and Negative Affect." *Journal of Personality and Social Psychology* 47:1105–17.

Dimberg, Ulf. 1990. "Facial Electromyography and Emotional Response." *Psychophysiology* 27 (5): 481–94.

Downs, Anthony. 1957. *An Economic Theory of Democracy*. New York: Harper and Row.

Edwards, Kari. 1990. "The Interplay of Affect and Cognition in Attitude Formation and Change." *Journal of Personality and Social Psychology* 59 (2): 202–16.

Ekman, Paul, ed. 1982. *Emotion in the Human Face*. 2d ed. Cambridge, England: Cambridge University Press.

———. 1992. "An Argument for Basic Emotions." *Cognition and Emotion* 6 (3/4): 169–200.

Elster, Jon, ed. 1986. *Rational Choice*. New York: New York University Press.

———. 1989. *Nuts and Bolts for the Social Sciences*. Cambridge, England: Cambridge University Press.

———. 1993. *Political Psychology*. Cambridge, England: Cambridge University Press.

———. 1999. *Alchemies of the Mind: Rationality and the Emotions*. Cambridge, England: Cambridge University Press.

Erikson, Robert S., Michael B. MacKuen, and James A. Stimson. 1998. "What Moves Macropartisanship? A Response to Green, Palmquist, and Schickler." *American Political Science Review* 92 (4): 901–12.

Eysenck, Michael W., and Angela Byrne. 1992. "Anxiety and Susceptibility to Distraction." *Personality and Individual Differences* 13 (7): 793–98.

Fabrigar, Leandre R., Penny S. Visser, and Michael W. Browne. 1997. "Conceptual and Methodological Issues in Testing the Circumplex Structure of Data in Personality and Social Psychology." *Personality and Social Psychology Review* 1 (3): 184–283.

Ferejohn, John A., and James H. Kuklinski, ed. 1990. *Information and Democratic Processes*. Urbana: University of Illinois Press.

Finifter, Ada. 1972. *Alienation and the Social System*. New York: Wiley.

Fiorina, Morris P. 1981. *Retrospective Voting in American National Elections*. New Haven: Yale University Press.

———. 1996. "Rational Choice, Empirical Contributions, and the Scientific Enterprise." Pp. 85–106 in *Rational Choice Theory: Economic Models of Politics Reconsidered*, ed. Jeffrey Friedman. New Haven: Yale University Press.

Fishbein, Martin, and Icek Ajzen. 1975. *Belief, Attitude, Intention and Behavior: An Introduction to Theory and Research*. Reading, Mass.: Addison-Wesley.

Fiske, Susan T. 1988. Conversation with author.

Fiske, Susan T., and Mark Pavelchak. 1985. "Category-based versus Piecemeal-Based Affective Responses: Developments in Schema-Triggered Affect." In *The Handbook of Motivation and Cognition: Foundations of Social Behavior*, ed. R. Sorrentino and E. Higgins. New York: Guilford.

Fowles, Don C., Margaret J. Christie, Robert Edelberg, William W. Grings, David T. Lykken, and Peter H. Venable. 1981. "Publication Recommendations for Electrodermal Measurements." *Psychophysiology* 18 (3): 232–39.

Gazzinga, Micheal S. 1992. *Nature's Mind: The Biological Roots of Thinking, Emotions, Sexuality, Language, and Intelligence*. New York: Basic Books.

———. 1998. *The Mind's Past*. Berkeley: University of California Press.

George, Mark S., Terence A. Ketter, Priti I. Parekh, Barry Horwitz, Peter Herscovitch, and Robert M. Post. 1995. "Brain Activity during Transient Sadness and Happiness in Healthy Women." *American Journal of Psychiatry* 152 (3): 341–51.

Gibson, James L. 1998. "A Sober Second Thought: An Experiment in Persuading Russians to Tolerate." *American Journal of Political Science* 42 (3): 819–50.

Goleman, Daniel. 1995. *Emotional Intelligence: Why It Can Matter More Than IQ*. New York: Bantam.

Goode, Erica. 1998. "New Hope for the Losers in the Battle to Stay Awake." *New York Times*, 3 November, C1, C8.

Gray, Jeffrey A. 1984. "The Hippocampus as an Interface between Cognition and Emotion." In *Animal Cognition*, ed. M. L. Roitblar, T. G. Bever, and M. S. Terrace. Hillsdale, N.J.: Lawrence Erlbaum.

————. 1985. "A Whole and Its Parts: Behaviour, The Brain, Cognition, and Emotion." *Bulletin of the British Psychological Society* 38:99–112.

————. 1987a. "The Neuropsychology of Emotion and Personality." Pp. 171–90 in *Cognitive Neurochemistry*, ed. S. M. Stahl, S. D. Iversen, and E. C. Goodman. Oxford, England: Oxford University Press.

————. 1987b. *The Psychology of Fear and Stress.* 2d ed. Cambridge: Cambridge University Press.

————. 1990. "Brain Systems That Mediate Both Emotion and Cognition." *Cognition and Emotion* 4 (3): 269–88.

————. 1991. "Fear, Panic, and Anxiety: What's in a Name?" *Psychological Inquiry* 2 (1): 77–88.

Gray, Jeffrey A., and Neil McNaughton. 1996. "The Neuropsychology of Anxiety: Reprise." Pp. 61–134 in *Perspectives on Anxiety, Panic and Fear*, ed. D. A. Hope, no. 43. Lincoln: University of Nebraska Press.

Green, Donald P., and Bradley Palmquist. 1995. "How Stable Is Party Identification?" *Political Behavior* 43 (4): 437–66.

Green, Donald P., and Jack Citrin. 1994. "Measurement Error and the Structure of Attitudes: Are Positive and Negative Judgments Opposites?" *American Journal of Political Science* 38 (1): 256–81.

Green, Donald P., and Peter Salovey. 1999. "In What Sense Are Positive and Negative Affect Independent?" *Psychological Science* 10 (4): 304–06.

Green, Donald P., Bradley Palmquist, and Eric Schickler. 1998. "Macropartisanship: A Replication and Critique." *American Political Science Review* 92 (4): 883–99.

Green, Donald P., Peter Salovey, and Kathryn M. Truax. 1999. "Static, Dynamic, and Causative Bipolarity of Affect." *Journal of Personality and Social Psychology* 76 (5): 856–67.

Green, Donald P., Susan Lee Goldman, and Peter Salovey. 1993. "Measurement Error Masks Bipolarity in Affect Ratings." *Journal of Personality and Social Psychology* 64 (6): 1029–41.

Grunert, Klaus G. 1996. "Automatic and Strategic Processes in Advertising Effects." *Journal of Marketing* 60 (4): 88–100.

Haggard, E. A., and F. S. Isaacs. 1966. "Micromomentary Facial Expressions as Indicators of Ego Mechanisms in Psychotherapy." Pp. 154–65 in *Methods of Research in Psychotherapy*, ed. C. A. Gottschalk and A. Averbach. New York: Appleton-Century-Crofts.

Hamill, R., T. D. Wilson, and R.E. Nisbett. 1980. "Insensitivity to Sample Bias: Generalizing from Atypical Cases." *Journal of Personality and Social Psychology* 39:578–89.

Hastie, Reid. 1986. "A Primer of Information-Processing Theory for the Political Scientist." Pp. 11–39 in *Political Cognition*, ed. Richard Lau and David Sears. Hillsdale, N.J.: Lawrence Erlbaum.

Hastie, Reid, and Bernadette Park. 1986. "The Relationship between Memory and Judgment Depends on Whether the Task Is Memory-Based or On-Line." *Psychological Review* 93:258–68.

Heath, Robert G. 1986. "The Neural Substrate for Emotion." Pp. 3–35 in *Biological Foundations of Emotion.* Vol. 3 of *Emotion, Theory, Research, and Experience*, ed. Robert Plutchik and Henry Kellerman. Orlando: Academic Press.

Hess, Ursula, Arvid Kappas, Gregory J. McHugo, John T. Lanzetta, and Robert E. Kleck. 1992. "The Facilitative Effect of Facial Expression on the Self-Generation of Emotion." *International Journal of Psychophysiology* 12:251–65.

Hobbes, Thomas. [1651] 1968. *Leviathan*, ed. C. B. Macpherson. London: Penguin Books.

Hogarth, Robin M., and Melvin W. Reder, eds. 1987. *Rational Choice: The Contrast between Economics and Psychology.* San Diego: Academic Press.

Holmes, Stephen. 1995. *Passions and Constraint: On the Theory of Liberal Democracy.* Chicago: University of Chicago Press.

Hume, David. 1739–40. *A Treatise of Human Nature.* London: Penguin Books.

Huntington, Samuel P., and Jorge I. Dominquez. 1975. "Political Development." In *Handbook of Political Science*, ed. Fred Greenstein and Nelson Polsby. Reading, Mass.: Addison-Wesley.

Ingram, Rick E. 1989. "Affective Confounds in Social-Cognitive Research." *Journal of Personality and Social Psychology* 57 (4): 543–54.

Iyengar, Shanto, and Donald Kinder. 1987. *News That Matters: Television and American Public Opinion.* Chicago: University of Chicago Press.

Izard, Carroll E. 1972. *The Face of Emotion.* New York: Appleton-Century-Crofts.

———. 1977. *Human Emotions.* New York: Plenum.

———. 1992. "Basic Emotions, Relations among Emotions, and Emotion-Cognition Relations." *Psychological Review* 99 (3): 561–65.

James, William. 1883. "What Is Emotion?" *Mind* 9:188–204.

———. 1894. "The Physical Basis of Emotion." *Psychological Review* 1:516–29.

Jamieson, Kathleen Hall. 1992. *Dirty Politics: Deception, Distraction, and Democracy.* New York: Oxford University Press.

Janis, Irving L. 1982. *Groupthink.* 2d ed. Boston: Houghton Mifflin.

Janis, Irving L., and Leon Mann. 1977. *Decision Making.* New York: Free Press.

Jennings, Dennis L., Teresa M. Amabile, and Lee Ross. 1982. "Information Covariation Assessment: Data-Based versus Theory-Based Judgments." Pp. 211–30 in *Judgment under Uncertainty: Heuristics and Biases,* ed. Daniel Kahneman, Paul Slovic, and Amos Tversky. New York: Cambridge University Press.

Jervis, Robert. 1997. *System Effects: Complexity in Political and Social Life.* Princeton: Princeton University Press.

Jones, Bryan D. 1994. *Reconceiving Decision-Making in Democratic Politics: Attention, Choice, and Public Policy.* Chicago: University of Chicago Press.

Kahneman, Daniel, and Amos Tversky. 1984. "Choices, Values, and Frames." *American Psychologist* 39:341–50.

Kahneman, Daniel, Paul Slovic, and Amos Tversky. 1982. *Judgment under Uncertainty: Heuristics and Biases.* Cambridge: Cambridge University Press.

Kelley, Stanley, and Thad Mirer. 1974. "The Simple Act of Voting." *American Political Science Review* 68:572–91.

Key, V. O., Jr., and M. C. Cummings. 1966. *The Responsible Electorate: Rationality in Presidential Voting, 1936–1960.* New York: Vintage.

Kinder, Donald R. 1994. "Reason and Emotion in American Political Life." Pp. 277–314 in *Beliefs, Reasoning, and Decision-Making: Psycho-Logic in Honor of Bob Abelson,* ed. Roger Schank and Ellen Langer. Hillsdale, N.J.: Lawrence Erlbaum.

Kinder, Donald R., and David O. Sears. 1981. "Prejudice and Politics: Symbolic Racism versus Racial Threat to the Good Life." *Journal of Personality and Social Psychology* 40: 414–31.

Kinder, Donald R., and D. Roderick Kiewiet. 1981. "Sociotropic Politics: The American Case." *British Journal of Political Science* 11:129–61.

Kinder, Donald R., and Lisa D'Ambrosio. 1996. "War, Emotion, and Public Opinion." Unpublished manuscript. Ann Arbor: University of Michigan.

Kinder, Donald R., and Lynn M. Sanders. 1990. "Mimicking Political Debate with Survey Questions: The Case of White Opinion on Affirmative Action for Blacks." *Social Cognition* 8 (1): 73–103.

Kinder, Donald R., and Thomas R. Palfrey, ed. 1993. *Experimental Foundations of Political Science.* Michigan Studies in Political Analysis. Ann Arbor: University of Michigan Press.

Kinder, Donald R., Robert P. Abelson, and Susan T. Fiske. 1979. "Developmental Research on Candidate Instrumentation: Results and Recommendations." Technical report submitted to the Board of Overseers, National Election Studies in Ann Arbor, MI. Ann Arbor: Center for Political Studies, Institute for Social Research.

Krosnick, Jon A., Laura Lowe, and Joanne M. Miller. 1997. "The Impact of Threat and Opportunity on Public Activism." Unpublished manuscript. Columbus: Ohio State University.

Kuhn, Thomas. 1982. *The Structure of Scientific Revolutions.* Chicago: University of Chicago Press.

Kunst-Wilson, William R., and Robert B. Zajonc. 1980. "Affect Discrimination of Stimuli Cannot Be Recognized." *Science* 207:557–58.

Lang, Annie, ed. 1994. *Measuring Psychological Responses to Media*. Hillsdale, N.J.: Lawrence Erlbaum.

Lang, Peter J., M. M. Bradley, and B. N. Cuthbert. 1990. "Emotion, Attention, and the Startle Reflect." *Psychological Review* 97:377–95.

Lanzetta, John T., and Basil G. Englis. 1989. "Expectations of Cooperation and Competition and Their Effects on Observer's Vicarious Emotional Responses." *Journal of Personality and Social Psychology* 56 (4): 543–54.

Larsen, Randy J., and Edward Diener. 1992. "Promises and Problems with the Circumplex Model of Emotion." Pp. 25–59 in *Emotion*, ed. Margaret S. Clark. Newbury Park, Cal.: Sage.

Lau, Richard. 1986. "Political Schemata, Candidate Evaluations, and Voting Behavior." In *Political Cognition*, ed. Richard Lau and David Sears. Hillsdale, N.J.: Lawrence Erlbaum.

Lau, Richard R., Lee Sigelman, Caroline Heldman, and Paul Babbitt. 1999 "The Effects of Negative Political Advertisements: A Meta-Analytic Assessment." *American Political Science Review* 93 (4): 851–75.

Lazarus, Richard S., and Beatrice N. Lazarus. 1994. *Passion and Reason: Making Sense of Our Emotions*. New York: Oxford University Press.

Le Bon, G. 1986 [1896]. *The Crowd: A Study of the Popular Mind*. London: Unwin.

LeDoux, Joseph. 1987. "Emotion." Pp. 419–59 in *Higher Functions of the Brain, Part 1*. Vol. 5 of *Handbook of Physiology. Section 1. The Nervous System*, ed. Fred Plum. Bethesda: American Physiological Society.

———. 1992. "Brain Mechanisms of Emotion and Emotional Learning." *Current Opinion in Neurobiology* 2:191–98.

———. 1993. "Emotional Memory Systems in the Brain." *Behavioural Brain Research* 58:68–79.

———. 1996. *The Emotional Brain: The Mysterious Underpinnings of Emotional Life*. New York: Simon and Schuster.

Levenson, Robert W., and Anna M. Ruef. 1992. "Empathy: A Physiological Substrate." *Journal of Personality and Social Psychology* 63 (2): 234–46.

LeVine, Robert A., and Donald T. Campbell. 1972. *Ethnocentrism: Theories of Conflict, Ethnic Attitudes and Group Behavior*. New York: Wiley.

Libet, Benjamin. 1985. "Unconscious Cerebral Initiative and the Role of Conscious Will in Voluntary Action." *The Behavioral and Brain Sciences* 8:529–66.

Libet, Benjamin, Curtis A. Gleason, Elwood W. Wright, and Dennis K. Pearl. 1983. "Time of Conscious Intention to Act in Relation to Onset of Cerebral Activity (Readiness-Potential)." *Brain* 106:623–42.

Libet, Benjamin, Dennis K. Pearl, David Morledge, Curtis A. Gleason, Yoshio Morledge, and Nicholas Barbaro. 1991. "Control of the Transition from Sensory Detection to Sensory Awareness in Man by the Duration of a Thalamic Stimulus." *Brain* 114:1731–57.

Libet, Benjamin, Elwood W. Wright, Bertram Feinstein, and Dennis K. Pearl. 1979. "Subjective Referral of the Timing for a Conscious Sensory Experience." *Brain* 102:1597–1600.

Lodge, Milton G., and Ruth Hamill. 1986. "A Partisan Schema for Political Information Processing." *American Political Science Review* 80:505–20.

Lodge, Milton G., Kathleen M. McGraw, and Patrick Stroh. 1989. "An Impression-Driven Model of Candidate Evaluation." *American Political Science Review* 83:399–420.

MacLoud, Colin, and Andrew Mathews. 1988. "Anxiety and the Allocation of Attention to Threat." *Quarterly Journal of Experimental Psychology* 40 A (4): 653–70.

MacKuen, Michael B., Robert S. Erikson, and James A. Stimson. 1989. "Macropartisanship." *American Political Science Review* 83 (4): 1125–42.

Madison, James, Alexander Hamilton, and John Jay. [1787] 1961. *The Federalist Papers*, ed. Jacob Cooke. Cleveland: World.

March, James G. 1978. "Bounded Rationality, Ambiguity and the Engineering of Choice." *Bell Journal of Economics* 8:587–608.

Marcus, George E. 1988. "The Structure of Emotional Response: 1984 Presidential Candidates." *American Political Science Review* 82 (3): 735–61.

———. 1991. "Emotions and Politics: Hot Cognitions and the Rediscovery of Passion." *Social Science Information* 30 (2): 195–232.

———. Forthcoming. *The Sentimental Citizen: Emotion in Democratic Politics.*

Marcus, George E., and Michael B. MacKuen. 1993. "Anxiety, Enthusiasm and the Vote: The Emotional Underpinnings of Learning and Involvement during Presidential Campaigns." *American Political Science Review* 87 (3): 688–701.

Marcus, George E., and Michael B. MacKuen. 2000. "Emotions and Politics: The Dynamic Functions of Emotionality." In *Citizens and Politics: Perspectives from Politial Psychology*, ed. James Kuklinski. New York: Cambridge University Press.

Marcus, George E., Sandra L. Wood, and Elizabeth Theiss-Morse. 1998. "Linking Neuroscience to Political Intolerance and Political Judgment." *Politics and the Life Science* 17 (2): 165–78.

Marcus, George E., John L. Sullivan, Elizabeth Theiss-Morse, and Sandra Wood. 1995. *With Malice toward Some: How People Make Civil Liberties Judgments.*Political Psychology, ed. James Kuklinski. New York: Cambridge University Press.

Marcus, George E., W. Russell Neuman, Michael B. MacKuen, and John L. Sullivan. 1996. "Dynamic Models of Emotional Response: The Multiple Role of Affect in Politics." Pp. 33–59 in *Research in Micropolitics*, ed. Michael Delli Carpini, Leonie Huddy, and Robert Y. Shapiro. Greenwich, Conn.: JAI.

Maslow, Abraham H. 1954. *Motivation and Personality.* New York: Harper.

Masters, Roger, and Denis Sullivan. 1989. "Nonverbal Displays and Political Leadership in France and the United States." *Political Behavior* 11 (2): 123–56.

———. 1993. "Nonverbal Behavior and Leadership: Emotion and Cognition in Political Attitudes." In *Explorations in Political Psychology*, ed. Shanto Iyengar and William McGuire. Durham: Duke University Press.

May, Cynthia P., Michael J. Kane, and Lynn Hasher. 1995. "Determinants of Negative Priming." *Psychological Bulletin* 118 (1): 35–54.

McHugo, Gregory J., Lanzetta John T., Denis G. Sullivan, Roger D. Masters, and Basil Englis. 1985. "Emotional Reactions to Expressive Displays of a Political Leader." *Journal of Personality and Social Psychology* 49:1512–29.

Millar, Murray G., and Abraham Tesser. 1986a. "Effects of Affective and Cognitive Focus on the Attitude-Behavior Relation." *Journal of Personality and Social Psychology* 51 (2): 270–76.

———. 1986b. "Thought-Induced Attitude Change: The Effects of Schema Structure and Commitment." *Journal of Personality and Social Psychology* 51 (2): 259–69.

Millar, Murray G., and Karen U. Millar. 1990. "Attitude Change as a Function of Attitude Type and Argument Type." *Journal of Personality and Social Psychology* 59 (2): 217–28.

Miller, Warren E. 1991. "Party Identification, Realignment, and Party Voting: Back to the Basics." *American Political Science Review* 85 (2): 557–68.

Mishkin, Mortimer, and Tim Appenzeller. 1987. "The Anatomy of Memory." *Scientific American* 256:80–89.

Moreland, Richard L., and Robert B. Zajonc. 1979. "Exposure Effects May Not Depend on Stimulus Recognition." *Journal of Personality and Social Psychology* 37 (6): 1085–89.

Mueller, Dennis C. 1979. *Public Choice.* New York: Cambridge University Press.

Mueller, John. 1992. "Democracy and Ralph's Pretty Good Grocery: Elections, Equality, and the Minimal Human Being." *American Journal of Political Science* 36 (4): 983–1003.

Mutz, Diana Carole. 1998. *Impersonal Influence: How Perceptions of Mass Collectives Affect Political Attitudes.* Cambridge Studies in Political Psychology and Public Opinion. Cambridge: Cambridge University Press.

Nadeau, Richard, Richard G. Niemi, and Timothy Amato. 1995. "Emotions, Issue Importance, and Political Learning." *American Journal of Political Science* 39 (3) 558–74.

Neisser, Ulric. 1963. "The Imitation of Man by Machine." *Science* 139:193–97.

Nelson, Thomas E. 1998. "Group Affect and Attribution in Social Policy Opinion." *Journal of Politics* 61 (2): 567–84.

Neuman, W. Russell. 1981. "Differentiation and Integration: Two Dimensions of Political Thinking." *American Journal of Sociology* 86:1236–1268.

———.1986. *The Paradox of Mass Politics: Knowledge and Opinion in the American Electorate.* Cambridge: Harvard University Press.

Neuman, W. Russell, Marion R. Just, and Ann N. Crigler. 1992. *Common Knowledge: News and the Construction of Political Meaning.* Chicago: University of Chicago Press.

Nisbett, Richard, and Lee Ross. 1982. *Human Inference: Strategies and Shortcomings of Social Judgment.* Englewood Cliffs, N.J.: Prentice-Hall.

Nørretranders, Tor. 1998. *The User Illusion,* trans. Jonathan Sydenham. New York: Viking.

Nye, Joseph S., Jr., Philip D. Zelikow, and David C. King, ed. 1997. *Why People Don't Trust Government.* Cambridge: Harvard University Press.

Osgood, Charles E., George J. Suci, and Percy H. Tannenbaum. 1957. *The Measurement of Meaning.* Urbana: University of Illinois Press.

Page, Benjamin, and Robert Y. Shapiro. 1992. *The Rational Public.* Chicago: University of Chicago Press.

Panksepp, Jaak. 1989. "The Neurobiology of Emotions: Of Animal Brains and Human Feelings." Pp. 5–26 in *Handbook of Social Psychophysiology,* ed. H. Wagner and A. Manstead. Chichester, England: Wiley.

———. 1991. "Affective Neuroscience: A Conceptual Framework for the Neurobiological Study of Emotions." Pp. 59–99 in *International Review of Studies on Emotion,* ed. Kenneth T. Strongman. New York: Wiley.

———. 1998. *Affective Neuroscience: The Foundations of Human and Animal Emotions,* ed. Richard J. Davidson, Paul Ekman, and Klaus Scherer. Series in Affective Science. New York: Oxford University Press.

Patterson, Orlando. 1991. *Freedom.* Vol. 1 of *Freedom in the Making of Western Culture.* New York: Basic Books.

Patterson, Thomas. 1993. *Out of Order.* New York: Knopf.

Pesso, Albert. 1969. *Movement in Psychotherapy.* New York: New York University Press.

Pesso, Albert, and John Crandell, ed. 1990. *Moving Psychotherapy: Theory and Application of the Pesso System/Psychomotor Therapy.* Cambridge: Brookline Books.

Petty, Richard E., and John T. Cacioppo. 1986. *Communication and Persuasion: Central and Peripheral Routes to Attitude Change.* Springer Series in Social Psychology. New York: Springer-Verlag.

———. 1996. *Attitudes and Persuasion: Classic and Contemporary Approaches.* Boulder, Colo.: Westview.

Plutchik, Robert. 1980. *Emotion: A Psychoevolutionary Synthesis.* New York: Harper and Row.

Plutchik, Robert, and Henry Kellerman, ed. 1989. *The Measurement of Emotions.* Vol. 4 of *Emotion, Theory, Research, and Experience.* San Diego: Academic Press.

Popkin, Samuel L. 1991. *The Reasoning Voter: Communication and Persuasion in Presidential Campaigns.* Chicago: University of Chicago Press.

Pratto, Felicia, and Oliver P. John. 1991. "Automatic Vigilance: The Attention-Grabbing Power of Negative Social Information." *Journal of Personality and Social Psychology* 61 (3): 380–91.

Putnam, Robert D. 1993. *Making Democracy Work: Civic Traditions in Modern Italy.* Princeton: Princeton University Press.

———. 1995. "Bowling Alone: America's Declining Social Capital." *Journal of Democracy* 6:67–78.

Rahn, Wendy. Forthcoming a. "Affect as Information: The Role of Public Mood in Political Reasoning." In *Elements of Reason: Cognition, Choice, and the Bounds of Rationality*, ed. Arthur Lupia, Matthew McCubbins, and Sam Popkin. New York: Cambridge University Press.

————. Forthcoming b. "The Multiple Functions of Public Mood: How Feelings Change Minds and Influence Behavior." In *New Perspectives on the Changing Mind*, ed. Bryan D. Jones and Michael C. Munger.

Rahn, Wendy M., Brian Kroeger, and Cynthia M. Kite. 1998. "A Framework for the Study of Public Mood." *Political Psychology* 17 (1): 29–58.

Rahn, Wendy M., et al. 1990. "A Social-Cognitive Model of Candidate Appraisal." Pp. 136–59 in *Information and Democratic Processes*, ed. John Ferejohn and James Kuklinski. Urbana: University of Illinois Press.

Robinson, Robert G. 1995. "Mapping Brain Activity Associated with Emotion." *American Journal of Psychiatry* 152 (3): 327–29.

Rolls, Edmund T. 1999. *The Brain and Emotion*. Oxford: Oxford University Press.

Roseman, Ira. 1979. "Cognitive Aspects of Emotion and Emotional Behavior." Paper presented at the 87th annual convention of the American Psychological Association, New York, N.Y.

————. 1984. "Cognitive Determinants of Emotions: A Structural Theory." Pp. 11–36 in *Review of Personality and Social Psychology*, ed. P. Shaver. Beverly Hills: Sage.

————. 1991. "Appraisal Determinants of Discrete Emotions." *Cognition and Emotion* 5 (3): 161–200.

Roseman, Ira, Robert P. Abelson, and Michael F. Ewing. 1986. "Emotions and Political Cognition: Emotional Appeals in Political Communication." In *Political Cognition*, ed. Richard Lau and David O. Sears. Hilldale N.J.: Lawrence Erlbaum.

Rosenau, James N. 1997. *Along the Domestic-Foreign Frontier: Exploring Governance in a Turbulent World*. New York: Cambridge University Press.

Russell, James A. 1980. "A Circumplex Model of Affect." *Journal of Personality and Social Psychology* 39:1161–78.

Russell, James A., and James M. Carroll. 1999. "On the Bipolarity of Positive and Negative Affect." *Psychological Bulletin* 125 (1): 3–30.

Russell, James A., and Lisa Feldman Barrett. 1999. "Core Affect, Prototypical Emotional Episodes, and Other Things Called Emotion: Dissecting the Elephant." *Journal of Personality and Social Psychology* 76 (5): 805–819.

Russell, James A., Anna Weiss, and Gerald A. Mendelsohn. 1989. "Affect Grid: A Single-Item Scale of Pleasure and Arousal." *Journal of Personality and Social Psychology* 57 (3): 493–502.

Russell, James A., Maria Lewicka, and Toomas Niit. 1989. "A Cross-Cultural Study of a Circumplex Model of Affect." *Journal of Personality and Social Psychology* 57 (5): 848–56.

Rusting, Cheryl L., and Randy L. Larsen. 1995. "Moods as Sources of Stimulation: Relationships between Personality and Desired Mood States." *Personality and Individual Differences* 18 (3): 321–29.

Schacter, Daniel L. 1996. *Searching for Memory*. New York: Basic Books.

Schwarz, Norbert, and Gerald L. Clore. "Feelings and Phenomenal Experiences." Pp. 433–64 in *Social Psychology: Handbook of Basic Principles*, ed. E. Tory Higgins and Arie W. Kruglanski. New York: Guilford.

Sears, David O. 1990. "Symbolic Politics: A Socio-Psychological Analysis." Paper presented at the annual meeting of the International Society of Political Psychology, 11–14 July, Washington, D.C.

————. 1993a. "The Role of Affect in Symbolic Politics." Paper presented at a conference on political psychology, 14–17 June, University of Illinois at Urbana-Champaign.

————. 1993b. "Symbolic Politics: A Socio-Psychological Theory." Pp. 113–49 in *Explorations in Political Psychology*, ed. Shanto Iyengar and William J. McGuire. Durham: Duke University Press.

Sears, David O., and Carolyn L. Funk. 1990. "Self-Interest in Americans' Public Opinions." Pp. 147–70 in *Beyond Self-Interest*, ed. Jane J. Mansbridge. Chicago: University of Chicago Press.

Sears, David O., Carl Hensler, and Leslie Speer. 1979. "Whites' Opposition to "Busing": Self-Interest or Symbolic Politics?" *American Political Science Review* 73:369–85.

Sears, David O., Richard R. Lau, Tom R. Tyler, and Harris M. Allen, Jr. 1980. "Self-Interest vs. Symbolic Politics in Policy Attitudes and Presidential Voting." *American Political Science Review* 74 (3): 670–84.

Sen, Amartya. 1973. "Behavior and the Concept of Preference." *Economica* 40 (August): 241–59.

Simon, Herbert A.. 1967. "Motivational and Emotional Controls of Cognition." *Psychological Review* 74:29–39.

———. 1982. "Affect and Cognition: Comments." In *Affect and Cognition: The Seventeenth Annual Carnegie Symposium on Cognition*, ed. Margaret Sydnor Clark and Susan T. Fiske. Mahwah, N.J.: Erlbaum.

———. 1985. "Human Nature in Politics: The Dialogue of Psychology with Political Science." *American Political Science Review* 79 (2): 293–304.

———. 1986. "The Role of Attention in Cognition." Pp. 105–15 in *The Brain, Cognition, and Education*, ed. S. L. Friedman, K. A. Klivington, and R. W. Peterson. New York: Academic Press.

———. 1987. "Politics and Information Processing." *London School of Economics Quarterly* 1:340–70.

——— 1994. "Bottleneck of Attention. Connecting Thought with Motivation." In *Integrative Views of Motivation, Cognition and Emotion*, ed. W. D. Spaulding. Lincoln: University of Nebraska Press.

Smith, Adam. 1959. *The Theory of Moral Sentiments*. Indianapolis: Liberty Fund.

Sniderman, Paul M., Richard A. Brody, and Philip E. Tetlock. 1991. *Reasoning and Choice: Explorations in Political Psychology*. Cambridge: Cambridge University Press.

Sniderman, Paul M., Joseph F. Fletcher, Peter H. Russell, and Philip E. Tetlock, eds. 1996. *The Clash of Rights: Liberty, Equality, and Legitimacy in Pluralist Democracy*. New Haven: Yale University Press.

Somit, Albert, and Steven A. Peterson. 1999. "Rational Choice and Biopolitics: A (Darwinian) Tale of Two Theories." PS: *Political Science and Politics* 32 (1): 39–44.

Spenser, Edmund 1989 [1590] *The Faerie Queene*. London: Amereon.

Squire, Larry R. 1987. *Memory and Brain*. New York: Oxford University Press.

Stimson, James A. 1991. *Public Opinion in America. Moods, Cycles & Swings*. Boulder, Colo.: Westview Press.

Storm, Christine, and Tom Storm. 1987. "A Taxonomic Study of the Vocabulary of Emotions." *Journal of Personality and Social Psychology* 53 (4): 805–16.

Sullivan, Dennis, and Roger Masters. 1988. "Happy Warriors. Leaders' Facial Displays, Viewers Emotions, and Political Support." *American Journal of Political Science* 32 (2): 345–68.

Tellegen, Auke. 1985. "Structures of Mood and Personality and Their Relevance to Assessing Anxiety, with an Emphasis on Self-Report." In *Anxiety and the Anxiety Disorders*, ed. A. H. Tuma and J. D. Maser. Hillsdale, N.J.: Lawrence Erlbaum.

Tellegen, Auke, David Watson, and Lee Anna Clark. 1999a. "Further Support for a Hierarchical Model of Affect." *Psychological Science* 10 (4): 307–09.

———. 1999b. "On the Dimensional and Hierarchical Structure of Affect." *Psychological Science* 10 (4): 297–303.

Tesser, Abraham, and G. Clary. "Affect Control: Process Constraints versus Catharsis." *Cognitive Therapy and Research* 2:265–74.

Tesser, Abraham, and Leonard Martin. 1996. "The Psychology of Evaluation." Pp. 400–32 in *Social Psychology: Handbook of Basic Principles*, ed. E. Tory Higgins and Arie W. Kruglanski. New York: Guilford.

Thaler, Richard. 1991. *Quasi-Rational Economics*. New York: Sage.

Thayer, R. E. 1989. *The Biopsychology of Mood and Arousal*. New York: Oxford University Press.

Titchener, E. B. 1910. *A Textbook of Psychology*. New York: MacMillan.

Tomarken, Andrew J., Richard J. Davidson, and Jeffrey B. Henriques. 1990. "Resting Frontal Brain Asymmetry Predicts Affective Response to Films." *Journal of Personality and Social Psychology* 59 (4): 791–801.

Tomarken, Andrew J., Richard J. Davidson, Robert E. Wheeler, and Robert C. Doss. 1992. "Individual Differences in Anterior Brain Asymmetry and Fundamental Dimensions of Emotion." *Journal of Personality and Social Psychology* 62 (4): 676–87.

van Schuur, Wijbrandt. 1998. "From Mokken to Mudfold and Back: Distinguishing between Two Combined Mokken Scales and a Genuine Unfolding Scale." Pp. 45–65 in *In Search of Structure: Essays in Social Science and Methodology*, ed. M. Fennema, C. van der Eijk, and H. Schijf. Amsterdam: Het Spinhuis.

van Schuur, Wijbrandt, and Henk A. L. Kiers. 1994. "Why Factor Analysis Often Is the Incorrect Model for Analyzing Bipolar Concepts, and What Model to Use Instead." *Applied Psychological Measurement* 18 (2): 97–110.

Volkan, Vamik D. 1988. *The Need to Have Enemies and Allies*. Northvale, N.J.: Aronson.

Wagner, H. L., C. J. MacDonald, and A. S. R. Manstead. 1986. "Communication of Individual Emotions by Spontaneous Facial Expressions." *Journal of Personality and Social Psychology* 50:737–43.

Watson, David. 1988a. "Intraindividual and Interindividual Analyses of Positive and Negative Affect: Their Relation to Health Complaints, Perceived Stress, and Daily Activities." *Journal of Personality and Social Psychology* 54 (6): 1020–30.

———. 1988b. "The Vicissitudes of Mood Measurement: Effects of Varying Descriptors, Time Frames, and Response Formats on Measures of Positive and Negative Affect." *Journal of Personality and Social Psychology* 55 (1): 128–41.

Watson, David, and Auke Tellegen. 1985. "Toward a Consensual Structure of Mood." *Psychological Bulletin* 98:219–35.

———. 1999. "Issues in the Dimensional Structure of Affect—Effects of Descriptors, Measurement Error, and Response Formats: Comment on Russell and Carroll (1999)." *Psychological Bulletin* 125 (5): 601–10.

Watson, David, and Lee Anna Clark. 1991. "Self- versus Peer Ratings of Specific Emotional Traits: Evidence of Convergent and Discriminant Validity." *Journal of Personality and Social Psychology* 60 (6): 927–40.

———. 1992a. "Affects Separable and Inseparable: On the Hierarchical Arrangement of the Negative Affects." *Journal of Personality and Social Psychology* 62 (3): 489–505.

———. 1992b. "On Traits and Temperament: General and Specific Factors of Emotional Experience and Their Relation to the Five-Factor Model." *Journal of Personality* 60:441–76.

———. 1994. "The PANAS-X: Manual for the Positive and Negative Affect Schedule—Expanded Form." Unpublished manuscript. Iowa City: University of Iowa.

———. 1997. "Measurement and Mismeasurement of Mood: Recurrent and Emergent Issues." *Journal of Personality Assessment* 68:267–96.

Watson, David, and Lori McKee Walker. 1996. "The Long-Term Stability and Predictive Validity of Trait Measures of Affect." *Journal of Personality and Social Psychology* 70 (3): 567–77.

Watson, David, Lee Anna Clark, and Auke Tellegen. 1984. "Cross-Cultural Convergence in the Structure of Mood: A Japanese Replication and a Comparison with U.S. Findings." *Journal of Personality and Social Psychology* 47 (1): 127–44.

———. 1988. "Development and Validation of Brief Measures of Positive and Negative Affect: The PANAS Scales." *Journal of Personality and Social Psychology* 54 (6): 1063–70.

Watson, David, David Wiese, Jatin Vaidya, and Auke Tellegen. 1999. "The Two General Activation Systems of Affect: Structural Findings, Evolutionary Considerations, and Psychobiological Evidence." *Journal of Personality and Social Psychology* 76 (5). 820–38.

Watson, David, Lee Anna Clark, Curtis W. McIntyre, and Stacy Hamaker. 1992. "Affect, Personality and Social Activity." *Journal of Personality and Social Psychology* 63 (6): 1011–25.

Wattenberg, Martin P., and Craig L. Brians. 1999. "Negative Campaign Advertising: Demobilizer or Mobilizer?" *American Political Science Review* 93 (4): 891–99.

Wilson, Timothy D., and D. S. Dunn. 1986. "Effects of Introspection on Attitude-Behavior Consistency: Analyzing Reasons versus Focusing on Feelings." *Journal of Experimental Psychology* 22:249–63.

Wilson, Timothy D., and Jonathan W. Schooler. 1991. "Thinking Too Much: Introspection Can Reduce the Quality of Preferences and Decisions." *Journal of Personality and Social Psychology* 60 (2): 181–92.

Wilson, Timothy D., Sara D. Hodges, and Suzanne J. LaFleur. 1995. "Effects of Introspecting About Reasons: Inferring Attitudes from Accessible Thoughts." *Journal of Personality and Social Psychology* 69 (1): 16–28.

Wilson, Timothy D., D. S. Dunn, J. A. Bybee, D. B. Hyman, and J. A. Rotondo. 1984. "Effects of Analyzing Reasons on Attitude-Behavior Consistency." *Journal of Personality and Social Psychology* 47 (1): 5–16.

Wilson, William Raft. 1979. "Feeling More Than We Can Know: Exposure Effects without Learning." *Journal of Personality and Social Psychology* 37 (6): 811–21.

Zajonc, Robert B. 1980. "Feeling and Thinking: Preferences Need No Inferences." *American Psychologist* 39:151–75.

———. 1982. "On the Primacy of Affect." *American Psychologist* 39:117–23.

Zajonc, Robert B., Sheila T. Murphy, and Marita Inglehard. 1989. "Feeling and Facial Efference: Implications of the Vascular Theory of Emotion." *Journal of Personality and Social Psychology* 96 (3): 395–416.

Zaller, John R. 1992. *The Nature and Origins of Mass Opinion.* New York: Cambridge University Press.

Zaller, John R., and Stanley Feldman. 1992. "A Simple Theory of the Survey Response: Answering Questions versus Revealing Preferences." *American Journal of Political Science* 36 (3): 579–616.

Zevon, Michael, and Auke Tellegen. 1982. "The Structure of Mood Change: An Ideographic/Nomothetic Analysis." *Journal of Personality and Social Psychology* 43:111–22.

Zimmermann, Manfred. 1989. "The Nervous System in the Context of Information Theory." Pp. 166–73 in *Human Physiology,* ed. R. F. Schmidt and G. Thews. 2d ed. Berlin: Springler-Verlag.

Zuckerman, Marvin. 1991. *Psychobiology of Personality. Problems in Behavioral Sciences,* ed. Jeffrey A. Gray. Cambridge: Cambridge University Press.

Index